AF506176

Exporting Fascism

Italian Fascists and Britain's Italians in the 1930s

Claudia Baldoli

BERG

Oxford • New York

First published in 2003 by
Berg
Editorial offices:
1st Floor, Angel Court, 81 St Clements Street, Oxford, OX4 1AW, UK
838 Broadway, Third Floor, New York, NY 10003-4812, USA

Berg is an imprint of Oxford International Publishers Ltd.

Library of Congress Cataloging-in-Publication Data
Baldoli, Claudia.
Exporting fascism : Italian fascists and Britain's Italians in the 1930s /
Claudia Baldoli.
p. cm.
Includes bibliographical references and index.
ISBN 1-85973-756-0 (Cloth) – ISBN 1-85973-761-7 (Paper)
1. Italians–Great Britain–History–20th century. 2. Great Britain–Civilization–
Italian influences. 3. Fascism–Great Britain–History–20th century. 4. Fascism–
Italy–History–20th century. 5. Italy–Foreign public opinion, British. 6. Great
Britain–Relations–Italy. 7. Italy–Relations–Great Britain. I. Title.

DA125.I85B35 2003
327.1'4'09450941–dc21

2003010054

British Library Cataloguing-in-Publication Data
A catalogue record for this book is available from the British Library.

ISBN 1 85973 756 0 (Cloth)
      1 85973 761 7 (Paper)

Typeset by JS Typesetting Ltd, Wellingborough, Northants.
Printed in the United Kingdom by Biddles Ltd, Guildford and King's Lynn.

www.bergpublishers.com

Contents

Acknowledgements

I wish to thank MacGregor Knox for his suggestions and criticism as my PhD supervisor. Mario Isnenghi has been, throughout the years, a most valuable adviser and source of inspiration. Lucio Sponza has offered important comments on crucial points. I am grateful to the helpful and friendly archivists at the Archivio del Ministero degli Affari Esteri and at the Archivio Centrale dello Stato in Rome. I also would like to thank Martin Blinkhorn, Emilio Gentile, Roger Griffin, Jonathan Morris and Richard Overy for their suggestions at different stages of the research. Of course I remain the only one responsible for what follows. The scholarships offered by the University of Venice, the London School of Economics and the History Department at King's College London have made this research possible. Finally, special thanks to Pietro Di Paola, Peter Eade and the 'Brockley family' in London, and to my family in Italy, Maria, Mario and Giaime.

List of Abbreviations

ASMAE	Archivio Storico Ministero degli Affari Esteri, Rome
AP	Affari Politici
GB	Gran Bretagna
AL	Ambasciata di Londra
Gab	Archivio di Gabinetto del Ministro
AS	Archivio Scuole
DeF	Archivio De Felice
CG	Carte Dino Grandi
b.	busta
f.	fascicolo
sf.	sottofascicolo
ins.	inserto
ACS	Archivio Centrale dello Stato, Rome
SPD	Segreteria Particolare del Duce
Cart. Ris.	Carteggio Riservato
Cart. Ord.	Carteggio Ordinario
MinCulPop	Ministero della Cultura Popolare
NuPIE	Nuclei di Propaganda in Italia e all'Estero
DGSP	Direzione Generale Servizi della Propaganda
AG	Archivio Generale
CPC	Casellario Politico Centrale
CP	Carteggi di personalità
APr	Archivi privati
DDI	Documenti Diplomatici Italiani
PRO	Public Record Office, London
FO	Foreign Office
HO	Home Office
SUL	Sheffield University Library
BU	British Union
BLPES	British Library of Political and Economic Sciences
HLRO	House of Lords Record Office
BL	British Library

Introduction

The purpose of this book is to examine, with reference to the years of Dino Grandi's term as Italy's ambassador to London, the impact in Britain of the complex and shifting relationship between the Italian Fascist State, the foreign ministry, the embassy, the *Fasci*, the British Right and the Italian community. The analysis of Grandi's work in high diplomacy is thus integrated with the history of Italy's attempts to transform its emigrants in Britain into enthusiastic Fascists, and of the contacts between Fascist Italy and British sympathisers, notably the British Union of Fascists and the Conservative Italophiles.

In 1931 about 29,000 Italians lived in Britain, 20,000 of whom had been born in Italy. London constituted the largest community, hosting about 15,000 Italians, mostly concentrated in Clerkenwell and Soho. Since the nineteenth century, the Italians had mostly been employed in peddling and catering. However, during the 1930s the number of Italians who worked as peddlers diminished, while the number of those who started their own businesses increased. Second-generation immigrants, especially those who acquired British citizenship and could enter the liberal professions, tended to achieve social promotion. Yet those employed in catering and shopkeeping continued to be the vast majority. The Soho community, where most Italians worked in restaurants and hotels, hosted mainly emigrants from the valleys of Piedmont and Lombardy; while those in Clerkenwell mostly came from Emilia, Tuscany and Lazio (mainly from the Liri valley, in the Frosinone province) and worked as shopkeepers and ice cream sellers.[1] Stereotypes of the nineteenth-century Italian emigrant as a peddler and organ-grinder persisted well into the twentieth century. The consequence of this was the construction of a negative and weak sense of national identity.[2] In the analysis of the relationship between the communities and Fascism, which sought to eliminate those stereotypes, it is thus important to distinguish a political and ideological level (the few 'real' Fascists) from one of emotions and sentiments. Indeed, most emigrants accepted Fascism because its propaganda persuaded them, for the first time and against the host country's prejudices, that they were part of a renewed and superior civilisation. However, one of the aims of this book is to understand to what extent they were really willing to take part in Mussolini's project.

Efforts by Fascist institutions to create miniature Fascist Italies took place in London and in other British towns, as well as in other countries. News from the British 'Little Italies' appeared weekly in the newspaper of the *Fasci* in Great

Britain, *L'Italia Nostra*, which was published from 1928 to 1940. In cities such as Glasgow, Liverpool and Manchester, where Italian communities were relatively large, the *Fasci* founded organisations along the same lines of those instituted in London.

Wherever an Italian community existed, the *Fasci* Abroad sought to transform the Italians into Fascists. A few historians have attempted to draw a general map of their activity throughout the world.[3] But this activity took different forms according to a number of factors, such as the size of the communities, the different patterns of migration, the social, economic and geographic origin of the emigrants, and the attitude of local governments.[4]

The *Fasci* Abroad created Fascist organisations in other countries outside Italy, founded newspapers, and sought to take control of the administration of Italian schools abroad. During the 1920s, they had to face great difficulties, such as the existence of established non-Fascist clubs and associations, anti-Fascist propaganda and the assimilation of many Italian emigrants. After ten years in power, thanks in part to the favourable international reputation achieved by Mussolini's government, the *Fasci* Abroad were able to begin the transformation of the Italian communities into 'Little Fascist Italies' and to remodel the Italians living abroad. The latter had to become conscious of the fatherland and of their role: to work for the fascistisation of their communities and to be ready to act if the fatherland needed them. Pre-existing Italian organisations melted into the *Fasci* and were now held to obey exclusively the orders of the New Rome. This goal was to be accomplished abroad by Italian diplomats and by the local *Fasci*, the first in relation to foreign governments, the second in relation to the local Italian communities. The book analyses the extent of Fascist success and treats the *Fasci*'s project as part of Mussolini's wider totalitarian experiment in the 1930s.

The activities of the Italian *Fasci* Abroad had two principal aims: to 'remake' the Italians abroad and to expand Fascism in other countries. Until the end of the 1920s, the principal ambition of the Fascist regime was to build a politically and spiritually united nation. Yet the idea of 'nation' was too narrow: 'our purpose is not the nation, but the empire', wrote Camillo Pellizzi, inspector of the *Fasci* in Britain and Ireland, in 1925.[5] The concept of empire did not only refer to the question of achieving colonies, as it did during the liberal period and according to pre-1914 nationalist doctrine. After 1930 in particular, the regime developed its 'revolutionary' belief also in the direction of a 'universal' vocation. As Emilio Gentile pointed out, Italy intended to be the spiritual vanguard of European civilisation. The Italian *Fasci* Abroad were the most important means for the diffusion of this kind of 'spiritual' imperial dream.[6]

From the early 1930s onward, the *Fasci* Abroad were able to begin the enterprise of indoctrinating the Italians abroad, and of transforming the 'Little Italies' into 'Little Fascist Italies'. At the same time, the *Fasci* pursued a double target:

propaganda among both Italians and foreigners. They attempted to convince the emigrants that the *Fascio* was the only representative of *italianità* abroad, and sought to create a new relationship between them and their fatherland. They presented the new Italy as a disciplined, classless nation that would eventually take the leadership of European countries under the flag of the corporativist state. The corporativist order, instituted between 1926 (with the creation of a ministry of corporations) and 1934 (when actual corporations were established), despite being a non-functional bureaucratic apparatus, became one of the most successful pieces of Fascist propaganda, both among Italians abroad and foreigners. The corporativist system, which theoretically brought together employers, Fascist State and workers, represented the Italian way out of the economic depression, and the image of a classless society.

Sometimes, the theme of the 'education' of Italians seemed to be linked with the attempt to expand Fascism among the native population. This attempt to expand Fascism extended to Britain as well. *L'Italia Nostra* seized every opportunity to demonstrate that the British parliamentary system was decadent and that British politicians were becoming aware of this. The Italian government also established contacts with the British Union of Fascists. Yet the role of Count Dino Grandi, the Italian ambassador in London from 1932 to 1939, in relation to the expansion of Fascism in Britain is still unclear. As Paolo Nello wrote in his biography of Grandi, the latter did not seem to believe in the concept of universal fascism.[7] Nevertheless, until 1935 he held that Mussolini should continue to finance Mosley's movement, and developed personal and political relations with British fascists, although he did not appear to have held all of them in high esteem. During the first half of the 1930s, and in his letters to Mussolini in this period, Grandi also claimed repeatedly that fascism was expanding its influence in Britain. It is likely that the main purpose behind these letters was to flatter Mussolini, and that they did not reflect a belief that fascism would eventually come to power in Britain. Yet this hypothesis needs to be verified.

The book also investigates the issue of fascist solidarity during the 1930s, and concentrates on the effects of European fascism on Anglo-Italian relations. The British Foreign Office appeared to have been aware of Mussolini's speeches on European fascism since the early 1930s. In November 1933, after the celebration of the anniversary of the March on Rome, the British ambassador to Rome, Eric Drummond, noticed that, according to Mussolini, the 'revolution' had evolved from a national to a world plan. It was evident that the Duce considered that his prophecy that in ten years' time Europe 'would either be Fascist or fascistised', was becoming a reality. According to Drummond, Mussolini genuinely hoped that in the new era Fascist Italy would represent the example for the rest of the continent.[8] The attempt to establish a new fascist European order seemed to develop particularly during the years preceding the Second World War, but was evident from the beginning of the 1930s. The book analyses the contacts between Italian and British fascists in Britain as part of that attempt. The books published by the 'Greater Britain Publications' and the Home Office files at the Public Record Office confirm that, in the second half of the 1930s, Mosley's movement drew closer to Nazi Germany than to its first patrons in Rome. During the Ethiopian War in particular, Grandi's relationship with the BUF cooled, and the ambassador increasingly became interested in contacts with British Conservative Italophiles who supported Italy throughout the 1930s. The book therefore concentrates on the role of the BUF in seeking to create Anglo-Italian fascism in 1932–4, analyses the reasons for its failure, and focuses on the contacts between Fascism and the British Italophiles during the following years up to the outbreak of the Second World War, with due regard for the effects of international events such as the Spanish Civil War and for internal shifts in Italian policy, such as the adoption of anti-Semitism.

Finally, this book aims to contribute to the existing literature on Anglo-Italian relations by analysing the role of the *Fasci* abroad within the context of Italy's foreign policy. One of the few works on Anglo-Italian foreign relations during the Fascist period, by Richard Lamb, expresses the opinion that Mussolini was strongly pro-British until the Ethiopian War, and that he both feared and disliked Hitler.[9] Lamb has also insisted that the attitude of the British foreign secretary, Anthony Eden, toward Ethiopia and the Spanish Civil War threw Mussolini into Hitler's arms, and that if British recognition of Italy's annexation had been granted, the alliance between Italy and Germany would never have happened. An earlier book by Rosaria Quartararo advanced a similar interpretation. Nazi Germany was merely an instrument, a threat, designed to convince Britain to accept Italian policy in the Mediterranean; until 1940 Britain remained Italy's 'only constant point of reference'.[10] According to Renzo De Felice, Mussolini's only firm principle was the necessity of imperialism and of war as a means of measuring the value of a country – yet Mussolini was never sure on which side Italy should fight in case of war.[11] As Enzo Collotti has pointed out, these attempts to demonstrate that Fascist Italy was a victim of external pressures simply ignore the regime's grandiose war aims, its cultural aspects, and the links between domestic and foreign policies. A major weakness in those interpretations is indeed the perception of foreign policy as somehow separate from the cultural and propagandistic features of the regime. Indeed, a common aspect of both German and Italian regimes was the importance of military education and the inculcation of the 'fascist spirit' at all levels of the society, from school to sport to work organisations. Both regimes considered war as not merely part of politics, but as the basic element of life.[12] From this point of view, Fascism's revisionist foreign policy aims could never have been realised through an alliance with France and Britain, and therefore the 'Pact of Steel' with National Socialist Germany in May 1939 was logical and not merely accidental.[13] Germany was clearly preparing for war and Italy intended to participate in the conflict; its ultimate target in a new war could only be Britain and France, responsible since 1919 for Italy's 'mutilated victory', and especially their domination of the Mediterranean.[14] By analysing Grandi's role in London and by linking the cultural and political history of the Italian *Fasci* in Britain, this book hopes to contribute to the debate on Italian foreign policy.

Notes

1. See Umberto Marin, *Italiani in Gran Bretagna* (Rome: Centro Studi Emigrazione, 1975); Terri Colpi, *The Italian Factor: The Italian Community in Great Britain* (Edinburgh: Mainstream, 1991); Vittorio Briani, *Il lavoro italiano all'estero negli ultimi 100 anni* (Rome: Italiani nel mondo, 1970); Lucio Sponza, *Italian Immigrants in Nineteenth-Century Britain: Realities and Images* (Leicester: Leicester University Press, 1988). The autobiography of Charles Forte, *Forte. Autobiography of Charles Forte* (London: Sidgwick & Jackson, 1986), provides information on relatively integrated and professionally successful Italians in Britain in the 1930s.
2. Marco Porcella, 'Premesse dell'emigrazione di massa in età prestatistica', in *Storia dell'emigrazione italiana. Partenze*, edited by Piero Bevilacqua, Andreina De Clementi and Emilio Franzina (Rome: Donzelli, 2001), p. 40; Franzina, 'Partenze e ritorni', ibid., p. 609.
3. Enzo Santarelli, 'I fasci italiani all'estero (Note ed appunti)', *Studi urbinati di storia filosofia letteratura*, XLV (1971), 1–2, 1323; Domenico Fabiano, 'I fasci italiani all'estero', in Bruno Bezza (ed.), *Gli italiani fuori d'Italia. Gli emigrati italiani nei movimenti operai dei paesi d'adozione* (Milan: Angeli, 1983), 235; Emilio Gentile, 'La politica estera del partito fascista. Ideologia e organizzazione dei Fasci italiani all'estero (1920–1930)', *Storia Contemporanea*, XXVI (1995), 6, 897–956; Luca de Caprariis, 'Fascism for export? The Rise and Eclipse of the *Fasci Italiani all'Estero*', *Journal of Contemporary History*, XXXV, 2 (April 2000), 151–83; Nicola Labanca, 'Politica e propaganda: emigrazione e fasci all'estero', in Enzo Collotti, *Fascismo e politica di potenza. Politica estera 1922–1939* (Milan: La Nuova Italia, 2000), pp. 137–72; Patrizia Dogliani, *L'Italia fascista (1922–1940)* (Milan: Sansoni, 1999), pp. 323–42; João Fábio Bertonha, 'Emigrazione e politica estera: la "diplomazia sovversiva" di Mussolini e la questione degli italiani all'estero, 1922–1945', *Altreitalie*, July-December 2001, pp. 39–53; Emilio Franzina and Matteo Sanfilippo (eds), *Il fascismo e gli emigrati. La parabola dei fasci italiani all'estero* (Rome-Bari:

Laterza, 2003). Renzo Santinon, *I fasci italiani all'estero* (Rome: Settimo Sigillo, 1991) is an apologia for Fascism abroad without historiographical value.

4. Luigi Bruti Liberati, *Il Canada, l'Italia e il fascismo* (Rome: Bonacci, 1984); Mauro Cerutti, *Fra Roma e Berna. La Svizzera italiana nel ventennio fascista* (Milan: Angeli, 1986); Gianfranco Cresciani, *Fascismo, antifascismo e gli italiani in Australia, 1922–1945* (Rome: Bonacci, 1979); Anna Maria Martellone, *La 'questione' dell'immigrazione negli Stati Uniti* (Bologna: Il Mulino, 1980); Anne Morelli, *Fascismo e antifascismo nell'emigrazione italiana in Belgio* (Rome: Bonacci, 1987); Philip V. Cannistraro, *Blackshirts in Little Italy: Italian Americans and Fascism, 1921–1929* (West Lafayette: Bordighera, 1999).

5. Camillo Pellizzi, *Fascismo-Aristocrazia* (Milan: Alpes, 1925), p. 172.

6. Emilio Gentile, *La grande Italia. Ascesa e declino del mito della nazione nel ventesimo secolo* (Milan: Mondadori, 1997), p. 182.

7. Paolo Nello, *Un fedele disubbidiente. Dino Grandi da palazzo Chigi al 25 luglio* (Bologna: Il Mulino, 1933), p. 228.

8. 'Celebration of anniversary of the March on Rome', Drummond to Simon, 3 November 1933, PRO, *FO* 371/16800, C9749/163/22.

9. Richard Lamb, *Mussolini and the British* (London: Murray, 1997), p. 96. Lamb's use of Italian sources is extremely sketchy, he is remarkably selective in his use even of documents available in English, and his argument is not supported by evidence.

10. Rosaria Quartararo, *Roma tra Londra e Berlino. La politica estera fascista dal 1930 al 1940* (Rome: Bonacci, 1980), p. 35.

11. Renzo De Felice, *Mussolini il duce. I. Gli anni del consenso 1929–1936* (Turin: Einaudi, 1974), p. 340; see in particular the chapters 'Alla ricerca di una politica estera fascista' and 'Mussolini e l'Europa'.

12. Collotti, *Fascismo e politica di potenza*, p. 338; p. 475.

13. Enzo Collotti and Lutz Klinkhammer, *Il fascismo e l'Italia in guerra. Una conversazione fra storia e storiografia* (Rome: Ediesse, 1996); Denis Mack Smith, *Mussolini's Roman Empire* (New York: Penguin, 1977); MacGregor Knox, *Mussolini Unleashed, 1939–1941* (Cambridge: Cambridge University Press, 1982) and *Common Destiny: Dictatorship, Foreign Policy, and War in Fascist Italy and Nazi Germany* (Cambridge: Cambridge University Press, 2000); H. James Burgwyn, *Italian Foreign Policy in the Interwar Period 1918–1940* (Westport: Praeger, 1997).

14. Knox, *Fascism: Ideology, Foreign Policy, and War*, in Adrian Lyttelton (ed), *Liberal and Fascist Italy, 1900–1945* (Oxford: Oxford University Press, 2002), p. 110.

1

The 'Education of the Italians' in Britain, 1932–34

> The ten million Italians dispersed around the world are no longer a detached appendix of the fatherland, but the fatherland itself, which through them expands in the world the elements of its power and glory.[1]

The attempt to establish contacts between Italy and its emigrants was not a Fascist invention. During the liberal period some institutions sought to safeguard patriotic feelings among Italian communities abroad. The Dante Alighieri Society was the most thorough, and its activity did not end with the Fascist regime. On the particular question of Italian schools abroad, it was necessary for the *Fasci* Abroad to establish a relationship with the two institutions already involved in these matters: the Dante Alighieri Society and the Catholic Church. A comparison with the activities abroad of liberal Italy can help in understanding the institution of *Fasci* Abroad as an example of the peculiarity of Fascist foreign policy.

The main purpose of the London *Fascio* was to appear to the Italian community as the defender of Italian traditions, and to transform this community into a little Fascist Italy. This chapter takes Italian schools and summer camps for children as typical institutions for the 'education of Italians'. In particular, it concentrates on the propaganda disseminated by the Fascist newspaper in Britain, and analyses the attempt of the *Fascio* to create the images of a 'new Italy' and a 'new Italian'. The chapter does not deal extensively with the results, but largely with the means of Fascist propaganda.

The *Fasci Italiani all'Estero* and the London *Fascio*

Differences between liberal and Fascist foreign policies did not arise from any major contrast in the character of their colonial imperialisms; the Fascist regime aimed at similar targets as the liberal state. Mussolini's ambitions in the Balkans and Africa were not particularly Fascist; the prime ministers Francesco Crispi (1887–91 and 1893–96) and Sidney Sonnino (1906 and 1909–10) had followed similar aims.[2] Historians generally agree that Italian imperialism began with Crispi, and persisted with King Vittorio Emanuele III and Foreign Secretary Antonino Di

San Giuliano, who encouraged Prime Minister Giovanni Giolitti to declare war on Turkey in 1911. Moreover, Italian interest in Tripoli dated back almost as far as the period of unification.[3] Federico Chabod described Crispi as the first opponent, since unification, of a peaceful and moderate Italian foreign policy. Yet he underlined the fact that Crispi's imperialism could not be compared with twentieth-century nationalist or Fascist types. Because of his concern for the greatness of Italy, Crispi was a Fascist 'precursor', but still he remained a 'son of the French Revolution'; Britain was his chief model, and he had no nationalist 'doctrine'.[4] Mussolini's politics were however formed above all in the Great War. The *Fasci di Combattimento* were created in order to defend Italy's victory in the Great War and to counter Italian socialists and the Allies who had 'mutilated' Italy's victory. They claimed that Fascism would build a new nation; Mussolini's newspaper *Il Popolo d'Italia* insisted on the myth of empire as early as 1920.[5]

The myth of the rebirth of Italy meant that once it had seized power, Fascism would seek to 'remake' the Italians, both within and outside Italy. Unlike the liberal state, Fascism succeeded – at least for some years – in the mobilisation of the Italian people and the popularisation of imperialism, and developed a strong linkage between domestic and foreign policy. In an essay on the peculiarities of Fascist foreign policy, Enzo Collotti has emphasised the importance of the project for the 'fascistisation' of Europe during the 1930s, and has suggested that the principal ingredient of Mussolini's foreign policy was the relationship between propaganda, diplomacy and politics.[6]

For its use of patriotic propaganda abroad, the Dante Alighieri Society may be considered a liberal precursor of the Italian *Fasci* Abroad. The Society was set up in Rome in 1889 in order to 'sponsor' Italian language and culture in the *terre irredente*, the lands occupied by Austria. As Richard Bosworth has suggested, their purpose was not only cultural, but also political and strongly anti-Austrian.[7] The Society did not limit its irredentism to the Trentino and Trieste, but aimed to extend it to every part of the world where Italian emigrants lived. The speeches of Pasquale Villari, president of the Society from 1896 to 1903, were significant for their accent on 'cultural imperialism'. In his opinion, any land where Italians lived had to be considered *irredenta*, at least culturally if not politically.[8] From this point of view emigration, usually regarded as a negative event because of the loss of vital energies to the fatherland, now acquired a positive aspect as a 'pacific' form of expansionism, an 'imperialism with clean hands'.[9] In particular, the Society was interested in the expansion of *italianità* in the Adriatic (especially in Albania), and in the Mediterranean; in 1908 it founded branches in Tripoli and Cyrenaica. Italian Nationalists promoted similar aims during the years preceding the Great War. One of them was Luigi Villari, Pasquale's son and a future Fascist propagandist in London, who argued in 1910 that, although the best outlet for emigration would be colonies, in the meantime the *Associazione Nazionalista Italiana* had to defend the

Italian language abroad and support Italy's national prestige among the emigrant communities.[10] Salvemini's difficulty, toward the end of the 1920s, in having to argue against the son of his highly esteemed professor (he could not even write Luigi's surname without seeing Pasquale's image praying him to keep silent) showed not only how the Fascists exploited Pasquale Villari, but also how *italianità* was stifled and absorbed into the Fascist conception of Italy's power.[11]

The activity of the *Fasci* Abroad was organised along the same lines as the Dante Alighieri Society. Yet while the latter saw the Italian abroad principally as an emigrant, the *Fasci* supported a radically different conception. Until Fascism came to power, the emigrant was assisted according to his status and needs: the Dante Alighieri Society took care of the illiterate; the various *Mutuo Soccorso* organisations assisted the poor; and the religious could find help at the *Italica Gens*, the *Bonomelli* and the *Opera di Don Guanella*. As Cornelio Di Marzio, general secretary of the *Fasci* Abroad from December 1926 to January 1928, observed, 'every illness had its cure: every poison its antidote'. Here Fascism made the real difference: 'no one was ever interested in the healthy, normal, independent citizen', who, however, had 'to be re-made'. Under Fascism *italianità* was no longer to be a cure for the emigrant's ailments, but an authentic anthropological revolution.[12]

Unlike the Dante Alighieri Society and the Nationalists, the *Fasci* soon became an integral part of Italian foreign policy. The first *Fasci* Abroad appeared in 1921, and the Grand Council of Fascism officially recognised their existence in February 1923. In 1934, a propaganda pamphlet introduced by the general secretary of the *Fasci* Abroad, Piero Parini, reported that there existed 460 *Fasci*, 269 *Sezioni Fasciste*, 220 *Fasci Femminili* and 74 *Case d'Italia* throughout the world with a total membership of 173,630.[13]

In 1925, Camillo Pellizzi, delegate to the *Fasci* of Great Britain and Ireland from 1922 to 1925, wrote that the activity of the *Fasci* was mainly directed toward the 'fascistisation' of the Italians abroad, rather than convincing foreign countries to adopt Fascism. The purpose was to 'discipline' the Italians and to encourage them to join the 'great Fascist enterprise of the national Risorgimento'. In their dealings with foreigners, the *Fasci* Abroad claimed that they limited themselves to negative actions: to correct false interpretations of events in Italy and to promulgate understanding of Italian problems and virtues.[14] The documents held in the Archivio Centrale dello Stato in Rome nevertheless demonstrate that *Fasci* Abroad activity was not really restricted to purely defensive campaigns. In 1924 Giuseppe Bastianini (a former *squadrista* from Perugia, secretary of *Fasci* Abroad between 1923 and 1926 and ambassador to London from 1939) addressed a memorandum to the representatives in France and Britain. He insisted that Fascists abroad had to create social links with local citizens, especially journalists, politicians, industrialists and intellectuals in order to convince them that Fascist 'style and thought' was the one that could better fit their aspirations.[15]

Social and public diplomacy of this kind was exactly what Luigi Villari tried to conduct in London between 1926 and 1934. This was quite evident from the memorandum he wrote to Mussolini at the end of his term of office. During the summer of 1925 the *Regio Commissariato dell'Emigrazione* had sent him to London, where he discovered the existence of a 'poisonous' anti-Fascist campaign carried on both by Italian and British anti-Fascists. He reported the situation to Mussolini, who decided that Villari should relocate to London and counterattack. Villari was to take orders directly and only from the Duce, not from the embassy or from the *Fascio*. As Villari described it to Mussolini, his propaganda technique involved letters and articles in British newspapers, the publication of books, and a well-developed social 'diplomatic' net among the various British clubs.[16]

The London *Fascio* had been the first founded outside Italy, in 1921.[17] The conservative and patriotic newspaper of the community, *La Cronaca*, founded in June 1920 by a group of ex-officers (*Unione Reduci Militari Italiani*), changed its name in July 1922 to *L'Eco d'Italia*, and was bought by the *Fascio* in August 1926. An anti-Fascist newspaper, *Il Comento*, existed from 1919 to 1924. Some conservative and non-Fascist Italians started the publication of *L'Italiano*, but that paper expired in December 1928. A new weekly Fascist newspaper, *L'Italia Nostra*, took the place of *L'Eco d'Italia* in September 1928 and was published until June 1940; the secretary of the London *Fascio* was also the director of this newspaper. *L'Italia Nostra* remained the only newspaper of the Italian community during the 1930s. News and comment on Italy and London normally occupied pages one to four; the fifth reported news from 'Little Italies' in other British provinces. A sixth page usually contained reviews of Italian books and stories about aviation (in which the *Fascio* informed the community about great Italian achievements in the air), and a seventh page, called 'La Voce d'Italia', listed Italian radio programmes. The final page was reserved for advertisements, both for those looking for work and for Italian products and restaurants.

During the 1930s, active anti-Fascists in the London community were very few. Most Italian political exiles had chosen to find refuge in other countries (especially in France and in the United States) rather than in Britain, because they considered British government to be very conservative and sympathetic to Italian Fascism.[18] Opposition to the *Fascio* within the community existed mainly in the 1920s, in particular until the period of Giacomo Matteotti's murder in Rome in 1924. The anti-Fascist newspaper *Il Comento* focused on events in Italy and warned about the danger of the growing dictatorship. Founded in 1919, the newspaper had sought to coordinate anti-Fascist militants in London and had accused the Italian authorities of sympathising with the Fascists even before the March on Rome. After it was shut down in 1924, the anti-Fascists, with no means and divided among themselves, could do very little to fuel anti-Fascist feeling in the community.[19] It was especially in the 1930s, and in particular during the Ethiopian war, that most of the

Italians in London expressed their enthusiasm for the dictatorship. In 1936 the anarchist Silvio Corio contributed, together with his companion Sylvia Pankhurst, to the foundation of an anti-Fascist fortnightly: *New Times and Ethiopia News*. The paper, which lasted until 1956, was created to support Ethiopia against Italy's invasion, but, as will be discussed in Chapter 3, was in fact an expression of the British Left and received help from very few Italians.

The development of *Fasci* in Britain owed much to the former foreign secretary, Dino Grandi, who became ambassador to Britain in July 1932. His presence in London was significant for the establishment of a new, closer relationship between the Fascist authorities and the Italian community. The previous Italian ambassador to London, Antonio Chiaramonte Bordonaro, had begun his diplomatic career during the liberal period, and had been close to the liberal prime minister of 1919–20, Francesco Saverio Nitti. But when Fascism came to power he decided to remain in service and was rewarded in 1926 with the appointment as general secretary of the ministry, in succession to Mussolini's would-be diplomatic mentor, Salvatore Contarini. In 1927 Mussolini decided that Grandi, at that time under-secretary for foreign affairs, should have a free hand in the 'fascistisation' of the diplomatic corps, and sent Chiaramonte Bordonaro to London.[20] When the latter died, in June 1932, Grandi immediately took his place as 'London exile', after Mussolini's press campaign to support Hitler during the German elections had nullified Grandi's efforts to negotiate with Pierre Laval.[21] The growth of Nazism in Germany, the need to act outside the League of Nations and to fascistise foreign policy led to the shift of 1932 and to Grandi's dismissal. While for Grandi Fascism remained an exclusively Italian phenomenon,[22] Mussolini wanted to satisfy the requests of the leaders of the Partito Nazionale Fasciste (PNF), requests which the Duce began to see as priorities, from the education of the younger generation to the propositions coming from universal Fascist militants.[23] At the same time, Grandi's appointment to Britain imposed a radical fascistisation on the London embassy, considering not only Chiaramonte Bordonaro's liberal past, but also the latter's nature as a bureaucrat-diplomat rather than a Party militant-diplomat. That the general direction was toward radicalisation, not only within the foreign ministry but also among the *Fasci* Abroad, was evident in the case of the London *Fascio*. Shortly before Grandi's arrival, when the *Fascio* needed a new secretary, Chiaramonte Bordonaro suggested to Parini that Tullio Sambucetti could be the new secretary. Sambucetti was one of the community notables; he contributed to cultural features in *L'Italia Nostra*, was founder and secretary of the organisation *Friends of Italy* and organiser of many conferences and trips to Italy. Chiaramonte Bordonaro also reminded Parini that Sambucetti, a resident in London since 1901 and a Fascist since 1922, had been secretary of the *Camera di Commercio* and was presently the director of Italian Studies at the London Polytechnic. But in the year of the Fascist regime's *decennale*, these qualities were no longer enough. Parini, who had met Sambucetti during several visits to London, considered him too old at 58, 'a nice man', but 'a bit boring, old-fashioned, the typical language teacher for educated ladies'. His 'Fascist, therefore modern, sensitiveness', was 'rather poor'.[24] Parini thus decided to entrust the younger and more intransigent Carlo Camagna with the secretaryship of the *Fascio* in June 1932.

Terri Colpi has suggested that, unlike his predecessor, Grandi regularly mixed with the Italian population in London, and that his mission seemed deliberately to address the issue of how 'to turn the British Italian community into a showpiece of fascist "corporatist" theory'.[25] A careful examination of Grandi's papers at the Archivio Centrale dello Stato in Rome and of *L'Italia Nostra* confirms this last statement. In a programmatic letter to Mussolini of 20 August 1932, Grandi told the Duce that his intention was to appear as a 'father' to the Italian community. He described the situation he found in London. In particular, he emphasised the absence of an organisation among Italian cooks and waiters, although they numbered many thousands and were spread almost everywhere throughout the city. He also promised to improve the situation of the Italian hospital, which appeared to have been deserted even by Italians because of its poor condition. He also underlined the importance of showing Italian movies in London cinemas.[26] At the beginning of August, he started his London mission with 'a noble act of *cameratismo fascista*', showing up at Victoria station, where 200 Italian children from all over the country were gathered for the departure of a train to summer camps in Italy. Grandi stressed that his first thoughts after his arrival in Britain were devoted to the Italian community there; he arrived at Victoria station with 200 bags of sweets, 'patriotically adorned, each with a tricolour flag'.[27] Throughout the following years, he appeared to enjoy the role as father of the community, which became in his thoughts his own 'church'. In 1934 he began organising classical music concerts, performed by Italian musicians, in the embassy. In a letter to Parini he explained his concern that the community could have fun at those parties, at which he offered food and drinks; he asked the secretary of the *Fasci* Abroad to send photographs of the Duce and small books for the children: 'I apologise for this, but . . . I have become a priest, and you are the bishop of the diocese . . . it is necessary that the church cut a fine figure!'[28]

In September 1932, the month after Grandi's arrival in London, the London *Fascio* moved from its previous seat to the *Club Cooperativo*, where, since 1909, many of the institutions of the community had been located. With this manoeuvre, the *Fascio* intended to give 'the first example of the brotherly collaboration that, more than anything else, was necessary to the Italian community in London'.[29] Grandi's intention was to bring together the dispersed forces of the community in order to control them and serve as their patron. Indeed, the directorate for Italian schools and the most influential community institutions had their seat at the *Club Cooperativo*.[30]

The Italian Language and Schools in London: the *Fascio*, the Dante Alighieri Society, and the Church

The *Fasci* Abroad made great efforts and spent huge sums of money on the organisation of Italian schools abroad, which were considered the most important institutions for the defence of cultural traditions. Parini traced the origins of the schools back to the age of Crispi:

> the Italian schools abroad, which number today more than 300,000 pupils in almost 2,000 schools, may proudly look at the day when a statesman, who had been the thoughtful and passionate forerunner of a virile Italy, Francesco Crispi, created the first and scanty group of schools outside the frontiers.[31]

The stress on tradition was addressed in the first instance to second-generation emigrants born in Britain and more likely to assimilate. Those emigrants were likely to care less about sending their children to Italian schools. According to the London *Fascio*, it was an obligation for all Italian families to send their children to Italian schools, unless parents wanted them to forget their own language and traditions and therefore make them 'feel foreigners twice over', in both Britain and Italy.[32]

Education of children in Italian schools was in some respects openly Fascist. Elena Salvoni remembered that

> in the late twenties there was a strong movement towards health and fitness so every morning we were out in the grounds doing exercise, all in unison, jumping up and down and waving our arms about. At the end of each session we had to march past the doctor and his wife with our right arms raised and fists clenched; we did as we were told and had no idea that this was the Fascist salute which was to have such sinister significance later in our lives . . . For weeks one particular year we were drilled for a parade before Mussolini's daughter.[33]

The principal subjects taught in the first year of the primary schools were conversation, Italian language, recitation, moral education, singing, craftwork, drawing and hygiene. Conversation included discussions about the children's families, their own role in the family, their ancestors and the veneration of ancestors in their family. The language classes began with simple concepts of grammar. Recitation and singing normally focused on learning short poems and songs of a patriotic or Fascist nature (for example *I bimbi d'Italia si chiaman Balilla*). Moral education varied from the teaching of religious values to education in the respect for personal property (the idea of 'mine' and 'yours'), and to various notions such as respect for others and parental love. The subjects remained the same in the second year, but fascistisation increased. If hygiene lessons were very general in the first year (such as 'the clean child'), they concentrated in the second year on Fascist efforts to improve the Italian people's hygiene (such as summer camps in Italy and Britain, and the Duce's care of public health). Language classes introduced dictation of texts such as 'Duce, you are the Light of Italy'. To some texts, such as 'I love and respect the Duce', children were asked to make comments and reflections. While first-year drawing and craftwork lessons required the children to draw or construct images of children, in the second year they switched to images of Roman lictors.[34] New subjects appeared in the third and fourth years, namely history and geography, which were to become more and more important throughout the 1930s, especially after the conquest of Ethiopia. While after 1935 the teaching of history and geography increasingly focused on Italy's role in the world, between 1932 and 1934 it concentrated mainly on the Italian peninsula itself, although with constant references to ancient Rome.[35]

In order to maintain a high level of *italianità* in the schools, it was fundamental that directors and teachers should be Fascist. Every year, on 1 September, Piero Parini met the directors of Italian schools abroad, in order 'to give them the appropriate instructions for the coming school year'. Whenever possible, Parini organised an appointment for them with the Duce as well.[36] According to a British inquiry of 1934, the Italian foreign ministry dealt directly with the employment of teachers for Italian schools abroad; this made it clear that the intention was propagandistic rather than merely educational. In 1934, the Dominion Office observed that the Italian foreign ministry *modus operandi* was to 'engage teachers sound in the Fascisti faith to proceed to various countries and there organise schools for the teaching of the Italian language and Italian culture. These teachers are in no sense employed in consular work but in teaching and possibly in propaganda work'. The Italian foreign ministry paid their salaries.[37] According to the British, these teachers were under the orders of the Italian *Fasci* Abroad, and 'a special appropriation in the Ministry of Foreign Affairs budget' existed under the heading 'Foreign Schools'. The British regarded this method of furthering and maintaining Italian culture among Italian colonies abroad as a peculiarly Fascist conception.[38]

In the organisation of schools, the Dante Alighieri Society and the Catholic Church assisted the activity of the *Fasci*. Before 1922, Italian schools abroad were under the jurisdiction of these two institutions. A professor of Italian Literature at University College, Count Antonio Cippico, had founded the London section of the Dante Alighieri Society in 1912. Camillo Pellizzi had been interested in the 'fascistisation' of the Society since 1922. In his opinion, Fascists had to become members of the Society in order to form the majority and to preside over its assembly. But things turned out to be more complicated. Due to 'conflicts', the Society ceased its activity until 1932, when Pellizzi finally became its president.[39] In some British cities the Dante did not exist until the early 1930s, and was founded directly by the Fascists. In 1934 Gigi Maino, an Italian journalist who had worked in Britain for one year and was a representative of the Society, set up Dante's committees in Glasgow, Edinburgh and Cardiff. Before leaving the country, he made arrangements with the consuls in Liverpool and Bristol for the opening of committees in those cities as well.[40]

Although there were sometimes problems and conflicts over jurisdiction between the *Fasci* Abroad and the Dante Alighieri Society, the latter now claimed in its statute that its aim was 'safeguarding and spreading the Italian language and culture outside the kingdom and maintaining everywhere a high feeling of *italianità* according to the spirit of the Fascist Revolution'. Some of the highest authorities of the regime were part of the national council of the Society – representatives of the national executive of the PNF, of the Ministries of Press and Propaganda and National Education, of the National Institute of Fascist Culture, of the *Opera Nazionale Balilla*, of the *Opera Nazionale Dopolavoro* and of the Institute LUCE.[41] In 1932, at a national congress in Rome, Piero Parini applauded the Society for joining the *Fasci* Abroad and reaffirming *italianità* in the world, and for 'preparing new and major conquests'. The members of the Society appeared to be quite xenophobic in their speeches. On that occasion, a member of the Dante, Professor Giulio Quirino Giglioli talked about lands that were currently part of other states, but were geographically nevertheless Italian; he inveighed against the 'mania' of using foreign words in Italy, and advocated a law that would finally forbid them.[42] By the early 1930s, the Dante Alighieri Society appeared completely fascistised, and served thereafter as an instrument in the hands of the *Fasci* Abroad.

In the attempt to persuade Italian families in London to send their children to Italian schools, the *Fascio* could rely on Catholic support as well. Despite the occasional friction that characterised Church–State relations within Italy, there seemed to be no antagonism between the *Fascio* and the Catholic churches in London. Funerals, weddings and baptisms amalgamated Catholic tradition with the new Fascist choreography. During the first half of the 1930s, the most relevant example was the funeral of Chiaramonte Bordonaro, which was celebrated with a Catholic–Fascist ritual. But this tendency was also evident in ceremonies for more humble Italians. For instance, in 1934, the clerico-Fascist priest Henry Hughes celebrated a mass for the death of a young *avanguardista*. The mass for the martyrs was introduced in Italy on the first anniversary of the March on Rome, representing the hoped future union between Church and State through 'a concrete attempt to combine the familiar liturgy of Catholicism with the emerging ritual forms of Fascism'.[43] By 1934 it was an established ritual. At the moment of the Eucharist, the most sacred part of the liturgy, a *piccola italiana* made a short speech, and the *capogruppo* called the name of the dead. The young Fascists answered: '*Presente!*' raising their arms in the Roman salute.[44]

The *Fascio* organised non-Catholic feast days such as the *Befana Fascista* and the *Natale di Roma* in order to gain popularity within the community and to add something new and peculiar of its own to the existing religious ones. Yet at the same time, it joined in with Catholic ceremonies and eventually tried to patronise them. All in all, affirmed Henry Hughes from the pages of *L'Italia Nostra*, Fascism had 'saved' the Vatican, as a result of the Lateran Pacts between Mussolini and Pope Pius XI in 1929. The newspaper documents the endeavour of the *Fascio* to assert its authority over the Church's activities, although the stress on loyalty to the Catholic religion seemed to be fundamental for the *Fasci* abroad. Indeed it was intended as a way of preserving *italianità*. Mussolini knew that the Catholic emigrant always felt himself to be Italian: 'the Catholic who says his prayers in Italian and believes in the Roman God cannot be dissuaded, and remains with us'.[45]

Henry Hughes was the typical clerico-Fascist, whose ultimate purpose was to keep alive in the Italian community in London both the Catholic religion and patriotic feeling. He wrote articles and even the occasional moral tale in the *Fascio* newspaper. He told stories about unknown heroes of the Great War who went along a profound and tormented spiritual path (at one and the same time political, literary and religious) from Freemasonry and Internationalism to Catholicism and Nationalism. The conclusion (and purpose) of his tales was a very practical one: how could the Italian community preserve the greatest achievement of Fascism, 'the spiritual and religious unity of the Italian people'? Was this possible by sending children to Protestant schools, where they would acquire a mentality that was not Italian? 'No! To maintain the Italian community of London strong, respected, admired, we must stay all together . . . and together also spiritually'.[46]

In this crusade against the Protestant school, even the spectre of Moscow could be exploited. Britain was said to be at a turning point: Rome or Moscow? Fascism or Communism? Catholicism or Protestantism (which would eventually lead to atheism)? 'And the Italians in London . . . on which side are they? There is no reason to ask! None the less, do not forget that Italian children will be men in 25 years' time. And if we go on sending them to Protestant schools, later on . . . will they be on the side of Rome, or of Moscow?'[47]

The 'New Italy'

The existence of two Italies, one in the fatherland and one spread out all over the world was not simply a matter of rhetoric or propaganda for the regime. The expansion of Fascism within 'Italy abroad' required the effort of ambassadors, intellectuals and propagandists, as well as individuals without a clear institutional role such as Luigi Villari. Such expansion also encouraged the founding of newspapers and the publication of books.

If it was to succeed, the project of 'fascistisation' of the Italians abroad had to take into consideration pre-existing conditions and cultural patterns. This was true also of the experiment to 'remake the Italians' in Italy, where Fascist intellectuals sought to make the new ideal type of Italian conform with the cultural features of the liberal state.[48] In the case of the 'education of the Italians' outside Italy, the Fascist mission became more difficult because of the cultural variations produced by contact with foreign countries. But it was still possible to manipulate nostalgic feelings through reference to roots and traditions which the Fascists hoped would increase national pride.

Many of the tales in *L'Italia Nostra* focused on the subject of travels to the fatherland. In 'Return to the village', an Italian man on a train journey to Lake Garda met a 35-year-old woman who had lived in Paris since she was a teenager, after following her boyfriend there. Although she had become a successful singer in Paris, her heart could not bear the distance from her beloved village on the lake, Salò, and she decided to return there and live as a peasant. Descriptions of the beauty of the landscape were clearly meant to stimulate homesickness especially among emigrants who came from the Lake Garda area.[49]

In another tale, an Italian, who had emigrated when a small child, travelled to Rome and suddenly heard someone speaking the dialect of his region, the Marche. As in the case of the Proustian *madeleine*, he started remembering everything:

> it was the voice of my land . . . I suddenly turned, while a wave of emotion took me over. My memory went back to my homeland, to the small mansion on the bank of the friendly river, to the small field deprived of the strong arms that used to cultivate it, to the little cemetery that embraces and looks after the remains of my ancestors.[50]

In order to emphasise the role of the *Fascio* as the only representative of patriotism in Britain it was necessary to build a new relationship between the emigrants and the fatherland. They had to perceive the Fascist government as the first Italian regime to take care of its emigrants, and the first to gain both interest and respect from other countries.[51] They also had to realise that Fascism was an epochal event in which they could participate. They had to feel that they belonged to a nation, and at the same time that they were also rightfully part of a larger history. Fascism could attempt to reach emigrant hearts precisely because it presented itself as a new regime that despised the rules of international democracy and appeared to promote the emigrants' own sentiments.

In a book written in 1939, Giuseppe Bastianini gave an idea of the populist approach employed by the *Fasci* Abroad and of the Fascist attempt to present Italy as different from any other state. He stated that both the diplomatic work carried on for years around the problem of emigration and the efforts made by economists, diplomats and journalists had all been useless. In Bastianini's view, it would have been enough to call an Italian worker who emigrated to America or France fifty or forty years ago and ask him to say in his own language what he does as an emigrant, to have the precise definition . . . To give a definition of this man we have to penetrate his soul and listen to the words he thinks and does not say when he asks for jobs from foreigners.

Under Fascism the emigrants were to be recognised in terms of their 'personality' and in terms of their rights as workers. The first indication of this difference, as so often with the Fascist regime, was a change in vocabulary: 'the Duce wanted to eliminate the word "emigrant" from the dictionary', to replace it with *'italiani all'estero*.[52]

The Italian Fascist newspaper in London provided a great many examples of this new relationship between the emigrants and their home country, which now had to be regarded as a paternal and protective figure. According to Terri Colpi, Italians were integrated into the economic and social structure of the host country, but not assimilated, since their traditional values, patterns of behaviour and attitudes were still Italian; 'Mussolini was the first to give them the sense of belonging that they longed for'. Except for some anti-Fascists, 'the vast majority of the Italian community in Britain embraced Fascism in a whole-hearted manner. The basic principles of Fascism', honour, family and fatherland, 'were, after all, the very principles by which most of them lived their lives and therefore a slogan and sentiment which they could readily identify'.[53] Salvemini's experience among Italians in North America, where he arrived in 1929, confirmed such an hypothesis: most emigrants were

hard workers, linked to their families by heroic bonds of sacrifice. Arrived in America, illiterate, shoeless and with bags on their shoulders, they had to face unheard-of diffi-culties and suffering, despised by everybody because they were Italians. And now they heard, even from Americans, that Mussolini had made Italy a great country, where no one was unemployed, where everyone had a bath at home, where trains were on time, and that Italy was respected and feared of in the world. Whoever challenged this view, not only destroyed their ideal fatherland, but also hurt their personal dignity. Italy and the Italian government and Mussolini were in their imagination an indivisible whole; to criticise Mussolini meant to fight Italy and to offend them as individuals.[54]

The experiences described in the diaries of three Italians living in London during this period are interesting in this connection. Elena Salvoni, born in London in 1920 of Italian parents, attended an Italian school, went to the Catholic Church every Sunday, and participated in the Italian procession for the Feast of Madonna del Carmelo every year. She nevertheless remembered that 'as working-class families none of us in the Clerkenwell vicinity had felt the need of Mussolini's protection; it was more for the elitist professions in Britain, a bit like the

Freemasons'.[55] The same indifference toward the *Fascio* was perceptible in the autobiography of Charles Forte, who was also born in England.[56] It was a different matter for Calisto Cavalli, who was born in Lugagnano, in the province of Piacenza, fought in the Great War and emigrated to London in 1920. When he wrote his memoirs, he said he had never been a member of the *Fascio*, although he sympathised with Fascism, because it defended principles such as 'Family' and 'Morality'.[57]

The greatest difficulty for the *Fascio* was to convert to Fascism those Italians who were born in England. As Piero Parini wrote in *L'Italia Nostra* in 1933,

> it was said sometimes that one can love his fatherland even without knowing it. This is not totally true. Men who left the Italian soil thirty, forty years ago can well – even if they had never gone back – maintain the image of an old house in their soul . . . but what about the young ones?[58]

The London *Fascio* made remarkable efforts to attract the Italian working classes in particular. Although its diplomatic and social relationships were restricted to its Italian and British upper-class members, the Fascists insisted on collaboration between classes and tried to gain popularity among the working classes with expedients such as improvements to the Italian hospital. In 1932, for example, they established a surgery for children in need.

The new Italy was thus presented as a classless nation. *L'Italia Nostra* declared that socialist rhetoric was sentimental and old-fashioned compared with the practical achievements of Fascism. Thanks to reduced-fare trains, the most humble workers could enjoy Italy's artistic and natural treasures. This was the '*sole dell'avvenire*' that the democratic parties had not been able to realise, a failure that Italians living abroad, where democratic parties still existed, could easily perceive for themselves.[59] In this respect, the corporativist state was the masterpiece of Fascist propaganda abroad. It was presented, and was viewed by British fascists as well, not simply as an economic system but as a universal idea, as historical evidence of the predestined expansion of Fascism abroad. 'It is not just an experiment; the corporativist state is today a living and lively creature that has found in our Italy the fertile soil for its expansion'.[60] British interest in the corporate system was continually emphasised as proof that fascism would replace democracy in England as well.[61]

In January 1933, the London Italian Fascist Enrico Discoli commented on news about the distribution of land to the unemployed in Britain as a 'significant event, which confirms the repercussions of Fascist policy in Britain as well'. He interpreted this act as a 'new direction in British politics, which can possibly move toward fascism, once the last doubts surrender to the mathematical evidence of facts'.[62] In April 1933, the British fascist Harold Goad wrote in the Italian newspaper that Britain had a lot to learn from Italy about trade unionism, certainly much more than from Russia, 'not least because the Italian race is, from historical tradition, much closer to ours'.[63] The Italian government appeared to hold British publications on Fascism in high regard. For instance, in 1934, a letter from Mussolini's press office to the Italian embassy in Washington suggested that *The Working of a Corporate State*, jointly written by Harold Goad and Muriel Currey, was a most appropriate book for the diffusion of fascism abroad. The office sent two copies of it to the embassy.[64]

To explain the political meaning of the new system, the London newspaper employed intellectuals such as Camillo Pellizzi to expound, among other issues, the alleged qualitative difference between the liberal and fascist concepts of social assistance. The notion of state assistance was to replace the liberal one of 'charity' and 'philanthropy'; this was regarded as the first step toward 'national solidarity'. It was typical of Pellizzi to insist on the idea of Fascism as a movement towards something else, a system in a state of continuous revolution.[65] The Fascists in London frequently emphasised the question of social assistance as a means of promoting demographic growth. In 1932, the Party had employed 1.5 million lire for Italian mothers living abroad who travelled to Italy to have their children '*in Patria*'.[66] In the same year, the chargé d'affaires in Italy, John Murray, reported to the British foreign secretary, Sir John Simon, that 'much stress was perceptible in regard to birth rate' in Italy, and that this was directly connected with the idea of empire building.[67] Mussolini, in speeches in the 1920s, had made explicit the links between demographic growth, the military education of the new Italian and the concept of Italian expansion in the world.[68]

In 1932, whilst Italy was celebrating the *decennale* of the Fascist Revolution, the newspaper carried articles and interviews describing the impressions of Italian emigrants who had had the opportunity to visit Rome, and also explaining how life in Italy had changed after ten years of Mussolini's government. *Bonifiche, treni popolari* and family subsidies were among the chief issues, but it was mainly Italy's 'spiritual' rebirth that impressed Italians abroad. 'Going back to Rome today', wrote an Italian Londoner and a reader of *L'Italia Nostra*,

> one can well say that the Capital has been reborn. One can talk about Mussolini's Rome not only because of its new town planning but also and especially for its spirit . . . And to day the city has rapidly acquired a new character: not Roman, but Italian . . . It is destined that Rome must receive its shape from one man. The Rome of Augustus, the Rome of Sixtus V, and now the Rome of Mussolini . . . That is, for those who knew it before, the greatest example of what has been achieved in Italy in the last ten years.[69]

Thanks to the rebirth of the myth of imperial Rome, all Italians, wherever in the world they happened to live, could feel a renewed sense of their history. Their new destiny would be immediately manifest as soon as they went to see Rome:

> Respect and adoration for imperial Rome is a rule in our Fascist character. Mussolini has restored the remains of ancient Rome, and has satisfied a desire among those Italians who had regained the sense of their history and therefore of their destiny.[70]

In order to understand how the nation was imagined, it is worthwhile examining how Fascist Italy presented itself, and in particular its past. It is likely that British interest in Fascism (and therefore in Italy) led emigrants to a new curiosity about their own country.[71] For example, Fascists complained that Italy's contribution to the Great War was regularly underestimated, and Italian authors challenged the British version of wartime history in books in English on Italy's 1915–18 war effort.[72] Most of the time, the means used by the *Fascio* were merely defensive, in an attempt to contradict what they considered to be 'British lies'. *L'Italia Nostra* denounced what it regarded as deliberate falsehoods presented by some British historians,[73] and kept its readers informed about Fascist conferences on themes such as 'how we have to reply to our English friends who boast that they have won the war alone', or about the necessity of demonstrating to British public opinion 'how Italy had fought in the war'. Both military officers and university professors spoke at such conferences. Sometimes it was a British fascist sympathiser who lectured on Italian history, such as Sir John Marriot ('a distinguished historian of our national Risorgimento'). He took part in a series of lectures entitled 'The Rise of Modern Italy', and spoke about 'Domestic Problems in Italy: Fascism, the Church and the State'. In one lecture he explained the Italian contribution to the Great War and described Mussolini as the 'saviour of modern civilisation', concluding with a definition of the Lateran Pacts as the 'greatest event of our century'.[74]

Historical stories in *L'Italia Nostra* built upon this propaganda, usually focusing on the *Risorgimento* and the Great War. As in Fascist conferences and school programmes, the Great War represented the 'founding myth' in its Italian conception of 'our war' and its rootedness in Italy's previous history. Another myth was that of the anonymous hero, with whom anyone could identify, as part of a mass mysticism.[75] The heroism of unknown soldiers and unreserved commitment to the fatherland were thus the main themes. In 'Doctor Antonio', a tale written in 1855 by Giovanni Ruffini, an Italian exile of the Risorgimento and a friend of Giuseppe Mazzini, which was published in weekly instalments in *L'Italia Nostra* over several months, a humble Italian doctor attempted for many years to win the love of a good-natured rich English woman. She usually went on holiday to Liguria with her father, a proud English patriot, who had many prejudices against the Italians and was therefore the main obstacle to their love. Eventually Antonio succeeded in demonstrating to him the qualities of the Italian people, and he moved with his daughter to Naples. It was the year 1848 and the demonstrations for Italy's independence had begun. Although she tried to persuade him to stay, Antonio decided to take part in the events. With the sound of shooting outside the house, he declared his eternal love to her; nevertheless, he said, 'my first love is to the Fatherland'. After the patriots' defeat, he was put in jail; she became ill and died gazing at the castle where he was imprisoned, while inside he suffered and prayed for his country.[76] A similar fate befell Marziale Bellarosa, a fictitious tragic hero of the Great War, who died happy because he was promoted to the rank of corporal after having accomplished his last, extremely dangerous and fatal action.[77]

On several occasions it was possible for the Italian community in London to assist at the OGIE (*Organizzazioni Giovanili Italiane all'Estero*, Italian Youth Organisations Abroad) athletic exhibitions and watch, during the same demonstration, in the presence of the authorities, Italian films on either the Great War or Fascist Italy. In 1932, during the *decennale* celebrations, the *Fascio* showed two movies in London and in the British provinces. One was about Italian life under Fascism and one showed a speech by Mussolini in Turin.[78] The following year the *Fascio* presented *Parla il Duce*, another film of Mussolini speeches.[79] The film given the most emphasis was *Camicia Nera*, a drama written by Gioacchino Forzano and shown in London in April 1933, in Liverpool in June, and in Birmingham in July.[80] *L'Italia Nostra* published the comments from children of Italian schools who were brought to see the film. Like the ones written by their contemporaries in Italy, children's accounts described Mussolini's actions as 'close to magic';[81] the effects of the invention of the myth is evident in their writings:

> Before seeing '*Camicia Nera*' I already loved the Duce, but after having seen it I love our wonderful Duce even more, who has created so many beautiful works: huge hospitals, buildings, bridges, streets and schools. He transformed a village afflicted by malaria into a big and beautiful town! Many Italians will live there, including some from abroad who wish to return to the Fatherland.

Not only did the children express admiration and love, but also a sort of 'self-identification'. One child wrote: 'the part I liked most is this: when the small child put the Italian flag on his door'; another one dreamt of having taken part in the events: 'how much I would have liked to be a Fascist at that time, to see the glorious March on Rome! One thing I liked most was the first publication of *Il Popolo d'Italia* and the journalists who sold it'. Another one expressed his emotional participation: 'When did the miracle happen? Oh, when the image of the Fatherland appeared in front of that poor ill soldier. Italy, Italy, he shouted! Oh, I myself answered his voice with my voice!'[82]

The British-Italian League was frequently involved in the organisation of these events. When the historian George Trevelyan founded it in 1916, the major aim of the League, which included both Italian and British members, was to deepen mutual understanding and friendship between the two allied countries. The pamphlets published by the League during the war years were clearly influenced by Italian 'democratic' interventionism, the irredentism of Cesare Battisti and the patriotism of Leonida Bissolati,[83] who had supported the theory of the Great War as the last war of the Italian Risorgimento. After the war, unlike Bissolati but like Mussolini, they supported Italy's claims to Dalmatia and the myth of the 'mutilated victory'.[84] At the beginning of the 1930s, the former ambassador to Rome, Rennell Rodd, was president of the League; in 1933, when he resigned from his embassy in Rome, Ronald Graham took his place. During the first half of the 1930s, the League participated in almost every Fascist social and cultural event.

The League was also involved in the celebration of anniversaries such as the commemoration of the fiftieth anniversary of the death of Garibaldi in 1932. On that occasion, it organised a ceremony in London which appeared to have had a considerable echo in Italy. This suggested a direct relationship between the Italian *Fasci* Abroad and the British-Italian League. As Graham reported to Simon, 'much prominence was given in press to lunch and lecture arranged by Anglo-Italian Society in London, and there is no doubt British participation in celebration was greatly appreciated in Rome'. What struck Graham particularly was Mussolini's speech during the unveiling of the monument on the Janiculum hill, which presented the new Italy as the practical realisation of Garibaldi's dream, and the blackshirts as the direct successors of the redshirts:

> If the bronze horseman above us could come to life and open his eyes, I am glad to hope that he would recognise the descendants of his redshirts in the soldiers of Vittorio Veneto and in the blackshirts who for ten years, in an even more popular and fruitful form have carried on his work.[85]

Since they had presented themselves, in 1922, as the 'Italy of Vittorio Veneto', the Fascists used the celebration of 4 November as an occasion to show that Fascism and the Nation – Fascism and Little Italy in London – were a unique body. At the commemoration in 1933 they claimed that the whole community was 'united in comradeship, beating as a single heart for the fatherland and the Duce'. The Great War and the March on Rome were celebrated on the same day. The Fascists organised a parade through London and a mass in which they paid homage to dead heroes of the war and of the March on Rome. The intention was to institutionalise a unique memory of both events.[86]

Besides the celebration of Christmas, the *Fascio* tried to set up new feast days in Britain: the *Befana Fascista* (Epiphany, represented in Italy as an old good witch) and the *Natale di Roma*. The latter had become, on 19 April 1923, the first public holiday introduced by Mussolini's government, and continued throughout the regime to replace the 1 May celebrations. The Birth of Rome was a new feast for the Italian workers: it intended to bring work and patriotism together, and suggested that Fascism was looking back at ancient Rome as its inspiration for the nation's rebirth and for a successful future of expansion.[87] The Epiphany, the Italian traditional occasion for gifts for children at the end of the Christmas holidays, was an opportunity for Grandi to appear as the 'father' of the community. Every year the newspaper published photographs of him among hundreds of children from the Italian schools. Children received gifts from the *Fascio*, and this brought it a certain prestige among the families of the community. During the Epiphany of 1933, Grandi reminded the children that even the *Befana* was 'new': 'she no longer has the wrinkled, although smiling, face of the old toothless woman coming down from the chimney hood, but the fresh young face of a young Italian woman, living symbol of the Italy of tomorrow'.[88]

The 'New Italians'

From the articles in *L'Italia Nostra*, it is possible to perceive a fundamental dichotomy between two archetypes of 'the Italian'. On the one hand, the regime called on the emigrant, for the first time, to take his part in history as a son of a reborn nation that professed its descent from Imperial Rome and claimed to be initiating a new era in world history. The Fascists had to convince the Italians that they were themselves unknown heroes of this mythical age; Italians abroad, as well as in Italy, had to be educated to accept these myths from childhood. The Italian *Fasci* in Britain not only created the same organisations that existed in Italy (*Balilla, Piccole Italiane, Avanguardisti*),[89] but also ventured to establish a direct connection between the Italians and their fatherland. In this sense, the major Fascist contribution was the summer camps in Italy for the children of Italian workers abroad. Their significance lay less in actual participation (only a minority of the children could join the camps) than in the propaganda that derived from those who could. In 1935, the British ambassador in Italy, Eric Drummond, noticed that

> those who have been privileged to visit the camps would, I think, agree that the work undertaken is of great benefit to the children and reflects much credit on the Fascist authorities. It is none the less true, as has been reported in the past, that these camps are of very considerable propaganda value, particularly amongst the children's mothers.[90]

Propaganda from the community newspaper revealed the qualities required of the new Italians. After visits and excursions, the month spent in the peninsula came to a climax with participation in a major athletics contest in Rome during which the Duce reviewed over 40,000 young Italians. The London *Fascio* underlined the military aspect of the education given to Italian children from abroad. Military officers acted as trainers at the camps, and the newspaper talked about an '*esercito infantile*' (a children's army). The final purpose was the creation of '*comunanza e fraternità di vedute*' (agreed views) among Fascist children and to avoid the 'dispersion' of the 'qualities of the race'. The young had to acquire the 'shape' of the new Italian, the Fascist shape. The Italian *Fasci* Abroad considered summer camps as a kind of 'factory', in which the new Italy produced new Italians according to its requirements.[91]

Against this military, virile and mythical dimension, the newspaper promoted an ideal that brought Italians back to their unexceptional daily and family life. In this case, the Fascist newspaper evoked the fatherland only as a distant image, and insisted on homesickness ('*nostalgia*'). Italians outside Italy had to live and work for the sake of their families alone; they had to be religious, honest and hard working. According to the newspaper, one of the most rooted elements of '*nostalgia*' which afflicted the 'good Italian worker, *quello bonaccione e virtuoso* who has nothing else in his head but his family, his shop, and his work', was the Sunday bowls match. Love and harmony within the family would enable the emigrants to work hard, conscious, 'every day, every hour', that they were there not to earn great sums of money, which would not make them happy, but 'to secure a carefree old age'.[92]

The emphasis on this non-political aspect was probably due to the need to convince the British that the Fascists believed in and respected the first precept of the Italian *Fasci* Abroad, according to which Fascists abroad had to obey the laws of the country in which they lived and to undertake not to interfere in local politics.[93] Moreover, by saying that Italian Fascists were not involved in politics, they intended to distinguish the 'good' Italian from the 'subversive' anti-Fascists. The anti-Fascist was represented as irreligious, '*facinoroso*' – a person harbouring criminal plans with the deliberate intention of creating disorder, both anti-patriotic and immoral. 'The anti-Fascists are neither workers nor honest people. They act in the darkness, hide and kill like common criminals'.[94] Almost every week the newspaper published articles on the '*vili armi del fuoruscitismo*' all over the world: murders, assaults, the infliction of serious injuries and so on. In 1932 the Italian *Fasci* Abroad published a book with a preface by its secretary Piero Parini listing numerous cases of violence by anti-Fascists against Italian Fascists living abroad.[95]

Another possible explanation for this dichotomy in the representation of the Italians abroad is a generational one. While Fascist emigrants had to be an example of honesty and morality, their sons, the new generation, had to take action, in order to become the pioneers of Fascism and of Italian expansion in other countries. Ideally this would begin at birth: their mothers went to Italy to give birth in the fatherland; in their childhood they were enrolled in Italian organisations and joined summer camps (uniting them with their mother country for the second time since their birth); then they would become *Avanguardisti* and finally blackshirts, soldiers of Fascism abroad. Their mission, it seems, was no longer restricted by the need to be loyal to other countries' laws, since from all appearances Fascist education would persuade them that they must fulfil a revolutionary duty. Camillo Pellizzi, who promoted the idea of spiritual revolution in order to build a new civilisation based on the expansion of *italianità* in the world, had stated this in precise terms as early as 1924. Italian Fascists abroad were not to be merely propaganda agents but apostles of a new religion.[96] This aspect was not concealed from British public opinion; the London *Fascio* also organised summer camps in England: the first 'Mussolini camp' appeared in 1933 at Maidstone in Kent. *L'Italia Nostra* announced the news with fervent enthusiasm, proclaiming that the children were now 'called to a new life'. This suggested that they were no longer part of the country in which they lived; the Fascist newspaper emphasised the presence at the camp gates of a group of curious people as 'one of the many beautiful lessons our youngest give to the British, a lesson that teaches that the Italian of today is very different from the old one'.[97] Grandi's decision to visit the camp seems to have been planned in order to attract both British visitors and the local press.[98]

Both the organised tours to Italy and the summer camps were significant for the development of the myth of the Duce abroad. As in Italy, the myth of the Duce had to stimulate 'fantasies, dreams, expectations, in a word all the thoughts and feelings that take the name of imagination and are interlaced with but do not coincide with the data of experience'.[99] Since he became prime minister in 1922, Mussolini had been touring Italy, visiting towns and areas where previous prime ministers had never been. He had established a 'physical' contact with the Italians, and a sense of omnipresence, helped by the distribution of his portraits and photographs in every public space.[100] The newspaper published photographs of the Duce swimming, jumping difficult obstacles on his horse and working in the fields. Besides Rome, Predappio, the village where Mussolini had been born, became a station of 'ideological tourism' and pilgrimage.[101] In 1933, 1,400 Italian children from abroad visited both Mussolini's parents' graves and the house where he had been born.[102]

The newspaper's accounts of summer camps did not end when the camps shut for the winter, but went on for months, covering the impressions of the visitors, as well as carrying compositions written by children who had participated in the camps. Even more than for the Fascist children who lived in Italy, Mussolini was represented as a father and Italy as a mother: while the children's mothers had remained abroad, another mother, the mother of all, welcomed them as soon as they crossed the border. As in the perfect Fascist family, that image was matched by the virile representation of the Duce as the father of all.[103] The peak of enthusiasm was reached with the description of the 'salute to the Duce' during the group's visit to the Foro Romano. Its purpose was to foment emotion, above all love of Italy and of the Duce. This love could blend Italy and Mussolini together in a unique body: 'talking about the Italian people You have said, Duce, that its future is the only reason of Your life. Well, we do not have any other wish than to be the very reason of Your life, which means to be "Italy"'. The *avanguardisti* gratefully thanked him for the new country: 'We have seen fertile lands, reclaimed marshland, reborn towns, new great buildings near the ancient ones; assisted maternity, protected childhood, people and state in one single body, the beauty of the places sacred by work and spirit'. The conclusion was a promise, first suggested by Pellizzi in 1924: the promise to be ready to rally to the fatherland in case of need: 'Duce, do not forget us: we will not forget You. Duce, if the country needs us, call us, we will come!'[104]

Conclusion

Grandi's appointment to the London embassy in 1932 was the beginning of an intense period of 'fascistisation' of the Italian community. His attitude toward the community was different from that of his predecessor as ambassador, Chiaramonte Bordonaro. Grandi acted as a local 'duce', seeking to appear as both the highest authority and the 'father' of the Italians in London. During the first two years of his ambassadorship, the London *Fascio* incorporated most of the Italian community's social clubs and institutions into its own organisation. The two most influential organisations that already existed among the emigrants, the Dante Alighieri Society and the Catholic Church, both appeared by then to be 'fascistised'.

The documents held at the Public Record Office and at Archivio Centrale dello Stato, and the Italian Fascist newspaper in London suggest that Fascist propaganda activities abroad were centralised and directed from Rome. Directors and teachers of Italian schools abroad were employed by the Italian foreign ministry. Propagandists such as Luigi Villari took their orders directly from Mussolini, and the director of *L'Italia Nostra* was also the secretary of the London *Fascio*.

The study of the London *Fascio* activities and the comparison with the organisations of liberal Italy abroad demonstrate that Mussolini's foreign policy was fundamentally different from that of previous governments. The London *Fascio* not only attempted to establish a link between Italy and its emigrants, but also sought to convince Italians in Britain that *Fascism* was a synonym for *italianità*. Fascist 'education' in the early 1930s primarily involved the organisation of Italian schools and summer camps for children where the 'new Italy' endeavoured to transform Italian children into pioneers of the Fascist Revolution outside Italy. The Fascist newspaper insisted on the 'spiritual' rebirth of Italy, and the London *Fascio* organised lectures and published books in order to outline a new history of the nation, tracing its roots back to the Roman Empire, the Risorgimento and the Great War. They presented the corporativist state as a proof of a newly realised classless society which they claimed they would bring into being in the Italian community in London as well.

The number of Italians in Britain that fully embraced Fascism is far from certain. According to Roberta Suzzi Valli,[105] the London *Fascio* achieved the greatest degree of public support from the Italian community during the Ethiopian War, and especially following Britain's sanctions against Italy. The war can be considered as a turning point in Anglo-Italian relations, and its impact will be studied in Chapters 3 and 4, which will focus on Italian propaganda in Britain and on the relationship between Italian and British fascists in 1935–6. However, as the next chapter will explain, the Italian authorities in London sought contacts with British fascists even before the war, in the attempt to expand fascism in Britain as part of a wider attempt to create a European fascist movement.

Notes

1. *Guida generale degli italiani a Londra* (London: Edward Ercoli & Son, 1933), p. 58. Unless otherwise stated, translations from the Italian are my own.
2. Rosaria Quartararo, *Roma tra Londra e Berlino. La politica estera fascista dal 1930 al 1940* (Rome: Bonacci, 1980), p. 31; H. James Burgwyn, *Italian Foreign Policy in the Interwar Period 1918–1940* (Westport: Praeger, 1997), p. xii.
3. Christopher Seton-Watson, 'British Perceptions of the Italo-Turkish War 1911–1912', in Enrico Serra and Cristopher Seton-Watson, *Italia e Inghilterra nell'età dell'imperialismo* (Milan: Angeli, 1990), pp. 111–45; Enrico Serra, 'I diplomatici italiani, la guerra di Libia e l'imperialismo', ibid., pp. 146–64.
4. Federico Chabod, *Storia della politica estera italiana dal 1870 al 1896*, vol. II (Bari: Laterza, 1965³), p. 600.
5. See Giorgio Rumi, *Alle origini della politica estera fascista (1918–1923)* (Bari: Laterza, 1968).
6. Enzo Collotti, *Il fascismo nella storiografia. La dimensione europea*, in Angelo Del Boca, Massimo Legnani and Mario G. Rossi (eds.), *Il regime fascista. Storia e storiografia* (Rome and Bari: Laterza, 1995), pp. 17–44.
7. Richard J. B. Bosworth, *Italy, the Least of the Great Powers: Italian Foreign Policy before the First World War* (Cambridge: Cambridge University Press, 1979), p. 49.
8. See Pasquale Villari, *Scritti e discorsi per la Dante* (Rome: Società Dante Alighieri, 1933); the editor of the book was Felice Felicioni, former *squadrista* of Perugia and one of the principal champions of the transition of the Dante to Fascism. See also Patrizia Salvetti, *Immagine nazionale ed emigrazione*

nella Società 'Dante Alighieri' (Rome: Bonacci, 1995), p. 82. On the idea of 'cultural imperialism', see the beautiful pages by Lucien Febvre on the Roman colonisation of the Rhine (*Il Reno*, Rome: Donzelli, 1998).

9. Beatrice Pisa, *Nazione e politica nella Società 'Dante Alighieri'* (Rome: Bonacci, 1995), p. 286.

10. On the *Associazione Nazionalista Italiana*, see Franco Gaeta, *Nazionalismo italiano* (Rome and Bari: Laterza, 1981, first ed. 1965); Francesco Perfetti, *Il movimento nazionalista in Italia (1903–1914)* (Rome: Bonacci, 1984). The idea that colonies were the solution to the problem of emigration was not supported only by the nationalist right, but also by the democratic poet Giovanni Pascoli, who defined Italy as 'the great proletarian'.

11. Gaetano Salvemini, *Memorie di un fuoruscito*, in *Scritti vari (1900–1957)*, edited by Giorgio Agosti and Alessandro Galante Garrone (Milan: Feltrinelli, 1978), p. 623.

12. Cornelio Di Marzio, *Fascisti all'estero*, in Giuseppe Luigi Pomba (ed), *La civiltà fascista illustrata nella dottrina e nelle opere* (Turin: Utet, 1928), p. 646. On the Fascist idea of anthropological revolution, see Silvio Lanaro, *Patria. Circumnavigazione di un'idea controversa* (Venice: Marsilio, 1996), p. 52; Emilio Gentile, *La grande Italia. Ascesa e declino del mito della nazione nel ventesimo secolo* (Milan: Mondadori, 1997), p. 173.

13. Murray to Simon, 25 November 1934, PRO, *FO* 371/18439, R6643/5270/22: 'Fascist organisation among Italians living abroad'.

14. Camillo Pellizzi, *Fascismo-Aristocrazia* (Milan: Alpes, 1925), p. 148.

15. 'Segreteria Generale dei Fasci italiani all'estero – A tutte le delegazioni dell'Europa centrale con particolare riferimento alle delegazioni di Francia e Inghilterra', 3 June 1924, ACS, *SPD, Cart. Ris.*, b. 37, f. 242/R: 'Bastianini Giuseppe'.

16. 'Missione di Luigi Villari a Londra 1926–1934' (no date), ACS, *MinCulPop, NuPIE*, b. 37, f. 193: Villari Luigi.

17. For information on the London *Fascio* in the 1920s, see Roberta Suzzi Valli, 'Il fascio italiano a Londra. L'attività politica di Camillo Pellizzi', *Storia Contemporanea*, XXVI (1995), 6, pp. 957–1001.

18. Gaetano Salvemini, *Memorie*, p. 584.

19. Alfio Bernabei, *Esuli ed emigrati italiani nel Regno Unito 1920–1940* (Milan: Mursia, 1997), pp. 75–83; Edward Anderson, *Towards Fascism: the Italian Community and the Italian Press in London, 1920–1922*, MA dissertation, Birkbeck College, 2002.

20. Fabio Grassi Orsini, *La diplomazia*, in Del Boca, Legnani and Rossi (eds.), *Il regime fascista*, pp. 278. According to Bosworth, *Least of the Great Powers*, p. 109, Chiaramonte Bordonaro was a victim of Mussolini's desire to 'fascistise' the diplomatic service.

21. MacGregor Knox, *Il fascismo e la politica estera italiana*, in Richard J. B. Bosworth and Sergio Romano, *La politica estera italiana (1860–1985)* (Bologna: Il Mulino, 1991), p. 314. On Grandi's dismissal, see also Renzo De Felice, *Mussolini il duce*. I. *Gli anni del consenso 1929–1936* (Turin: Einaudi, 1974), pp. 393–418.

22. De Felice, ibid., p. 377; H. James Burgwyn, 'Grandi e il mondo teutonico: 1929–1932', *Storia Contemporanea*, XIX (1988), 2, p. 209; Paolo Nello, *Un fedele disubbidiente. Dino Grandi da Palazzo Chigi al 25 luglio* (Bologna: Il Mulino, 1993), p. 228.

23. De Felice, *Mussolini il duce*, p. 408.

24. Chiaramonte Bordonaro to Parini, 29 April 1932; Parini to Chiaramonte Bordonaro, 9 May 1932, ASMAE, *AL*, b. 775, f. 2, sf. 'PNF Londra'.

25. Terri Colpi, *The Italian Factor: The Italian community in Great Britain* (Edinburgh: Main Stream, 1991), p. 90.

26. Grandi to Mussolini, 20 August 1932, ACS, *CP*, *Apr*, *Carte Grandi*, *Fondo E. Susmel*, b. 9, f. 1.

27. 'S. E. l' Ambasciatore Dino Grandi inizia la sua missione londinese con un nobile gesto di cameratismo fascista – Entusiastiche dimostrazioni d'affetto e di devozione alla stazione di Victoria', *L'Italia Nostra*, 5 August 1932, n. 186, p. 1.

28. Grandi to Parini, no date but March 1934, ACS, *MinCulPop*, *DGSP*, *AG (1930–1943)*, b. 118, f. 'Gran Bretagna 1933', sf. 'Concerti di musica italiana in Inghilterra'.

29. *Guida generale*, pp. 98–9.

30. Among them: *Associazione Nazionale Combattenti* (veterans association), *Associazione Nazionale Alpini*, *Loggia Italia* (Freemasonry), *Associazione Culinaria* (cooking society), *Mutuo Soccorso* (workers association), *Associazione dei Parrucchieri* (hairdressers society), Italian Sporting Club.

31. Piero Parini, 'La cultura italiana e gli italiani all'estero', *Il Legionario*, 29 April 1933, n. 17, p. 3.

32. 'La riapertura delle scuole italiane', *L'Italia Nostra*, 23 September 1932, n. 192, p. 5.

33. Elena Salvoni, *Elena: A life in Soho* (London: Quartet Books, 1990), pp. 32–3. Salvoni misrepresented the Fascist 'Roman salute' by describing instead the communist 'clenched fist'. Edda Mussolini Ciano visited Italian schools in London in June 1934.

34. Programmes of the Italian schools in London for the school year 1932–1933, first and second classes, ASMAE, *AS (1929–35)*, III/3, b. 814.

35. Ibid.

36. Piero Parini to Alessandro Chiavolini, 19 August 1932, ACS, *SPD*, *Cart. Ord.*, b. 13, f. G.3: 'Fasci Italiani all'Estero 1925–1941'.

37. Dixon (Dominion Office) to Batterbee (Downing Street), 14 September 1934, PRO, *FO* 371/18439, R5270/5270/22: 'Contact between Italy and her emigrants'.

38. Chancery to Southern Department, 26 October 1934, PRO, *FO* 371/18439, R6000/5270/22: 'Activities in the United Kingdom of Italiani all'Estero section of Italian Ministry of Foreign Affairs'.

39. 'Il camerata C. Pellizzi presidente del comitato di Londra della Dante Alighieri', *L'Italia Nostra*, 7 July 1932, n. 182, p. 4. See also *Guida generale*, p. 86. By 1932, Italian schools were located in Clerkenwell, Oxford Street, Southwark, King's Cross, Hackney, Marylebone and Stratford (ibid., p. 89).

40. Gigi Maino to foreign ministry, 15 March 1934, ACS, *MinCulPop, DGSP, AG (1930–1943)*, b. 119.

41. Renzo Santinon, *I fasci italiani all'estero* (Rome: Settimo Sigillo, 1991), pp. 253–4.

42. 'La difesa dell'italianità oltre confine nei voti del congresso della Dante', *L'Italia Nostra*, 7 October 1932, n. 194, p. 1.

43. Mabel Berezin, *Making the Fascist Self: the Political Culture of Interwar Italy* (Ithaca-London: Cornell University Press, 1997), p. 87.

44. 'Fervida giovinezza italiana – Il commosso tributo degli italiani di Londra ai funerali dell'avanguardista Michele Ceresa – l'intervento delle autorità. Il solenne corteo attraverso le vie del Soho. Il rito fascista. Le corone', *L'Italia Nostra*, 2 March 1934, n. 265, p. 1.

45. O. Pedrazzi, 'Un emigrante', *L'Italia e il mondo*, November 1926, p. 6, quoted in Gianfausto Rosoli, 'Santa Sede e propaganda fascista all'estero tra i figli degli emigrati italiani', *Storia Contemporanea*, 1986, 17 (2), p. 315.

46. Henry Hughes, 'Chiesa e Patria', *L'Italia Nostra*, 3 February 1933, n. 209, p. 3. See also 'Per le nostre scuole – Cattolicismo e italianità', ibid., 17 February 1933, n. 212, p. 3.

47. Hughes, 'Per le nostre scuole – Roma o Mosca?', *L'Italia Nostra*, 10 March 1933, n. 215, p. 3.

48. From a cultural point of view, see the studies of Mario Isnenghi, *L'educazione dell'italiano. Il fascismo e l'organizzazione della cultura* (Bologna: Cappelli, 1979), and of Simonetta Soldani and Gabriele Turi (eds.), *Fare gli italiani: scuola e cultura nell'Italia contemporanea. 2. Una società di massa* (Bologna: Il Mulino, 1993).

49. 'Ritorno al villaggio', *L'Italia Nostra*, 19 February 1932, 3.

50. 'Cose tristi del passato', *L'Italia Nostra*, 4 March 1932, 3.

51. See Aldo Berselli, *L'opinione pubblica inglese e l'avvento del fascismo (1919–1925)* (Milan: Angeli, 1971).

52. Giuseppe Bastianini, *Gli italiani all'estero* (Milan: Mondadori, 1939), pp. 36–8, p. 45. In 1927 the *Direzione Generale degli Italiani all'Estero* took the

place of the *Commissariato Generale dell'Emigrazione* (see Mario Isnenghi, 'Per una mappa linguistica di un "regime di parole". A proposito del convegno "Parlare fascista"', *Movimento operaio e socialista*, 2 (1984) as a comment to a meeting held in Genova on 22–24 March 1984 about the Fascist use of words: 'Parlare fascista. Lingua del fascismo, politica linguistica del fascismo').

53. Colpi, *The Italian Factor*, pp.86–8.

54. Gaetano Salvemini, *Memorie*, p. 625.

55. Salvoni, *Elena*, p. 44.

56. Charles Forte, *Forte. The autobiography of Charles Forte* (London: Sidgwick & Jackson, 1986), pp. 22–42.

57. Calisto Cavalli, *Ricordi di un emigrato* (London: La Voce degli Italiani, 1973).

58. Piero Parini, 'La Patria pei figli all'estero', *L'Italia Nostra*, 29 September 1933, n. 243, pp. 1–2.

59. 'Carri di tespi e treni popolari sulle strade d'Italia – Le realizzazioni del fascismo per la vita spirituale del popolo', *L'Italia Nostra*, 29 July 1932, n. 185, p. 2.

60. 'Stato e diritto del lavoro', *L'Italia Nostra*, 16 March 1934, n.267, p.1. See also Fausto Pitigliani, *The Italian Corporative State* (London: P. S. King & Son, 1933).

61. See Marco Palla, *Fascismo e Stato corporativo. Un'inchiesta della diplomazia britannica* (Milan: Angeli, 1991).

62. Enrico Discoli, 'La stampa inglese ed il fascismo', *L'Italia Nostra*, 13 January 1933, n. 207, p. 2.

63. Harold Elsdale Goad, 'La stampa inglese e l'Italia – Un articolo della *English Review* sul sistema corporativo italiano', *L'Italia Nostra*, 7 April 1933, n. 219, p. 1.

64. Harold Goad and Muriel Currey, *The Working of a Corporate State: A Study of National Cooperation* (London: Nicholson & Watson, 1932). Ufficio Stampa del Capo del Governo, Sezione Propaganda, to Italian embassy, Washington, 26 June 1934, ACS, *MinCulPop, NuPIE*, b. 27, f. 36: 'Goad Harold'. The file included another book by Harold Goad: *What is Fascism?: an Explanation of its Essential Principles* (Florence: Italian Mail and Tribune, 1929).

65. Camillo Pellizzi, 'Dieci lustri di fraterna attività benefica tra gli italiani di Londra – Il cinquantesimo anno dell'ospedale italiano 1884–1934 – Beneficienza liberale e solidarietà fascista', *L'Italia Nostra*, 24 November 1933, n.251, p. 1.

66. 'L'assistenza sociale e l'opera del partito – Un milione e mezzo per le madri italiane all'estero', *L'Italia Nostra*, 5 August 1932, n. 186, p.2.

67. Murray to Simon, 13 August 1932, PRO, *FO* 371/15986, C7031/2351/22: 'Birth rate in Italy'.

68. MacGregor Knox, *Il fascismo e la politica estera*, p. 291.

69. 'Roma di ieri e Roma di oggi – Impressioni romane di un italiano a Londra', *L'Italia Nostra*, 16 September 1932, n. 191, p. 3. See also 'La nuova Italia nelle impressioni di un italiano emigrato – L'opera costruttiva del Duce', ibid., 26 August 1932, n.189, p.1.

70. 'Roma imperiale e Roma del fascismo', *L'Italia Nostra*, 13 January 1933, n. 207, p.3.

71. See Alfio Bernabei, *Esuli ed emigrati italiani nel Regno Unito 1920–1940* (Milan: Mursia, 1997).

72. See Luigi Villari, 'Italy at War', in id., *The Awakening of Italy: The Fascista Regeneration* (London: Methuen, 1924), pp. 24–43; id., 'Italy and the World War (1914–1918)', in id., *Italy* (London: Ernest Benn, 1929), pp. 135–46; id., *The War on the Italian Front* (London: Cobden-Sanderson, 1932); Gino Gario, *Italy: 1914–18* (London: T. G. Norris, 1937); Camillo Pellizzi, *Italy* (London: Longmans Green, 1939). See the conception of the public use of history suggested by Jürgen Habermas, 'L'uso pubblico della storia', in Gian Enrico Rusconi, (ed.), *Germania: un passato che non passa. I crimini nazisti e l'identità tedesca* (Turin: Einaudi, 1987), and by Nicola Gallerano, 'Storia e uso pubblico della storia', in id. (ed.), *L'uso pubblico della storia* (Milan: Angeli, 1995), where it is defined as 'the activity that regulates and settles the relations between memory and oblivion, between what is worth and what is not worth remembering' (p. 22).

73. 'Il contributo italiano alla grande guerra – un nuovo volume inglese di grossolane menzogne', *L'Italia Nostra*, 12 August 1932, n.187, p. 2. It concerned a book written by 'one of the most famous sportsmen' of Britain, Vivian Nicholls: *Oars, Wars and Horses*, which contained 'shameless and coarse lies and insults against our brave soldiers'.

74. 'S.E. l'Ambasciatore all'University of London', *L'Italia Nostra*, 17 March 1933, n. 216, p. 4.

75. Isnenghi, *L'educazione dell'italiano*, p. 10; p. 29; Gentile, *Il culto del littorio. La sacralizzazione della politica nell'Italia fascista* (Rome and Bari: Laterza, 1993), p. 75.

76. 'Il dottor Antonio', *L'Italia Nostra*, 24 June 1932–8 September 1932. Giovanni Ruffini, *Doctor Antonio: A Tale* (Edinburgh: T. Constable & Co, 1855).

77. 'Marziale Bellarosa. Novella', *L'Italia Nostra*, 15 January 1932, pp. 3–6.

78. 'Un anno di vita italiana', *L'Italia Nostra*, 11 November 1932, n. 199, p. 4; 'Oltre 1500 persone al Portland Hall per la film "Il discorso di Torino"', ibid., 16 December 1932, n. 203, p. 1.

79. 'Domenica gli italiani di Londra celebreranno l'annuale fascista raccogliendosi entusiasticamente attorno ai simboli della patria – L'orazione di S.E.

Fani – Il film "Parla il Duce" – Le melodie d'Italia', *L'Italia Nostra*, 26 October 1933, n. 298, p. 1.

80. See 'Indici di films in Gran Bretagna', in ACS, *MinCulPop, DGSP, AG (1930–1943)*, b. 118, f. 'Gran Bretagna 1933'.

81. Simonetta Falasca-Zamponi, *Fascist Spectacle: the Aesthetics of Power in Mussolini's Italy* (Berkeley-Los Angeles: University of California Press, 1997), p. 68.

82. Gina Cattini, 12 years old, third class, school of St Peter, *L'Italia Nostra*, 12 May 1933, p. 1. A. Capella, third class, St Peter, and Maria Sartori, second class, St Peter, ibid. 19 May 1933, p. 3. Jolanda Bescaglia, fourth class, school of St Patrick, ibid. 26 May 1933, p. 3.

83. See Edward Bollough, *Irredentism and the War* (London: British-Italian League, 1917), and *The Trentino* (London: British-Italian League, 1917).

84. Lucy Re-Bartlett, *Italy, the Pioneer of Peace* (London: British-Italian League, 1921), p. 8.

85. Graham's translation of the speech. Graham to Simon, 7 June 1932, PRO, *FO* 371/15986, C4887/2496/22: 'Celebration of 50th anniversary of death of Garibaldi'.

86. 'Una giornata di travolgente passione italiana', *L'Italia Nostra*, 10 November 1933, n. 249, p. 1.

87. Falasca-Zamponi, *Fascist Spectacle*, pp. 91–3.

88. 'Una cerimonia di fede e di gioia – L'adunata di oltre mille bambini', *L'Italia Nostra*, 26 January 1934, n. 260, p. 1.

89. Note that the major authorities of the London colony were responsible for these organisations. For example, Olga Bossi, the consul's wife, was the head of the *Piccole Italiane*.

90. Drummond to Hoare, 9 July 1935, PRO, *FO* 371/19555, R4344/4344/22: 'Italian summer camps for Fascist children'.

91. 'La partenza dei giovani italiani per le colonie estive', *L'Italia Nostra*, 15 July 1932, pp. 1–2.

92. 'Spunti di nostalgie – Il giuoco delle bocce – Il più democratico e popolare giuoco italiano', *L'Italia Nostra*, 7 October 1932, n. 194, p. 3; 'La felicità è nella semplicità', ibid., 4 November 1932, n. 198, p. 5.

93. 'Fascists abroad must pay obedience to the laws of the country in which they live. Every day they must give examples of their obedience, if necessary, to the native citizens themselves' (from the statute of *Fasci Italiani all'Estero* of 28 January 1928, in Piero Parini, *Gli italiani nel mondo*, Milan: Mondadori, 1935).

94. 'Le prodezze dell'antifascismo in America', *L'Italia Nostra*, 8 January 1932, p. 1.

95. Parini, *Fasci italiani all'estero: 45 morti, 283 feriti* (Rome: Fasci Italiani all'Estero, 1932). The *fuorusciti* were Italian anti-Fascists who had to leave Italy and find refuge in other countries to avoid persecution and imprisonment.

96. See Camillo Pellizzi, *Problemi e realtà del fascismo* (Florence: Vallecchi, 1924).

97. 'Una bandiera tricolore nel Kent – Con la cerimonia dell'Alza Bandiera si è inaugurato domenica scorsa il "Campeggio Benito Mussolini"', *L'Italia Nostra*, 25 August 1933, n. 238, p. 1.

98. 'S.E. Grandi visita il campo Mussolini a Maidstone – la bella iniziativa fascista elogiata dall'ambasciatore', *L'Italia Nostra*, 8 September 1933, n. 240, p. 1.

99. Luisa Passerini, *Mussolini immaginario. Storia di una biografia 1915–1939* (Rome and Bari: Laterza, 1991), p. 3. See particularly part III, 'L'esplosione della biografia. 1933–1939', pp. 153–234.

100. Emilio Gentile, *Fascismo. Storia e interpretazione* (Rome and Bari: Laterza, 2002), p. 127; Falasca-Zamponi, *Fascist Spectacle*, p. 35.

101. Massimo Baioni, *Predappio*, in Mario Isnenghi, (ed.), *I luoghi della memoria. I. Simboli e miti dell'Italia unita* (Rome and Bari: Laterza, 1996), p. 505.

102. 'Terra di Leggenda – Pre' D'appio', *L'Italia Nostra*, 12 May 1933, n. 224, p. 3; 'Una visita a Predappio nuova di 1400 bimbi italiani all'estero', ibid., 1 September 1933, n. 239, p. 2.

103. See for example 'Le braccia aperte di mamma Italia', *Il Legionario*, 10 September 1932, n. 37, pp. 6–7; Claudia Baldoli, 'Le Navi. Fascismo e vacanze in una colonia estiva per i figli degli italiani all'estero', *Memoria e ricerca*, 6, 2000, p. 168.

104. 'Il ritorno dei cento ottanta giovani italiani che hanno trascorso un mese in patria – Entusiastiche scene – Racconti e ricordi – Le ultime giornate romane – la visita del Duce', *L'Italia Nostra*, 15 September 1933, n. 241, p. 1. See also 'Il grande pellegrinaggio delle colonie di Gran Bretagna alla città eterna – Come nacque l'idea del pellegrinaggio. L'omaggio al Duce – Manifestazioni e cerimonie. L'entusiastica adesione degli italiani di Londra e delle provincie', ibid., 12 January 1934, n. 258, p. 1.

105. Suzzi Valli, 'Il fascio italiano a Londra', *Storia Contemporanea*, p. 957.

2

Anglo-Italian Fascism, 1932–34

The historiography of British fascism has usually identified the contradiction between its support for continental fascism and its extreme nationalist propaganda in Britain as one of the major reasons for the BUF's failure.[1] This contradiction seemed also to have been Mosley's principal obsession throughout his life, for he underlined in his autobiography, published in 1968, that he had not copied Fascism or National Socialism. On the contrary, they were 'in the very air of Europe'.[2] Although he had copied symbols and attitudes from the Italian regime, the fascist phenomenon had characterised an entire period of the twentieth century in Europe, and had emerged first in Italy for mainly chronological reasons.[3] According to George Mosse, it was its emphasis on nationalism, and sometimes on different models of racism, that limited the expansion of European fascism.[4] Mosley's autobiography endorsed this idea, clearly with the intention of denying any relationship between his movement and Italian Fascism and, especially, German Nazism.[5] Mosley's principal biographer, Robert Skidelsky, argued that the BUF leader faced a complex undertaking in seeking to introduce his movement as British instead of an imitation of either the Italian or German model.[6] During the Ethiopian War in particular, Mosley's pro-Italian attitude showed that 'BUF beliefs appeared to derive from ideological sympathy with Italian fascism'.[7]

This chapter will explore three main points in focusing on Anglo-Italian relations between 1932 and 1934: the Italian attitude toward the BUF, and in particular the role of Dino Grandi; contacts between Italian and British fascists; and the cultural origins of British fascism and its relationship to Italian Fascism and to the idea of European fascist solidarity.

Dino Grandi and British Fascism

Grandi's role and attitude toward fascism in Britain has seemed ambiguous. Paolo Nello wrote in his biography of Grandi that the latter did not appear to believe in the concept of 'universal' fascism.[8] Nevertheless, until 1935 Grandi held that Mussolini should continue to finance Mosley's movement. He also developed personal and political relationships with British fascists, although he does not appear to have held all of them in high esteem. During the first half of the 1930s, in his letters to Mussolini, Grandi repeatedly claimed that fascism was expanding its influence in Britain. The leitmotiv of Italian hopes for the rise of fascism in Britain was that the country was on the brink of a political and economic crisis the 'old' parliamentary system could not master. The Italian newspaper in London, as well as the Italian press in general, repeatedly reported this belief, and Grandi constantly confirmed it in his letters to Mussolini. Division within the Conservative Party was indeed a fact, especially over the India question.[9] In this respect, some ultra-right-wing Conservatives went so far as to agree with some fascist claims, namely the need for a strong government and the application of a corporativist system both in the mother country and in the empire. In a letter to Mussolini, Grandi set forth the example of the former governor of Kenya (1925–31) Sir Edward Grigg, who, at a speech in Nottingham, advocated the possibility of applying the corporativist system to colonial government. In his opinion, the existence of a parliamentary system was itself an obstacle to the administration of colonies. He adduced two basic reasons in favour of his argument: the concept of *funzionalità*, which meant that only 'men of recognised competence' would govern; and the suppression of class war: 'take the example of Kenya. Here class war is becoming a race war; whites, Africans, Indians. Why could we not create new harmony and efficiency by adopting a corporativist system?'[10]

Assiduous propaganda from Italy matched the interest of those Conservatives in the corporativist system. Apart from numerous books on the subject, the Italian foreign ministry regularly sent to the London embassy an English edition of a bulletin entitled *New Notes on Fascist Corporations*. It was issued by the ministry of corporations in Rome and reported information on budget and syndicates, as well as speeches by the minister of corporations, in order to show the 'tenacious effort and stout resistance of the Italian people in face of the depressing influence of the [world economic] crisis'.[11] In particular, Grandi emphasised the renewal of conflict between Baldwin, Churchill, Lord Lloyd and Beaverbrook in 1933 as 'a new, serious symptom of disease and of disorganisation which is currently afflicting the most popular British party'.[12] Of course, as was expected from an ambassador, Grandi's public contacts did not include British fascists, but members of Parliament, ministers, journalists and members of the royal family.[13] In his letters to Mussolini, he wished to appear as a sort of 'ambassador of the Revolution', with three key features: the father – and 'duce' – of the new fascist 'Little Italies' in Britain described in Chapter 1; the respectable diplomat who dealt with the parliamentary and diplomatic establishment; and the supporter of the British Union of Fascists and of fascist revolution in Britain. Even when acting the second role, Grandi seemed to seize every opportunity to expound Italy's greatness – the advantages of having a Fascist dictatorship, and the coming sunset of the par-liamentary system in Europe. The fact that the most common British attitude toward Fascism in Italy was remarkably favourable[14] pushed him perhaps too far, as he was generally inclined to offer Mussolini an overall picture of Britain as an old country, where traditions were slowly but inevitably being challenged by new fascist ideas. In 1933, after a dinner with the Home Office minister John Gilmour and some members of the House of Lords, he reported to the Duce a conversation with Lloyd George, who, referring to the Four-Power Pact and to a speech by Mussolini at the Chamber, allegedly told Grandi: 'either the world decides to follow Mussolini or the world will be lost. Only your Leader has clear ideas and walks with confidence on the path marked by His own will'. 'Do you not find it strange', he then asked, 'that an old liberal like myself thinks and says such things about He who is the executioner of liberalism?' At this point Grandi allegedly replied to Lloyd George that his opinion of the Duce was not strange at all, what was strange was the fact that he insisted in believing himself an old liberal. In order to show that his propaganda role continued even among liberals, Grandi claimed to have added: 'it would be the greatest mistake . . . in the present revolutionary age . . . to classify our thoughts by using dead political terms'.[15] The crisis was so evident that no one, Grandi argued, could any longer ignore it:

> Even the old parliamentarians – MacDonald is probably the only exception – have become aware of it. They have recently started campaigning for the defence of parliamentarian institutions . . . This is for England, I mean the traditional, slow-moving England, intolerant of novelty, represented by *The Times*, a completely new language . . . As I said, this is the real crisis . . . What everybody is asking for is leadership, a road to follow and a guide.[16]

The growth of anti-Nazi opinion in Britain after 1933, described by the ambassador as 'anti-German hysteria' which, according to him, drew together different classes and parties,[17] had two main effects on Grandi's policy in Britain. Although he frequently mentioned to Mussolini that journalists and politicians always distinguished between Germany and Italy, it is evident that the British government began, as early as 1933, to worry about the ideological similarities and mutual expressions of solidarity between the two regimes.[18] Rosenberg's visit to Britain in June 1933 revealed Grandi's difficulties in having to deal with Britain and Germany at the same time.[19] The second aspect was a radicalisation of the fascism/anti-fascism dispute in Britain, followed by the intensification of Grandi's support for British fascism, as well as his expectations that some kind of fascist action was possible within the country:

> This country is the tortoise among the nations of the world. But like turtles, it will arrive, and I shall not be surprised by seeing tomorrow, perhaps after a violent domestic crisis . . . Mosley's blackshirts, Cripps' labour-fascists, and Lord Lyvington's young imperialists fighting alongside one another.

As usual, Grandi concluded the letter by emphasising his own revolutionary role in Britain: 'as to my own part, as ambassador of the Revolution, be sure that I shall never omit anything in teaching this English youth all You have taught me, namely everything that is necessary in order to carry out a serious Revolution'.[20]

In a long letter to the Duce, Grandi made clear that he distinguished two main 'fascist' types in England: Mosley's BUF and a segment of trade unionism. The Labour MP Sir Stafford Cripps organised the latter:

> The attitude of the Socialist League and its plan for the establishment of socialism are discussed in a recently published book, 'Problems of a Socialist Government'. From both this book and the propaganda of the Socialist League it seems evident that Cripps' neo-socialism is anti-parliamentary and anti-Marxist. Petrie has recently written that Cripps is an 'unconscious fascist' and both *Time and Tide* and *Evening Standard* have called him openly a 'fascist'.[21]

L'Italia Nostra was also concerned about Cripps, and appeared to be convinced of the existence of two principal fronts in British fascism, Cripps and Mosley:

> Several Trade Union leaders and intellectuals consider the parliamentary system as outdated: this is clear from both Mister Cole's studies and Sir Stafford Cripps' activity at the House of Commons. Thus the struggle against the parliamentary system seems to develop in Britain along two main lines: one led by some trade unionists and one by Mosley. It is too early to claim that fascism, as a concept and practice of a new civilisation, is taking over in Britain;

nevertheless, it was understandable that 'the time will come when it will be necessary to adopt a harmonic form of class collaboration which cannot be distant from Fascist corporativism'.[22]

Although the trade unionist corporativists were certainly useful to the Italian propaganda, it was the BUF – the only British movement organised along the lines of the Italian Fascist party – on which both the Italian government and the embassy mostly concentrated their efforts and support. Thus Grandi kept Mussolini well informed about the progress of Mosley's activities in England such as demonstrations, speeches and fights against Communists.[23] He was uncertain whether Mosley himself would become the future British dictator, but nevertheless saw Mosley as the leader of a British version of *squadrismo*. Although the latter was very weak if compared to the Italian *squadre* of ten years before, Grandi thought it possible to compare the two situations. This comparison was evident both by their practical organisation and activities, such as violent attacks on Socialist and Communist meetings and the participation of fascist students in anti-democratic action against the Student Unions at British universities,[24] and from the 'palingenetic' aspects of BUF propaganda and beliefs. Indeed, just like the Italian *squadristi*, the British fascists invoked the coming of a new type of society, to be built on the cultural achievements of an older and more glorious era in national history, not to restore the past, but to use it as the foundation of the national rebirth (or 'palingenesis').[25] The myth of national regeneration had likewise occupied a 'central place in Italian political and cultural history from the Risorgimento to Fascism'.[26]

As reported in an article in a German newspaper which the Italian foreign ministry circulated among some of its embassies abroad, it was enough to visit the BUF headquarters to find similarities to *squadrismo*: the room contained 'training instruments, boxing gloves and other tools'. Benches were located near the walls, possibly for the spectators; a wardrobe contained 'swords, masks and fencing clothes. Probably here in the evenings they proceed to the training of the black-shirts'.[27]

In Grandi's opinion, support for Mosley was a sensible action, especially 'at this moment in which the wave of reaction against German fascism (reaction that, in its alarmist hysteria is even ridiculous) makes his propaganda particularly difficult'. He seemed to be conscious that some British friends of Italy did not look favourably upon Mosley, apparently judging that he lacked credibility, and disliking 'the exaggerated welcome given to Mosley in Italy'. Nevertheless, Grandi reminded the foreign ministry under-secretary, Fulvio Suvich, that 'since last summer, when Mosley started his movement and no one took him seriously, I dared to hold a different opinion'. Certainly, Mosley had bad qualities. He was 'naive and frivolous', and his style of life was much discussed. Still, Grandi held that he also had good qualities: he was a great orator; 'he hits hard and has plenty of guts'. These good qualities outweighed the bad ones. 'I cannot say if it is Mosley who will be destined to lead the new English youth which is fermenting its spiritual revolt'; it was nonetheless clear to Grandi that Mosley had a mission in Britain. At the moment he was a kind of 'political Marinetti' surrounded by a mob; this fact, rather than discouraging him, was seen by Grandi as a proof of his voluntarism, and brought the ambassador's thoughts back to the age of *squadrismo*:

> Is it perhaps the case that Revolutions are made by saints and gentlemen? During the punitive expeditions I carried out in Bologna in 1920 those who hit harder were not the children of good families. Thus I am not worried by the knowledge that part of the money we give Mosley will be spent in the night clubs of London.[28]

From the papers of the Italian *Fascio* in London held at the foreign ministry archives in Rome it is evident that frequent contacts occurred between the Italian *Fascio* and the BUF. In November 1933, one year after the foundation of the BUF, a letter sent by the Secretary of the *Fascio*, Carlo Camagna, to Piero Parini urged that the situation created by these connections be remedied. The local *Fascio*, wrote Camagna, maintained that it was necessary to respect the Duce's guidelines to the *Fasci* Abroad, especially the rule that forbade interference in local domestic politics. He had therefore always kept 'a relationship of friendly politeness' with the British fascists, 'without getting involved in intimate and continuous relationships, and without having official contacts with the leaders'. A clarification of this issue had then become more and more urgent, since contacts between the two fascist parties had gone well beyond a formal and respectful relationship. According to Camagna, repeated invitations from the BUF had been followed by visits of Italian Fascists to the British fascists' headquarters; at the same time, BUF members often visited the Italian *Fascio*. Moreover, both groups participated in one another's public events. It was therefore understandable that Camagna sought 'precise directives' from the general secretary of the *Fasci* Abroad. Parini's answer was a letter to Grandi, asking the latter's views.[29] Apparently no useful answer was forthcoming, and that fact undoubtedly revealed how difficult the matter was. The Italians continued to hold two contradictory positions: on the one hand, a formal and apparent lack of interest, and on the other, in practice, close collaboration with and even financial support for British fascism.

Although it is apparent from Camagna, and sometimes from the BUF paper *The Blackshirt*, that the two fascist institutions often participated in common activities, very little mention of such activity appeared in *L'Italia Nostra*. The most striking example of this emerged during a crucial moment in the history of the BUF, in June 1934, after the famous meeting at Olympia at which BUF stewards violently counterattacked an anti-Fascist attempt to disrupt Mosley's speech. The event caused a decline in the BUF's support in England, both because it brought the loss of Rothermere's *Daily Mail*'s support and because of the comparison between the BUF and German Nazis suggested by the conjunction between the Olympia disturbances with Hitler's 'night of the long knives'.[30] *The Blackshirt* published repeatedly a series of pictures of weapons allegedly used by the anti-fascists, and argued that BUF *squadrismo* (although it did not call it that) was the only assurance of free speech in Britain. Eventually, it suggested that the Olympia disturbance was the end of one period and the beginning of another.[31] The importance of Olympia for the future development of British fascism was immediately evident to the Italian government, especially because it had brought Rothermere's retreat, which the Italians considered as an important step forward toward a genuine fascism in Britain:

> Sir Oswald Mosley was following with perseverance his genuinely fascist propaganda and corporativist programme while the *Daily Mail* continued to support the cause of the old parties and of the traditional system, and to express its confidence in parliamentarian institutions.[32]

According to the Italians, it was likely that British fascists would now have greater chance of achieving power on their own, rather than 'under the ambiguous protection of a defender of old and outdated democratic regimes'.[33] Significantly, *L'Italia Nostra* never mentioned the Olympia incident. Instead, the very next day, it reported the news of the first meeting held in Rome by the British fascists in Italy. The Italian branches of the BUF also gathered in other Italian towns to celebrate both the anniversary of the Italian entry into the Great War and King George's birthday. Both English and Italian sympathisers of Mosley's movement joined the event; the newspaper mentioned the participation of Mr William Jones, head of the BUF Rome branch, his collaborator Mr Anderson, the leader of the women's section Mrs Anna Warig, and some Italian Fascist authorities. Mr Jones explained the programme of the BUF in Great Britain, and the meeting concluded with the Italian and British national anthems.[34] Although contacts between the two fascisms seemed to be natural in Italy, Grandi, as the major sponsor of financial support to the BUF, was of course fearful of the possibility of a major scandal. As early as 1933, he had already warned Suvich:

> To commit [the Italian consul in London] Bossi to give money to Dundas is the same, in case of a scandal, as if the money was given directly by the embassy. I would also exclude the Secretary of the London *Fascio* for many other reasons, or any other Fascist who lives in London, who would not be able to avoid a police interrogation in case the bomb exploded (which is likely to happen, sooner or later).[35]

The best solution would be to send a 'traveller' from Italy who would remain in London for only few days and therefore would become 'practically impossible to catch'. Grandi was also concerned about the British fascist Ian Hope Dundas, one of the principal connections between Italy and the BUF, and a man of whom Grandi had a poor impression:

> This Dundas has already come too often to the embassy, showing business cards in front of employees, with the title of representative of the BUF, and even telling to those who did not want to hear that he was instructed by the Duce to come to the embassy, etc. In general he did not give the impression of a trustworthy person.[36]

Grandi believed Dundas's contacts with the embassy were something about which Rome should be concerned. Yet they were nothing compared with his receiving money directly from Italian diplomats in London, who would hence appear to 'break, according to these suspicious, susceptible and intractable people, the laws of hospitality'.[37]

Contacts between Italian and British Fascists

In 1933 the Italian embassy in Sweden sent the Italian foreign ministry an article which had appeared in a local social-democratic newspaper about Mosley's propaganda in Britain and the international aspects of BUF policy. According to the article, the most noteworthy factor in the development of the movement was – although it boasted it was purely British – its international character. The Swedish newspaper pointed out that Mosley had visited Mussolini the previous year in order to learn 'the forms and methods of organisation adopted in Italy', and had also recently met with Hitler in Munich. It also reported some particulars of his recent visit to Rome, and disclosed that he was organising 'study trips' for BUF members to fascist countries. Grandi also noticed that Mosley had concluded an article in one of the first issues of *The Blackshirt* with the words 'forward to World Fascism!'[38] in apparent reference to the book *Verso l'Internazionale Fascista* by the universal fascist Asvero Gravelli, published in 1932. The Stockholm *Social-Demokrat* assumed that British fascism was a proof of the existence of an international fascist front.[39] One month earlier, Mosley had indeed admitted, in a letter presumably addressed to the Italian embassy in London, that he had again visited Italy in order to study Fascism in its birthplace: 'we even had the honour of being received by His Excellency the Head of the government, whose work is now universally admired in England, and whom we fascists salute as the origin and inspiration of world Fascism'. He added with confidence that 'the last few weeks in Rome have carried a long stage forward the great conception of universal Fascism'.[40] Mosley's visit to Italy had indeed focused the attention of the Italian press on the British movement, and the Italian fascist newspaper in London saw the BUF as an interesting *incognita* in Britain's political life.[41] The PNF in Italy also appeared eager to maintain connections with Mosley at a local level. For instance, the Milan branch of the Party had some contacts with him during the first half of 1933 in order to discuss the possibility of Italian publications on British fascism. And in summer 1933 the same branch asked the Italian embassy in London to forward Mosley an invitation to address an Italian Fascist gathering in Milan.[42]

Political and social contacts between the Italian government and the BUF were fairly regular throughout 1933 and 1934. Apart from the official visits paid by some BUF figures to Italy (in particular, Mosley and Dundas),[43] numerous meetings occurred both in Italy and in England. Even more than the exchanges between Mosley and Mussolini, it was probably the social encounters between members that had real consequences for British and Italian fascists in terms of their adherence to the concept of universal fascism. Meeting fascists from other countries was presumably an exciting experience especially for young Italians who had been brought up in the most nationalistic environment and subject to nationalist propaganda. Moreover, the knowledge that those fascists, although foreigners, were ideological brothers, and the Italians' belief that they were an example to others, contributed a good deal to the spread of a fascist European spirit among young Fascists during the 1930s.

The BUF arranged tours to fascist countries for its members and for interested non-fascists; those pilgrimages lasted about a fortnight, and their purpose was to 'see something of the Hitler movement at first hand, as well as to see in Italy the actual working of a Corporate State'.[44] In April 1933 in Rome the Duce received a group of 200 British teachers, who were examining the Italian educational system and observing the working of Italian schools. Professor Vaughan Johnston greeted Mussolini on behalf of the participants and allegedly added that they were glad to meet 'the leader of the new Italy in Rome, which had always been the common mother of all nations and is today re-establishing its place of prestige and responsibility in the world'. The British fascists and the London *Fascio* had apparently organised this tour jointly, and an Italian fascist stationed in London, Gino Gario, who was also a reporter for *L'Italia Nostra*, accompanied the group to Rome.[45] One week later, Mr De Liege, official representative of the BUF in Italy, paid a visit to the Secretary of the PNF, Achille Starace, to transmit to him the greetings of the British Fascists.[46]

Invited by the BUF, during the summer of 1933, 27 university students from Aosta and Florence spent 15 days in London, where they stayed at Mosley's property in the countryside. As Grandi wrote to the Italian foreign ministry, the students had called on him at the embassy, accompanied by two representatives of the BUF. Although Mosley had been outside London as a consequence of his first wife's death, he soon returned to town in order to spend time with them during their last days in England, to offer them a lunch and to give a speech. Grandi considered these exchanges (a group of 30 British fascists had been in Aosta a few months earlier and another group was soon going to Florence) extremely useful; they established contacts and strengthened friendships.[47] Yet Grandi did not see, or did not want to give too much weight to, the fact that Mosley acted as a local 'duce' for the Italians, not only giving a speech but also reviewing them in a military fashion as Mussolini did in Italy. This was noticed by *L'Italia Nostra*, which set aside its usual precautions in talking about the BUF, and gave two enthusiastic accounts of the event.[48] The British Home Office also expressed concern over the relationship.[49]

The Catholic authorities in London also helped in the organisation of a tour of Rome for British unemployed workers. The visits lasted three days. On the first day, a visit to the Foro Mussolini, where they could attend mass demonstrations by *dopolavoristi* and *avanguardisti*; on the second day, a visit to a *dopolavoro* facility; on the third, the Colosseum and homage to the grave of Italy's unknown soldier.[50] One week later, the London headquarters of the BUF announced to the Italian embassy their intention to send a team of boy members of the BUF to Rome to play a football match against a team of the Italian Balilla.[51]

The British fascists' attitude to these events was sometimes ambiguous, since they had to claim to be above all a nationalist party. Yet their belief that Britain would be great again only in a fascist Europe encouraged these meetings. The BUF newspaper often claimed that Britain would be the next country to go fascist, and regarded the meetings as a guarantee of future peace in Europe once this had occurred; *The Blackshirt* continued to repeat the slogan of 'international fascism'. In the summer of 1934 a group of British blackshirts walked six miles to Bristol docks to exchange fascist greetings with the officers and crew of an Italian ship, the *Monte Bianco*. This meeting was followed by a second later in the same week, when two German vessels also arrived at Bristol and a reunion of Nazis and Italian and British fascists took place. *The Blackshirt* stated that informal gatherings such as these strengthened 'the good understanding' that already existed between fascists of different nations.[52]

A completely blank page in the history of British fascism is the one regarding its activities abroad. Information on BUF branches in Italy can be found mainly in the Foreign Office files at the Public Record Office and from Italian newspapers. Between 1933 and 1934 the BUF founded branches in Genoa, Turin, Bordighera, Milan, Rome and Florence. Most of the members appeared to be subjects of both countries, either British born in Italy or individuals with dual nationality, although some were British fascists sent to Italy for propaganda purposes. The Genoa BUF branch was probably the largest, because of the large number of British citizens who traditionally lived in Liguria. The branch boasted some dozen adherents, although the British consul in Genoa found it difficult to discover either the exact number or the identity of most of them.[53] Their local leader was a youth called Browne, while John Celli was believed to be at the head of the national movement. The latter was of Anglo-Italian origins and used to live in Genoa but, in 1934, resided in Milan and spoke English with a 'slightly foreign accent'. When Browne had visited England a couple of years previously, Mosley had encouraged him to organise the BUF in Italy. The financing of the party in Italy seemed to come mostly from the BUF headquarters in London.[54] In the view of Drummond at the Foreign Office, it seemed likely that it was easier for an Englishman to secure employment in Italy if he were a British fascist than if he were not.[55] These BUF members, it is important to note, saw themselves as *British* fascists who chose to offer their loyalty primarily to Mosley and only secondarily to Mussolini. When they met, they usually sent a telegram of greetings to both leaders. The most striking distinction between them and Italian Fascists was that they were Anglicans. As will be shown in Chapter 4, this was the main distinction also between BUF members – either in Britain or in Italy – and the British Italophiles, who were mostly Catholics but not BUF members, and simply found Italian Fascism appealing.

The main duty of BUF members in Italy was to support the struggle of their fellow-countrymen in Britain for the rise of fascism in that country, by seeking to fascistise British subjects living abroad. Although they did not have the chance, or the time, to have a British Pellizzi, the BUF in Italy perhaps fit the Italian conception of the pioneer abroad, working for his fatherland and for the expansion of fascism from outside. While in Italy, BUF members not only gathered at Anglican churches, but also 'enjoyed' the fascist atmosphere of the state in which they had the 'good fortune' to live: they dressed in black shirts, paid homage to Italian martyrs of the revolution and sang fascist songs. The Italians observed the BUF's use of the black shirt within Italy with obvious pride: 'it was not without emotion that we saw the old black shirt of our revolution worn by subjects of a country so far away, with such deeply based and jealously guarded traditions, and with such a severe sense of protocol'.[56] At a meeting in Genoa in 1934, after the morning service at the Anglican Church, black-shirted, they visited a plaque in memory of a dead hero of *squadrismo*, for fascist martyrs had no nationality, and afterward they visited a war memorial.[57] The First World War was another common memory for Italian and British fascists, for their countries had been allied during the war; indeed, Italian Fascist university youth groups in London had paid homage the Whitehall Cenotaph the previous summer.

The BUF had contacts with Germany as well as Italy, through visitors from Britain and permanent residents abroad. They had a liaison officer to the Nuremberg Nazi Party rally, and some of them frequently travelled to both Italy and Germany.[58] Although Mosley claimed in his autobiography that he personally went to Italy only twice and that he was hardly acquainted with Hitler, it is obvious that the continuous travels of BUF members to fascist countries, as well as the frequent visits of his second wife and of his sister-in-law to Hitler, Goebbels and Goering in Munich were not merely accidental or unconnected with the organisation of fascism in Britain.[59] Moreover, as MI5 records revealed, the BUF in Britain had contacts not only with the Italian *Fasci* Abroad, but also with the Nazi *Auslands-organisation*. The British security service indeed began to watch the BUF from 1934, primarily as a result of its contacts with Italians and Nazis. MI5 enquiries, started in April of that year, 'very soon showed that there was close sympathy and some personal contact between the members of the Ausland Organisation [sic] in London and some of the principal personalities at Mosley's headquarters'.[60]

The reports of the Italian press regarding British fascism in Italy and the more general relationship with the BUF were sometimes ambiguous, and reflected the difficulties of the Italian government in dealing at the same time with British fascism and the British embassy. Nevertheless, as the British ambassador noticed, enthusiasm for British fascism was the main approach. In 1934, to the surprise of the British consul in Turin, an Italian journalist described Lloyd George as 'at heart a fascist'.[61] In the same way, Rome considered the 'conversion' of John Beckett, a distinguished former Labour MP, to fascism, as an important political event, an example of the prospects of fascist success in Britain.[62] At the same time, Drummond emphasised an article by the London correspondent of *Il Giornale d'Italia*, Franzero, who appeared to take, in the ambassador's opinion, the only objective stance on the subject found in Italian newspapers. Franzero saw the results of the London City Council elections as the image of British popular discontent with the present democratic regime; however, those who affirmed that England would go fascist in a few years 'showed an absolute incomprehension of English political feeling'. The main reason was that the British fascists were trying to 'transplant a political theory without first adapting it to its surroundings'. A major obstacle was the 'British detestation of any form of militarism and uniforms', while it was 'superfluous (and hence irritating) to preach discipline to people who by nature were the most disciplined in the world'. According to Franzero, this did not mean that fascism would not take root 'in some form or other' in England. On the contrary, this possibility was evident, but thanks more to the influence of ideas such as corporativism and to popular disappointment with democracy than to Mosley's efforts.[63] Some British fascists who were not BUF members shared this criticism of Mosley: they were Conservative Italophiles who favoured the establishment of a corporativist state adapted to the British tradition. In general, the Italian government keenly supported Mosley's movement, although Italian Fascists, Mussolini included, had personal contacts with the Italophiles as well. As will be explained in the next chapter, Italians, Italophiles and BUF members had some opportunities to meet together, especially in London. However, admiration for Mosley continued to be the main attitude of the Italian press, included Franzero, who a few months later paid tribute to the fascination that Mosley allegedly exercised over the crowds that he addressed.[64]

The public meetings organised by the BUF in Italy rendered the Italian government particularly uncertain of the attitude it should maintain. Drummond noticed this in a letter to Simon in which he gave details of the meeting organised by the Roman branch of the BUF in June 1934 to celebrate the King's birthday. About 115 people attended that meeting, 'over half being women', and, according to the ambassador, only a few were regular members of the British community in Rome. The organiser of the Roman branch of the BUF, Mr William Jones, chaired the meeting. Representatives of the PNF and a considerable number of other Fascists and journalists also attended. Although the British embassy was obviously not present at the ceremony, they must have sent an observer; Drummond was indeed informed that the Italian authorities 'did not appear altogether comfortable during the meeting'. As the unknown observer suggested, this 'was due to the fact that they had attended on the assumption that the meeting was an official one to celebrate His Majesty's Birthday: they may consequently have been under the erroneous impression that His Majesty's Embassy would be officially represented.' The proceedings opened with a speech by Mr Jones in broken English (subsequently, reported Drummond, repeated in perfect Italian) expressing loyalty to the King and alluding to the aims and objects of British fascism. The reading of a message of encouragement to the Rome branch from the London headquarters of the BUF followed. The event ended with a concert and the singing of 'Giovinezza' and 'God Save the King'. Although according to the embassy's observer the atmosphere was 'flat in the extreme', the Italian journalists spoke 'of an "impassioned meeting, full of inaugural *gentilezza*" and of the "very cordial *camaraderie* which characterised this significant event and again united the faithful followers of Sir Oswald Mosley and Italian Fascism"'.[65]

The 'Roman' Roots of British Fascism and the Fascist International

The British fascists began to write their own history shortly after the foundation of the Party. The two main examples of BUF history-writing were a book by James Drennan published in 1934, and one focused on the leader, by Chesterton, published three years later.[66] These works have to be seen as histories of a pre-revolutionary age, written by men who seemed to believe that a revolution was shortly to come: 'we march forward to a victory which is inevitable', wrote the biographer of Mosley.[67] Drennan emulated the structure of Italian histories of the Fascist revolution by Chiurco, Balbo, Farinacci and (in Britain) Villari.[68] As well as those Italian accounts, which began by describing the transition from the 'old' Giolitti-Nitti-Facta's Italy to Mussolini's 'new' age, Drennan's book traced an ideal path that was to lead from the England of Baldwin and MacDonald to that of Mosley. Once they had demonstrated their political skills, both Mussolini and Mosley had emerged from the chaos of democracy in order to rescue their own countries. As in the Italian books, much of Drennan's narrative consisted of quotations from the leader's articles and speeches. Chesterton pointed out that Mosley, as Mussolini did in Italy, 'was planning the greatest adventure of his career, and the boldest move in the history of British politics'. His tasks were 'more tremendous than any body of men or women had ever been called upon to shoulder in British political history'.[69] *The Blackshirt* also aimed to appear as a sort of *Il Popolo d'Italia* during the years preceding the March on Rome. The faith that fascism would come was reinforced by the notion of universal fascism: *The Blackshirt* frequently reported fascist successes in other countries, and put forward the examples of Italy and Germany. Mosley was often called simply 'the Leader' and presented as the British 'duce'.[70]

However, although during the first half of the 1930s the BUF's main model was Italy, the first step for British fascism was to establish a British tradition. As with all fascist movements, the BUF aimed to appear as quintessentially national, and Mosley stated that 'if our policy could be summarised in two words, they would be "Britain First"'. Indeed, even BUF's criticism to liberalism and the parliamentary tradition was rooted in pre-1914 British politics; in particular, the BUF shared Lord Milner's ideas for a coalition government run by efficient technocrats as opposed to an elected parliament of politicians and to party strife.[71] Mosley was influenced by both right-wing protectionist social-imperialists and British social democrats (although he was always opposed to internationalism and Marxist socialism), particularly by the Fabians (George Bernard Shaw, H. G. Wells and Sidney Webb) and Robert Blatchford's criticism of the liberal Cobdenite tradition and party system.[72]

At the same time, the 'Modern Movement' could not be confined to Great Britain: 'it comes to all the great countries in turn as their hour of crisis approaches, and in each country it naturally assumes a form and a character suited to that nation'. According to Mosley, if the British crisis had happened to precede the Italian, fascism would have been a British invention, and Italy, followed again by all other countries, would have taken the British case as the example.[73]

A journalist from the *Rheinish-Westfälische Zeitung* who interviewed Mosley in 1933 asked the first question that every non-English person, according to Mosley, was likely to ask: 'is not the fascist idea too non-English, and will it be able to overcome the parliamentary tradition?' Mosley made clear that belief in an unchanging traditional English model was a misconception, based on the fact that the English nation had always been identified with the average middle-class Englishman. Yet history had shown that the English aristocracy 'had always produced people of daring spirit, who yearn for new adventures. It has given birth to men who have been able to overcome petrified dogmas'. Some changes in English history, asserted Mosley, confirmed his argument exactly: from the lively and prosperous Tudor age, Stuart decadence had allegedly followed. But from this decadence, the people of England had been saved by Cromwell, 'whose appearance can be considered as the first fascist age of England'.[74]

In order to demonstrate that fascism had some sort of roots in the British tradition, Mosley's first and most important act was to look for a usable past older than the age of Cromwell. On the first page, even before the contents list of both the 1932 and 1934 editions of *The Greater Britain*, he published a drawing of the *fascio littorio*, and gave the following explanation: 'Fasces are the emblem which founded the power, authority and unity of Imperial Rome. From the Rome of the past was derived the tradition of civilisation and progress during the past two thousand years, *of which the British Empire is now the chief custodian.*'[75] The Roman colonisation of the British Isles was thus regarded as the origin of British civilisation, and the fact that the Romans came from the Italian peninsula did not mean that it was a foreign civilisation, for the British Empire now constituted the continuation of the Roman Empire and of its mission in the world. Mosley insisted on these same points in a small book published in 1936, in which he sought to explain fascism through '100 questions asked and answered'. The fifth question in particular, explored once again the problem of the 'foreign' roots of British fascism:

'If you do not copy foreign ideas, why do you (1) wear a black shirt, (2) use the Italian Fascist salute, (3) use the Italian Fasces?': 'We wear a black shirt because the colour Black best expresses the iron determination of Fascism in the conquest of red anarchy. Symbolism in itself is nothing new in British politics . . . The salute is not Italian nor is it German, but the Germans also use it. It is the oldest salute of European civilisation and was used in early Britain many centuries before a Fascist Party was created in Italy. The Fasces, too, are a symbol used in Britain for the last 2,000 years and are to be found on most of our great monuments. The symbol was brought to Britain by our Roman ancestors, who were here for four centuries and their stock remained for ever. The Fasces are the symbol of the Roman Empire. What more fitting than that they should be used by the Empire which succeeded and surpassed the Roman Empire?[76]

Mosley's explanation in *The Greater Britain* continued: 'The bundle of sticks symbolises the strength of unity. Divided, they may be broken; united, they are invincible'. Since Mosley explained his theory of the origins of British fascism as a legacy of the Roman Empire, which he saw as the only common root of European civilisation, it seems plausible to argue that he did not simply copy Italy, nor did he merely seek a new symbol for Britain, but for Europe too. The 'Italy of the *fascio*' was in his view not simply a 'Britain', but a 'Europe of the *fascio*', which would be led by Britain because the British Empire was evidently the major successor of the Roman one.[77] The fact that this exercise was not very successful, that it did not appear persuasive to public opinion and that those Roman roots might only be invented roots – an invented tradition – does not make it simply 'laughable'.[78] First because, although unsuccessful, the BUF had been able to attract followers, and it would be difficult to understand why they had been attracted without assuming that they truly believed in the message of the book they considered their 'bible'. And second, the British appeal to a Roman tradition involved the idea (and the invention) of a common European 'fascist' past – and future – which is crucial not only in the study of the ideological roots of universal fascism, but also in terms of the cultural and political relationships between fascist movements, and fascist countries, during the 1930s.

A BUF member who left four volumes of memoirs[79] likewise suggested that Mosley was influenced by the knowledge that ties between his country and Italy were ancient ones. They were not limited to the Romans, but had continued throughout the centuries thanks to commerce and cultural exchanges, from the Christian missionaries of the Dark Ages to the humanists of the Renaissance. Although 'the spiritual regeneration of the young Germans who followed Hitler won his [Mosley's] firm approval', according to Bellamy, the roots of British fascism were Italian and not German: 'some aspects of Nazism, such as the rising tide of hatred against the Jews on the one hand, and the revival of the worship of Thor and Odin and the old Teutonic gods [. . .] evoked no response in him'.[80] Gravelli showed a great understanding of both the appeal of fascism in Britain and the difficult conditions in which the 'British comrades' were acting: 'foreign fascists are brothers who carry on fighting in a sceptical and ambiguous world, who often sacrifice their own youth and shed their young and patriotic blood'. It was indeed moving, in Gravelli's view, that men all over Europe were fighting for an idea that was born in Rome, 'proclaimed by Mussolini who is the spiritual father of the whole movement'. Gravelli considered it a duty for Italian fascists to support those foreign fascists 'who profess, as we do, their faith in the universality of Roman ideas'.[81] The first book issued by the 'foreign fascisms collection' of the publishing house La Nuova Europa was one on British fascism. The main reason for this was not the degree of BUF success (on the contrary, the Italians often underlined the difficulties of the struggle for change within British parliamentary traditions), but precisely the fact that, in contrast to other fascist movements such as the German, fascists in Britain gave their movement the name 'British Union of Fascists', and adopted as their symbol the *fascio littorio*, 'traditional symbol of the Roman civilisation, which they are proud to continue'.[82] Although their slogan was 'Britain First', they nevertheless recognised the universality of Italian, or, better, Roman, Fascism. In 1934 *L'Italia Nostra* proudly reported an opinion expressed by the British press magnate Rothermere in the *Daily Mail*, where he reminded his readers the alleged historical debt that Britain owed to Italy: 'if the British of the past had been as foolish as they are now, England would not have a banking system, a Roman law and would not even know about football, since all these necessary elements of civilisation are of Italian origin.'[83]

One of the organisers of the BUF women's branch, Mary Richardson, not only underlined the 'parallels between this new imperial Rome and the old Rome worthy of the notice of every Britisher'. She also emphasised the parallel between the Roman and the British empires, both of which would eventually be saved by fascism: 'old imperial Rome fell, to be rebuilt again by the power of Fascism. Britain shall not 'fall', for fascism has come before it is too late . . .'[84] However, the major admirer of Mussolini within the BUF was probably Francis J. Burdett. He was only 15 years old when he wrote a school essay dedicated to the life of the Duce.[85] The 16-page essay, which his teacher judged 'a very thorough piece of work', was then sent – it is not clear whether by him or by the school – to the Italian embassy in London, and rewarded with a signed and framed photograph of Mussolini. Burdett soon became a productive journalist, and wrote in the BUF press as well as in the *British-Italian Bulletin*, a supplement to *L'Italia Nostra* that began to appear in 1935. In his essay on the Duce, Burdett saw a

> curious analogy in connection with the fortunes of Rome and those of the Mussolini family: once Rome was mistress of the world, she was reduced by civil wars to 'a mere geographical expression', and a member of the Mussolini family is rapidly restoring her to her ancient glory. A Mussolini was once podesta of Bologna, the family was reduced

by civil wars until one of its members became a village blacksmith, Benito Mussolini has risen to be the ruler of Italy and the 'strong man of Europe'.[86]

Burdett was particularly impressed by the way in which Fascism, through *squadrismo*, faced the post-war chaos. He not only dedicated a few pages in his essay on this subject, but also insisted on it in his articles in *The Blackshirt*, where he liked to remember how

> the blood-red banner of the Soviet arose from the ruins of this once glorious people. The sinister red star of world chaos and destruction appeared to be directing the destinies of the nation . . . All seemed lost, all was hopeless confusion, and Italia Bella, the land of the poets, the land of the arts, the home of genius and romance was crushed and dying.

The 'old men' in power were unable to cope with red terror, and

> Europe mourned the approaching destruction *of the mother of her civilisation* . . . But a new spirit stirred among the mountains of the North. Like a faint and hardly perceptible breeze, springing from out the soil of the Romagna it spread to every part of the land. Wherever it appeared the ruin and smoke was cleared away [my italics].

Twelve years later, according to Burdett, Italy and Mussolini were 'one indivisible whole', and it was 'impossible to think of one without thinking of the other'. However, the dictator's tasks were not necessarily confined to Italy: 'this new and greater Caesar has arisen in the twentieth century to lead his country, and who knows, perhaps Europe, to her highest plane of civilisation'.[87]

John Beckett, another BUF leader who wrote his memoirs,[88] revealed that he had become a fascist thanks to his visit to Italy in 1929. He claimed to have found in the Fascist State the realisation of the Labour programme he had unsuccessfully sought to establish in England. Influenced by Labour propaganda, he had previously regarded Fascism 'as merely a brutal last resort of Capitalism, and did not, therefore, expect to be impressed by it as a social system'. He recalled that he met in Italy Anglo-Italians, Fascists, labour leaders, railway men and dockside workers:

> There was no doubt that the working people looked upon Mussolini as their man, and seemed quite certain that, in any reasonable dispute with the employers, the Fascist decision would always go in their favour. The Anglo-Italians confirmed this. They admitted that Fascism had made the Italians a different people, but they were not altogether friendly to Mussolini, considering that his working-class sympathies were too great. [89]

A subsequent visit to Italy in autumn 1933 confirmed the impression that 'here was a great new conception of civilisation'; nationalism for him brought no disadvantages. Like Mosley in his autobiography, Beckett decided to remove those parts of his text concerning links with the Nazis, although they are obviously evident in his unpublished draft manuscript:

> The conception of national unity in the interests of all classes, combined with the abolition of class privilege and the drastic severing of national credit and money power from international standards -, ~~of the German National Socialist movement~~ seemed to me to provide a basis for the use of the enormous potentialities of the twentieth century productive power to organise a life of reasonable comfort for the whole of its citizens.[90]

He generally deleted, either in pen or pencil, racist concepts, remarks about Hitler, and criticism of Mosley:

> ~~When one thinks of Germany one thinks of Hitler, but also of Goering, Goebbels, Hess and a dozen other first class men who have built their reputations with the growth of their movement.~~ Mosley, Forgan and Allen had all made their reputations in the old parties, and Joyce was the first new man I had seen occupying a prominent position.[91]

In general, at the beginning of the 1930s, British fascists described the German experiment as merely a Teutonic form of fascism. It was not as perfect as the Italian Corporativist State, but nevertheless a step forward toward European fascism. In 1933 British fascists seemed concerned by the fact that the issue of fascism had been obscured in Germany by the 'irrelevant Jewish question', which simply complicated the access to power of the Nazis.[92] On the contrary, the Jewish issue was unknown to the Italian, perfect form of fascism: 'If we must look abroad – as all the world look to-day – let us recall the single-mindedness of the Italian leader, who avoided conflict with Jews, with Church, with sectional interests of any kind, and thus established on unshakeable basis the Power of Fascism in Italy.'[93]

The Italian foreign ministry could not but notice that '*The Blackshirt* does not normally devote much attention to Hitler and admires only Mussolini, of whom Mosley continuously claims to be a follower'.[94] It also recalled that Mosley once told the correspondent of *Il Corriere della Sera* that the BUF program was Mussolini's, adapted to the local situation and to racial differences; 'Different fascisms cannot exist – he said – only one can; Mussolini's'.[95] James Drennan agreed in his history of the BUF, saying that Mussolini had been able to invoke the myth of Rome 'to obliterate the memories of centuries of Italian disunity'. On the contrary, 'the Nazis can only turn upon the nearest aliens in the streets to find consolation for the past and assurance for the future'.[96] Germany, unlike Italy and Britain, allegedly did not possess a Roman past. Still, choosing fascism, it chose to belong to a European tradition: 'Fascism – National Socialism – whatever we like to call it, is essentially a European movement – a political and spiritual transformation, having its roots and taking its expression from the oldest seats of

European culture.'[97] The sense of being part of a unique new spirit was indeed stronger than national distinctions. In an article in *The Blackshirt* in 1933, Mosley quoted a letter sent from a German Nazi to a BUF member, as it reflected not only the spirit that had saved Germany, but also a more general awakening:

> the victory of Fascism! . . . At every moment our policy will be misrepresented and our supporters vilified. Nevertheless, we shall advance to power quicker than the Germans. We have advanced more quickly than any Fascist movement in the world in so short a space of time, and we shall continue that rate of progress.[98]

A. C. Miles, former director of industrial propaganda and senior propaganda officer of the BUF, saw the influence of both Italian and German fascisms on the BUF as stronger than the nationalist aspect. He claimed that this apparent disparity between the declared ideals and the actual practice of the organisation had been the main reason for his leaving the party in 1936.[99] He also wrote that he realised thereafter the danger of fascism to democracy and to the future of the country, and that he became a member of a democratic group, which included both Catholics and Protestants, Jews, Conservatives, Liberals, Labourists, Socialists and even Communists, all determined to 'destroy the evil of fascism' on a non-sectarian basis. As an example of his main complaint against the BUF, he reported the case of a young British fascist, by profession a waiter, who, after learning that 1,800 Italian waiters were coming to London for the Coronation celebrations, 'conceived this to be a glorious opportunity for the Fascist Movement to demonstrate the sincerity of its slogan that British jobs should be given to British workers'. 'In his innocence', Miles recalled, the young man rushed to the headquarters and obtained an interview with Alexander Raven Thomson. He suggested him that the BUF should have started a campaign to retain those jobs for British waiters, 'more than 2,000 of whom were signing the unemployment books at the Catering Trades Employment Bureau in High Street, Soho'. To his surprise, Thomson replied that *'Italians were not aliens, the only aliens the Fascist knew were the Jews in the East End of London'*.[100] After that rebuff, Miles wrote, the waiter left the BUF. According to Miles, many of Mosley's assistant directors were foreigners, especially Germans, and dozens of Germans and Italians held official positions in the British movement.

The British fascists, in defending themselves against such accusations, insisted that their relationship with the Italians was due to friendship rather than to a surrender of British independence to Italy. A friendship between men who had in common 'a vast conception and a great ideal' raised 'no question of subordination', since fascism would one day 'unite Europe in a new civilisation'.[101] If Mosley claimed such an egalitarian alliance between fascist nations in 1933, his views appear to have changed a good deal between then and 1939, when he stated that although the 'National Socialist and Fascist creed' was universal, the British did not borrow ideas from foreign countries. They had no models abroad 'for a plain and simple reason': 'we are proud enough of our own people to believe that, once Britain is awake, our people will not follow, but will lead mankind'.[102] Only Germany retained a complementary role to that of Britain, due to the fact that it did not need an empire, since the new German believed that 'racial deterioration will result from such racial intercourse', and had 'another mission in the world rather than to elevate savages'.[103] Germany had another duty, the 'germanisation' of Eastern Europe and the elimination of the Jews.

The question of hierarchies within the hypothetical European fascist new order, which became acute during the Second World War, was nevertheless already perceptible, despite the frequent appeals to fascist solidarity, in the first half of the 1930s. In fact it had been present since the first attempts to constitute a fascist international at the congress in Montreux in December 1934, and at the three following meetings in Paris, in Amsterdam and again in Montreux, in 1935. The project of dissolving nationalistic principles into a *supra*-national vision not only appeared to be a difficult target, but also seemed to be obscured by the question of the relationship with Germany. The most striking fact was perhaps that neither the British nor the Germans joined the congresses.[104] The BUF also took up the Jewish question in October 1934. Complex reasons existed for the BUF's adoption of an anti-Semitic policy, which was not imported from the continent but based on ideas embedded in English culture and shared by members of the party well before 1934.[105] Yet in that year, the Jews had come to be regarded as the enemy also because they were anti-German. The BUF indeed did not consider the Jews merely an internal enemy, but a European anti-fascist enemy, the core of the anti-fascist international.[106] According to Roger Griffin, the participants at the CAUR congress in December 1934 did see common features that linked their ideas with the practical achievements of the Italian regime, which must have represented for them the example for a future fascist Europe.[107] It would nonetheless be misleading to think of an Anglo-German fascist alliance faced by a 'tolerant' and anti-anti-Semitic 'fascist international front', led by Italy, politically and ideologically opposed to Nazism.[108] Such an interpretation could not explain why Gravelli and most of the supposedly 'anti-Nazi' young intellectuals, who allegedly wanted to build a tolerant fascist international during the 1930s, happened to adopt anti-Semitism in 1938 and to fight on the German side in the Salò Republic. According to Ledeen, after the failure of the Four-Power Pact, feeling isolated by the British and the French, Mussolini gave a new direction to Italian foreign policy that led him to accept anti-Semitism and alliance with Germany. The 'new course' in Mussolini's foreign policy would have destroyed the projects for a fascist anti-Nazi Europe. Some critics of this view, based on both Italian and German sources, have demonstrated how Mussolini had started his search, well before 1935, for allies for a revolutionary foreign policy destined to create a new European order.[109] Moreover, it is possible to find in Gravelli's literature how Gravelli himself clearly included Germany in his plans for the fascist international before 1935. In 1933 he saluted Hitler's success, whose first acts had been to declare friendship with Italy, and destroy Marxism and a Reichstag that was 'ready to ally with France'. Indeed the only obstacle that disturbed peace in Europe, according to Gravelli, was France: 'it is France that obstructs any development of German and Italian actions, and that sought with its allies to gain from Italo-German losses'.[110] Gravelli also praised Hitler, and asserted that Italy and Germany had the same enemies and a common mission to work for the cause of civilisation. The two countries were so close that, in Gravelli's view, a German in Italy would never feel like a foreigner:

> Not only is German taught in Alto-Adige, but everywhere in Italy. It is no longer exceptional to German tourists to hear pure Italians speaking their own language all over Italy. Is it not the case that the common feeling of National Socialism and Fascism has linked as brothers the purest Italians with Italians of German language?[111]

Some of Gravelli's later anti-German articles should probably be seen as a product of fear of German leadership rather than of any anti-racist ideology. Although Gravelli did not stand, during the first half of the 1930s, for anti-Semitism, he basically saw it as resulting from the particularities of Germany's situation: 'Judaism has had in Germany a pernicious importance, especially because of its relations with international finance and with freemasonry'.[112] As Emilio Gentile has pointed out, racism, as a new ideology, was widespread among young fascists who believed in universal fascism even before 1938.[113] An interesting example was the publication in 1923 in Rome of two racist and anti-Semitic bulletins that stood for universal fascism and were thus published in different languages: *Romana* and *Veritas*. According to those bulletins, the major role of international fascism was to fight not simply against Bolshevism, but also against the 'Jewish-Masonic world organisation'.[114] Gravelli's position toward Germany became less favourable in 1935, and appeared to include the British fascists as well, perhaps because the BUF did not join the fascist international congresses and seemed to come closer to Germany. Behind all this, he could not hide what was likely to have been his real dread: 'opinions exist in Germany which seek to suggest that Berlin wants to replace Rome as the centre of Western civilisation'.[115]

As far as Anglo-Italian fascist relations are concerned, and despite Gravelli's fears, plans for a fascist Europe did not die out with the invasion of Ethiopia. The BUF built a whole campaign (the 'Mind Britain's Business') in support of Italy in Ethiopia. However, the BUF's increased closeness to Germany played a role in convincing Grandi that British Conservative Italophiles were now more useful than the BUF to the Italian cause. A CAUR mission to Britain in 1935 persuaded the Italians that the BUF would never become part of an international movement based on the 'universality of Rome'. A British CAUR committee was therefore consituted without Mosley's knowledge; its president was the Italophile Charles Petrie.[116] The *British-Italian Bulletin* attached to *L'Italia Nostra* saw the collaboration of many British Italophiles who were not BUF members.

Conclusion

Although a fascist international never came into existence, plans for it did exist. It is possible to study those plans, and ideas, not only in relation to the congresses held in 1934 and 1935, but also by investigating the relationships between fascists from different countries and studying the newspapers and books they wrote. Until 1935, the BUF not only regarded Italy as the main model, but also decided to refer to a common origin: the Roman Empire. Its ideologues and publicists distinguished between a Roman and a Teutonic form of fascism, and claimed to belong to the first. Contacts between Italian and British fascists were frequent both in Italy and in Britain. Dino Grandi, even though fears of a public scandal made him cautious, supported the BUF from the beginning. It may be that his letters to Mussolini were not always trustworthy especially when he claimed that the British parliamentary system was in crisis. Yet it is possible to show that his role in Britain was in fact in some sense revolutionary, since he did not behave simply as an ordinary ambassador. At the same time, helped by the activities of the London *Fascio*, he sought to convert the Italian community into a Fascist nation within a foreign society, and supported the creation of a British revolutionary movement within parliamentary Britain. Relationships between Italian and British fascism were however complicated by the advent of Nazi Germany, which raised the issue of the rank order of the (future) fascist countries. That problem was already perceptible before 1935, but loomed ever larger from that year onward.

Notes

1. Robert Benewick, *Political Violence and Public Order: A study of British Fascism* (London: Allen Lane, 1969), p. 134; see also Mike Cronin (ed.), *The Failure of British Fascism: The Far Right and the Fight for Political Recognition* (London and Basingstoke: Macmillan, 1996); Andrew Thorpe (ed.), *The Failure of Political Extremism in Inter-War Britain* (Exeter: University of Exeter, 1989).
2. Oswald Mosley, *My Life* (London: Nelson, 1968), p. 91.

3. Mario Isnenghi, *Intellettuali militanti e intellettuali funzionari*, now in *L'Italia del fascio* (Florence: Giunti, 1996), p. 147. See also Stein Ugelrik Larsen, Bernt Hagtvet and Jan Petter Myklebust (eds.), *Who Were the Fascists: Social Roots of European Fascism* (Oslo: Universitetsforlaget, 1980). The leading idea of this work was that fascism had been a European movement, and that it was not simply an imitation of Italian or German regimes.

4. George L. Mosse (ed.), *International Fascism: New Thoughts and New Approaches* (London: Sage Publications, 1979).

5. Nevertheless, when he published his autobiography, he still maintained his position that British government should have left Germany a free hand in Eastern Europe. They would have invaded Poland, perhaps crushed Communism fighting with Russia, and war would have never happened in Western Europe. Neither that nor the Holocaust was 'Britain's business'.

6. Robert Skidelsky, *Oswald Mosley* (London: Macmillan, 1975).

7. Richard Thurlow, *Fascism in Britain: A History, 1918–1985* (Oxford and New York: Blackwell, 1987), p. 107.

8. Paolo Nello, *Un fedele disubbidiente: Dino Grandi da palazzo Chigi al 25 luglio* (Bologna: Il Mulino, 1993), p. 228. According to both Renzo De Felice (*Mussolini il duce. I. Gli anni del consenso, 1929–1936*, Turin: Einaudi, 1974, p. 377) and H. James Burgwyn (*Grandi e il mondo teutonico: 1929–1932*, 'Storia Contemporanea', XIX (1988), 2, p. 209), Fascism always remained, in Grandi's view, 'an exclusively Italian fact'. On Grandi's diaries and memoirs (*Dino Grandi racconta l'evitabile Asse*, Milan: Jaka Book, 1984; *Il mio paese. Ricordi autobiografici*, Bologna: Il Mulino, 1985), see Luciano Casali, 'Tristi rottami di un triste passato', *Italia Contemporanea*, 1984 (155), pp. 93–9; MacGregor Knox, 'I testi "aggiustati" dei discorsi segreti di Grandi', *Passato e presente*, n. 13, 1987, pp. 98–117.

9. See Bruce Coleman, *The Conservative Party and the Frustration of the Extreme Right*, in Thorpe, *The Failure*, pp. 49–66; Carl Bridge, *Holding India to the Empire: The British Conservative Party and the 1935 Constitution* (London: Oriental University Press, 1986). For the British fascists' view, see William Joyce, *Fascism and India* (London: 1933); and, from a contemporary observer, the comments on Conservatives and India in W. A. Rudlin, *The Growth of Fascism in Great Britain* (London: 1935), p. 116.

10. Grandi to Mussolini, 28 November 1933, ASMAE, *AL*, b. 805, f. 1: 'Italia – Pubblicazioni sul fascismo'.

11. *New Notes on Fascist Corporations*, March 1932, n. 3, p. 1. Some issues of the bulletin can be found in the 'Carte Chiaramonte Bordonaro' in ASMAE, *AL*, b. 775, f. 1 (Rapporti politici – Italia), sf. 'Propaganda corporativa all'estero. Bollettino informazioni corporative'. This bulletin was also sent to libraries, universities, politicians and journalists.

12. Grandi to Mussolini, 2 May 1933, ASMAE, *AP*, *GB*, b. 6, f. 1 (Rapporti politici), sf. 3 (Situazione politica interna ed estera).

13. It is possible to find accounts of Grandi's social life in London in *L'Italia Nostra*, and Grandi's comments on such events in ACS, *CP*, *APr*, *Carte Grandi*, Fondo E. Susmel, b. 9, f. 1.

14. Stuart J. Woolf, 'British Attitudes towards Fascism, 1922–1940', in *Inghilterra e Italia nel Novecento* (Florence: La Nuova Italia, 1973), pp. 185–9; Aldo Berselli, *L'opinione pubblica inglese e l'avvento del fascismo (1919–1925)* (Milan: Angeli, 1971); Elena Fasano Guarini, 'Il 'Times' di fronte al fascismo (1919–1932)', *Rivista Storica del Socialismo*, 1965 (25), pp. 155–85.

15. Grandi to Mussolini, 22 June 1933, ACS, *CP*, *APr*, *Carte Grandi*, Fondo E. Susmel, b. 9, f. 1.

16. Grandi to Mussolini, 9 August 1933, ibid.

17. Grandi to Mussolini, 3 September 1933, *DDI*, 7, XIV, p. 150.

18. See Grandi to Mussolini, 9 March 1933, *DDI*, 7, XIII, p. 197; Grandi to Mussolini, 10 March 1933, ibid, p. 220.

19. Grandi to foreign ministry, 10 May 1933, ASMAE, *AP*, *GB*, b. 6, f. 1 (Rapporti politici), sf. 3 (Situazione politica interna ed estera); foreign ministry to embassies in Berlin, Paris, Moscow, Warsaw, and Brussels, 11 May 1933, ibid.

20. Grandi to Mussolini, 3 September 1933, *DDI*, 7, XIV, pp. 149–52.

21. Grandi to foreign ministry, 23 September 1933, ASMAE, *AP*, *GB*, b. 6, f. 1 (Rapporti politici), sf. 3 (Situazione politica interna ed estera).

22. Enrico Discoli, 'Il congresso di Bruxelles – Trade Unions e Fascismo', *L'Italia Nostra*, 4 August 1933, n. 235, p. 2.

23. 'Mosley va dedicandosi con sempre maggiore attività ad organizzazione e propaganda partito fascista inglese', Grandi to foreign ministry, 21 February 1933, ASMAE, *AP*, *GB*, b. 6, f. 1 (Rapporti politici), sf. 1 (Propaganda Mosley).

24. 'Propaganda Mosley per organizzazione partito fascista inglese', Grandi to foreign ministry, then sent to Italian embassies in Paris, Moscow, Berlin, Warsaw, Brussels, and Washington. ASMAE, *AP*, *GB*, b. 6, f. 1 (Rapporti politici), sf. 1 (Propaganda Mosley).

25. Roger Griffin, *The Nature of Fascism* (London: Pinter Publisher, 1991), p. 47; id., 'The Ugly Duckling', in Cronin, *The Failure*, pp. 144–5. The British fascist revolution would have raised from the 'values of a mythical golden age of Elizabethan England, projected into a future of modernity' (Thurlow, *Fascism in Modern Britain*, Gloucestershire: Sutton Publishing, 2000, p. 37).

26. Emilio Gentile, 'The Myth of National Regeneration in Italy: from Modernist Avant-Garde to Fascism', in *Fascist Visions: Art and Ideology in France and Italy*, edited by Matthew Affron and Mark Antliff (Princeton: Princeton University Press, 1997), p. 25.

27. 'Fascismo in Inghilterra', *Rheinish-Westfälische Zeitung*, 6 March 1933, in ASMAE, *AP*, *GB*, b. 6, f. 1 (Rapporti politici), sf. 1 (Propaganda Mosley).
28. Grandi to Suvich, 16 May 1933, *DDI*, 7, XIII, n. 615, pp. 675–7. Proof of payment to Mosley by the Italian government can be found in a letter by Suvich to Grandi, 14 February 1934, ACS, *CP*, *APr*, *Carte Grandi*, Fondo E. Susmel, b. 9, f. 1.
29. Camagna to Parini, 6 November 1933; Parini to Grandi, 15 November 1933. ASMAE, *AL*, b. 805, f. 2 'PNF – Attività propagandistica in GB', sf: 'Fascio di Londra'.
30. See Stephen Cullen, 'Political Violence: the Case of the British Union of Fascists', *Journal of Contemporary History*, 1993, 28 (2), pp. 245–67; Vindicator (pseud.), *Fascists at Olympia: a Record of Eye-Witnesses and Victims* (London: Gollancz, 1934).
31. 'Olympia had to come sooner or later. It is the real beginning of the struggle for political supremacy in Britain' (*The Blackshirt* n. 60, 15 June 1934). See also the other articles in issue n. 60: 'The truth about the Olympia disorder – Communist determination to kill Mosley', p. 1; 'Reason's triumph – Red terror smashed at Britain's biggest meeting', by A. K. Chesterton, p. 3; 'Leader's great appeal to Olympia audience – The people demand a new creed', p. 4.
32. *Movimenti fascisti esteri* (Rome: Ministero degli Affari Esteri, 1934), pp. 70–1.
33. Ibid.
34. 'Il primo convegno romano dei fascisti britannici', *L'Italia Nostra*, 15 June 1934, p. 2.
35. Grandi to Suvich, 16 May 1933, *DDI*, 7, XIII, n. 615, pp. 675–7.
36. Ibid.
37. Ibid.
38. 'Fascism and Peace', *The Blackshirt*, 17 April 1933, n. 5, p. 1.
39. 'L'internazionale fascista e la Gran Bretagna'. Regia Legazione d'Italia in Svezia to foreign ministry, 12 May 1933, ASMAE, *AP*, *GB*, b. 6, f. 1 (Rapporti politici), sf. 1 (Propaganda Mosley).
40. 'Atti Mosley'. Letter by Mosley, addressee unknown (probably the Italian embassy), 26 April 1933, ASMAE, *AL*, b. 800, f. 2 (Rapporti politici, GB, BUF).
41. 'La visita di Sir O. Mosley a Roma – Interessanti dichiarazioni sul fascismo inglese', *L'Italia Nostra*, 21 April 1934, 221, p. 2.
42. Ferri to Vitetti, 29 August 1933, ASMAE, *AL*, b. 800, f. 2 (Rapporti politici, GB, BUF).
43. See HO 144/20147. Ian Hope Dundas, 'chief of staff' of BUF, 'left England for Rome on 27/4/36 to act as liason between Italian fascists and BUF. Used

cover of *Daily Mail* correspondent' (MF674216/227); 'Un esponente del BUF a Milano', *L'Italia Nostra*, 19 January 1934, n. 259, p. 2.

44. 'Tours to Fascist countries', *The Blackshirt*, 1 April 1933, n. 4, p. 4.
45. 'Duecento insegnanti inglesi ricevuti dal Duce', *L'Italia Nostra*, 6 April 1933, n. 270.
46. 'Omaggio dei fascisti inglesi a S. E. Starace', *L'Italia Nostra*, 14 April 1933, n. 220, p.1.
47. Grandi to foreign ministry, 11 August 1933, ASMAE, *AL*, b. 800, f. 2 (Rapporti politici, GB, BUF).
48. 'Una iniziativa del GUF per lo "Scambio d'ospitalità" – Studenti italiani in Inghilterra – La visita all'ambasciatore ed al fascio', *L'Italia Nostra*, 11 August 1933, n. 236, p. 4; 'Gli universitari fascisti rendono omaggio al milite ignoto e sono passati in rivista da Sir Oswald Mosley', ibid., 18 August 1933, n. 237, p. 5.
49. 'British Union of Fascists and Italian Fascist Students in London', PRO, *HO* 144/19069 (486825/51).
50. 'Pellegrinaggio operai inglesi disoccupati', Grandi to foreign ministry, 24 October 1933, ASMAE, *AL*, b. 800, sf. 'GB. Pellegrinaggio a Roma disoccupati britannici'.
51. BUF to Italian embassy, 3 November 1933, ASMAE, *AL*, b. 800, f. 2 (Rapporti politici, GB, BUF).
52. 'Blackshirts meet Fascisti', *The Blackshirt*, 1 June 1934, n. 58, p. 9.
53. Ministero degli Esteri, *Il fascismo inglese* (Rome: 1934), p. 72; British consul in Genoa to Drummond, 20 March 1934, PRO, *FO* 371/18436, R1929/1929/22.
54. Ibid.
55. Drummond to Simon, 23 March 1934, ibid.
56. As reported by Drummond to Simon, 8 June 1934, PRO, *FO* 371/18436, R3343/1929/22.
57. British consul in Genoa to Drummond, 20 March 1934, ibid., R1929/1929/22.
58. Murray Stuart to Foreign Office, 11 September 1934, ibid., R5040/1929/22.
59. See Diana Mosley, *A Life of Contrasts: The Autobiography of Diana Mosley* (London: Hamilton, 1977); D. Pryce-Jones, *Unity Mitford. A Quest* (London: 1976); PRO, *HO* 144/19069 Metropolitan Police, Special Branch, Scotland House, 31 August 1933: 'Regarding the departure of Captain J. H. Holliman, of the British Union of Fascists, for Germany today (Thursday), he was accompanied by other members of the B.U.F. It is also understood that a member named THOMPSON, author of 'Civilisation', who is married to a German, left for Germany yesterday (31st of August). On Friday, 1st of September, a party of about 15 fascists is due to leave for Germany. Captain HOLLIMAN, who had a special uniform made for the occasion, is being

accredited as "O.C., Storm Troops". At Nuremberg the British fascists will attend a review of the Nazi troops, and will later go to Berlin'. (486825/ 53).

60. PRO, MI5, KV4/1, *The Security Service. Its Problems and Organisational Adjustments 1908–1945*, Vol. I (March 1946), Part 2. *The Nazi Threat, 1933– 1939*, (a). *The NSDAP and its Ausland Organisation*, p. 77.

61. Leonard Parish to Drummond, 20 April 1934, PRO, *FO* 371/18436, R2563/ 1929/22. The Italian foreign ministry also gave a considerable prominence to some interviews with Lloyd George, seeking to show that he believed it was time for a 'new system of government' in England (*Movimenti fascisti esteri*, p. 67).

62. Again, the Italian foreign ministry was fairly impressed by the fact that a politician already authoritative within the Labour Party became one of Mosley's closest collaborators (ibid).

63. Drummond to Simon, 23 March 1934, PRO, *FO* 371/18436, R1929/1929/22.

64. Drummond to Simon, 6 July 1934, ibid., R3879/1929/22.

65. Drummond to Simon, 8 June 1934, ibid., R3343/1929/22.

66. James Drennan, *B.U.F.: Oswald Mosley and British Fascism* (London: John Murray, 1934); Arthur Kenneth Chesterton, *Oswald Mosley: Portrait of a Leader* (London: Action Press, 1937).

67. Chesterton, *Portrait*, p. 127.

68. Italo Balbo, *Diario 1922* (Milan: Mondadori, 1932); Roberto Farinacci, *Squadrismo* (Rome: Ardita, 1933); G. A. Chiurco, *Storia della rivoluzione fascista, 1919–1922* (Florence: Vallecchi, 1929); Luigi Villari, *The Awakening of Italy: the Fascista Regeneration* (London: Methuen, 1924); id., *The Fascist Experiment* (London: Faber & Gwyer, 1926); id., *Italy* (London: Fisher, 1929).

69. Chesterton, *Portrait*, p. 108; p. 95.

70. 'Mosley! Leader of thousands!/ Hope of our manhood we proudly hail thee!/ Raise we this song of allegiance,/ For we are sworn and we shall not/ fail thee!/ Lead us! We fearlessly follow/ To conquest and freedom – or else/ to death!' ('Mosley!', *The Blackshirt*, 15 June 1934, n. 60, p. 6).

71. Thurlow, *Fascism in Modern Britain*, pp. 47–8; Thomas Linehan, *British Fascism, 1918–39. Parties, Ideology and Culture* (Manchester: Manchester University Press, 2000), p. 21.

72. Linehan, *British Fascism, 1918–39*, pp. 30–2.

73. Oswald Mosley, *The Greater Britain* (London: BUF, 1932), p. 13.

74. 'Fascismo in Inghilterra', *Rheinish-Westfälische Zeitung*, 6 March 1933, in ASMAE, *AP*, *GB*, b. 6, f. 1 (Rapporti politici), sf. 1 (Propaganda Mosley).

75. Mosley, *The Greater Britain*. My italics.

76. Mosley, *Fascism: 100 Questions Asked and Answered* (London: BUF, 1936).

77. Mosley's interest in Europe carried on even after the war, and is well documented in his writings. See in particular *My Answer* (Ramsbury: Mosley Publications, 1946); *The European Situation: the Third Force* (Ramsbury: Mosley Publications, 1950); *Automation: Problems and Solution. The Answer of European Socialism* (London: Sanctuary Press, 1956). See also chapter 23 ('The Post-War European Idea') in *My Life*, pp. 432–46, where he wrote about Europe 'as a nation'.

78. As defined by Richard Thurlow, *The Failure of British Fascism 1932–1940*, in Andrew Thorpe, *The Failure*, pp. 72–3.

79. Richard Reynell Bellamy, *We Marched with Mosley*, 4 vols., Holt, Norfolk, 1968: typescript, xeroxed copy, SUL, *Special Collections and Archives, BU Collection, Memoirs of Members of the BUF*, 5/6.

80. Ibid., p. 261.

81. *Il Fascismo inglese* (Rome: La Nuova Europa, no date, but probably 1933), p. 6.

82. Ibid., p. 7.

83. 'Fascismo in Gran Bretagna – Un'importante conquista', *L'Italia Nostra*, 19 January 1934, n. 259, p. 2.

84. 'Mary Richardson writes on – New Rome and Old', *The Blackshirt*, 28 September 1934, n. 75, p. 8.

85. *A Modern Stateman and His Work: Il Duce*, unpublished essay, SUL, *Special Collections and Archives, BU Collection, Memoirs of Members of the BUF*, 5/10/(b).

86. Ibid., p. 2.

87. F. E. Burdett, 'Giovinezza . . . Giovinezza', *The Blackshirt*, 16 November 1934, p. 8.

88. John Beckett, *After My Fashion: Twenty Post-War Years* (London: 1940): typescript, SUL, *Special Collections and Archives, BU Collection, Memoirs of Members of the BUF*, 5/1.

89. Ibid., p. 283.

90. Ibid., p. 345 (strikethrough in original).

91. Ibid., p. 349 (strikethrough in original). After the Ethiopian war both Beckett and Joyce left the BUF. Beckett launched a National Socialist League, close to Germany and strongly anti-Semitic. See Gisela C. Lebzelter, *Political Anti-Semitism in England, 1918–1939* (London and Basingstoke: Macmillan Press, 1978), p. 98; Francis Beckett, 'The Rebel Who Lost His Cause', *History Today*, 1994, 44 (5), pp. 36–42. On Joyce, see Colin Holmes, '"Germany Calling". Lord Haw-Haw's Treason', in *Twentieth Century British History*, 1994, 5 (1), pp. 118–21.

92. 'Anti-Semitism is no issue of Fascism, and is unknown to Fascism outside the Teutonic races. In Germany, anti-Semitism is a symptom, not of Fascism, but of Germany' ('Editorial', *The Blackshirt*, n. 7, 16 May 1933, p. 2).

93. *The Blackshirt*, 1 April 1933, n. 4, p. 1. However, the British fascists always underlined that anti-Jewish propaganda was not merely a German fault, for 'it must also be remembered that in Germany, Jews are conspicuously associated at one extreme with the Communist and the Socialist movements, and at the other extreme with International Finance'. According to *The Blackshirt*, the Germans should have distinguished those German Jews 'who have proved in the past their love of Germany and not their love of Moscow' (ibid).

94. *Movimenti fascisti esteri*, p. 64.

95. Ibid., p. 65.

96. Drennan, *BUF*, p. 220.

97. Ibid., p. 16.

98. *The Blackshirt*, March 1933, p. 2.

99. A. C. Miles, *Mosley in Motley* (London: 1937), p. 5.

100. Ibid., p. 6. Italics in original.

101. 'Visit to Rome – The "immense majesty" of Fascist peace', *The Blackshirt*, 1 May 1933, n. 6, p. 1. R. Gordon-Canning so described the imagined future Europe: 'Before you can build a nation, you must have villages, districts and towns, each with their local patriotisms. Out of these one welds a unified country where these local patriotisms give way before the greater patriotism to the unified country. Similarly, before building a united Europe or an united world, it is necessary to create a series of nations, each of whose basis are sound and well-balanced from the economic point of view' ('The authority of Fascism – Blackshirts principles that lead to world peace', *The Blackshirt*, 29 June 1934, n. 62, p. 2).

102. Mosley, *Tomorrow We Live* (London: BUF, 1939), p. 2.

103. Ibid., p. 72.

104. Italy, Holland, Switzerland, Ireland, Denmark, Norway and France did. See Gisella Longo, 'I tentativi per la costituzione di un'internazionale fascista: gli incontri di Amsterdam e di Montreux attraverso i verbali delle riunioni', *Storia Contemporanea*, XXVII (1996), 3, pp. 475–570.

105. Linehan, *British Fascism 1918–39*, pp. 187–200. See also Tony Kushner and Ken Lunn, *Traditions of Intolerance: Historical Perspectives on Fascism and Race Discourse in British Society* (Manchester: Manchester University Press, 1989); Lebzelter, *Political Anti-Semitism in England*; id, 'Anti-Semitism: a Focal Point for the British Radical Right', in *Nationalist and Racialist Movements in Britain and Germany before 1914*, edited by Paul Kennedy and Anthony Nicholls (London and Basingstoke: MacMillan, 1981), pp. 88–105.

106. Only in 1939 did British fascism accept the German biological explanations that the Jew was a foreigner, simply because he 'comes from the Orient and

physically, mentally and spiritually, is more alien to us than any Western nation' (Mosley, *Tomorrow*, p. 65).

107. Roger Griffin (ed.), *International Fascism: Theories, Causes and the New Consensus* (London: Arnold, 1998), p. 2.

108. As Michael Ledeen has suggested in *Universal Fascism: The Theory and Practice of the Fascist International, 1928–1936* (New York: Howard Fertig, 1972). It is possible to find a similar approach in a recent study on Gravelli, Davide Sabatini, *L'internazionale di Mussolini. La diffusione del fascismo in Europa nel progetto politico di Asvero Gravelli* (Tusculum: Grottaferrata, 1997).

109. Giorgio Rumi, *Alle origini della politica estera fascista (1918–1923)* (Bari: Laterza, 1968); Denis Mack Smith, *Mussolini's Roman Empire* (New York: Penguin, 1977); MacGregor Knox, 'In the Duce's Defence. Unconvincing Efforts to Blame the British for Mussolini's Alliance with Hitler', in *The Times Literary Supplement*, 26 February 1999, pp. 3–4; Knox, *Il fascismo e la politica estera italiana*, in Richard J.B. Bosworth and Sergio Romano (eds.), *La politica estera italiana (1860–1985)* (Bologna: Il Mulino, 1991); Lutz Klinkhammer and Enzo Collotti, *Il fascismo e l'Italia in guerra. Una conversazione fra storia e storiografia*, (Rome: Ediesse, 1996); H. James Burgwyn, *Italian Foreign Policy in the Interwar Period 1918–1940* (Westport: Praeger, 1997).

110. Asvero Gravelli, *Europa, con noi!* (Rome: Nuova Europa, no date, but 1933).

111. Ibid., p. 79.

112. Ibid., p. 138.

113. Emilio Gentile, *La Grande Italia. Ascesa e declino del mito della nazione nel ventesimo secolo* (Milan: Mondadori, 1997), p. 204.

114. 'Profils et grimaces', *Veritas. Bulletin hebdomadaire de la défense social*, IX (1932), n. 1–2, p. 3.

115. Gravelli, *Panfascismo* (Rome: Nuova Europa, 1935), p. 183. During the Second World War, the same fear brought Pellizzi back from the idea of European fascism to the concept of Nation: it was necessary, at that point, to fight for 'Italy's spiritual supremacy over Germany', 'otherwise even victory is useless and harmful for us' (quoted in Gentile, *La Grande Italia*, p. 208).

116. Note by the ministry of press and propaganda on the CAUR's mission to Britain of 12–26 June 1935, 6 August 1935, ACS, *MinCulPop, DGSP, AG*, b. 118.

–3–

Toward a Corporativist Community: the *Fasci Italiani all'Estero* in Britain, 1935–37

An unsigned, hand-written note of 1935, now in the *Gabinetto* files of the Italian foreign ministry, anticipated Italy's plans for Mediterranean domination, and for a future alliance with Germany:

> From now onward Britain will always be our most stubborn and dangerous enemy, because we challenge its supremacy over the Mediterranean . . . They are resolute in preparing to wage war on us. Therefore we must not trust their friendly proposals . . . On the other hand, Italy will never be great and powerful unless it is free in its own sea . . . Consequently we should, if possible, take the opportunity at this favourable moment . . . to provoke the British until they declare war on us . . . and to expel them from the Mediterranean and its adjacent territories. In order to do this, we first need to neutralise France, and I believe this can be done, considering its fear of Germany, only by offering our alliance and by explaining that it is also in its interest to humble British arrogance and expel the British from the Mediterranean, which is also a French sea. In case . . . France wanted to remain allied with Britain and our enemy, we must withdraw from the League of Nations and ally with Germany. It is urgent that we approach Germany so that we do not remain isolated in case of an Anglo-French coalition against us. The present unfair sanctions, wanted by Britain, demonstrate all this even more.[1]

The plan consisted of three main phases: preparation for war with Britain, 'the real enemy';[2] an attempt to turn France against Britain; and, if this did not work, alliance with Germany and withdrawal from Geneva. Some histories of Anglo-Italian relations during the Fascist period have suggested a different interpretation, arguing that Italian foreign policy until the outbreak of the Second World War was pro-French and pro-British, and that it became pro-German only at the very end, as a result of British pressure on Mussolini.[3] The propaganda and policy of the *Fasci italiani all'estero* in Britain and their relationship with both the Italian government and the London embassy can contribute to the resolution of this controversy.

The Ethiopian War and the conquest of empire had a major impact on the activity of the Italian *Fasci* in Britain. It determined a change in the structure and also in the role of the *Fasci* Abroad, which reflected the main directions of Italian foreign policy and of Anglo-Italian relations in those crucial years. This chapter attempts to link three main aspects: diplomatic relations between Rome and the London embassy, the creation of an anti-British tradition in Italy and the activity of the *Fasci* in Britain. These aspects seem to be tightly bound together: the new image of Britain in Fascist Italy reflected – and at the same time influenced – Mussolini's decisions in foreign policy, and the activity of the *Fasci* Abroad, especially in Britain (a country that both Rome and the London embassy already appeared to consider as the enemy), expressed those policies. In their attempt to achieve a further transformation of the Italian community, the activity of the *Fasci* thus contributed to the development of Anglo-Italian relations.

Italian Fascism and Britain during the Ethiopian War

As described in Chapter 1, until the end of 1934 the *Fasci* in Britain did not engage in direct anti-British propaganda, but focused on the fascistisation of the Italian communities as well as on the creation of a relationship with the British Union of Fascists. Even the problem of Malta provoked only one article of protest against British policy in *L'Italia Nostra*, and even then it was Lord Gerald Strickland's governorship that the newspaper attacked, rather than the policy of the British government.[4] The links with the BUF, although very numerous during those years, rarely appeared in the newspaper, which dealt with foreign policy issues only to extol the Duce's diplomatic achievements and to create the myth of Mussolini as Europe's principal leader.

At the beginning of 1935 *L'Italia Nostra* was still celebrating the Four-Power Pact of 1932 as the basis of the European balance of power. It supported an agreement between the Anglo-French-Italian triangle and Germany, through the elimination of the alleged 'injustice of Versailles' that purportedly condemned Germany to a permanent inferiority. It was now Germany that had to make the moves toward peace indicated by the Duce.[5] The London *Fascio* thought that Germany was a threat to European stability, although it usually blamed the British government for this, arguing that British politicians lacked Mussolini's grasp of the situation and had failed to adopt firm policies toward Germany. Grandi also appeared to share this opinion, drawing a parallel with British indecision in 1914; and it was precisely that indecision, he argued, which brought Europe into war. Hitler, as well as the Kaiser in 1914, expressed the passions rather than the interests of the German people, while John Simon represented the lazy and superficial optimism of a ruling class in decay.[6]

Nevertheless, at least until the Stresa conference of April 1935, *L'Italia Nostra* continued to warn that Germany was a real danger for Europe. The symbol and promise for the future was the Duce, who arrived at Stresa, 'fearless pilot', on a

Savoia-Marchetti seaplane and made a 'bold landing' on the lake.[7] However, the national newspaper of the *Fasci* Abroad, *Il Legionario*, suggested that uncertainty still dominated Anglo-Italian relations. First of all, despite Mussolini's spectacular landing, peace depended mostly on those who had not gone to Stresa, namely Germany and the Soviet Union, and secondly, the three powers who met at Stresa did not share the same views. It was especially important to note, continued the journal, the persistent and typical British inclination to remain isolated, which made collaboration difficult.[8]

The attitude of the *Fasci Italiani all'Estero* in general and of the *Fasci* in Britain in particular changed sharply from neutral to anti-British between June and July 1935. The sudden change might suggest that a decision had been taken at the general secretariat in Rome, and followed by the *Fasci* in Britain. However, anti-British articles appeared in *L'Italia Nostra* one week before those in *Il Legionario*, and the London paper soon became far more anti-British than *Il Legionario*.[9] This might seem surprising in a newspaper that had always avoided criticism of British politics and society that might have created problems for Italians living in Britain. Grandi suggested the need for a shift at the beginning of June, when he made it clear to Suvich that British policies were likely to change in response to two major developments soon expected from the Italian government: attack on Ethiopia and withdrawal from the League of Nations.[10]

The ministry prepared for these developments by organising pro-Italian propaganda. The most important channels were: a section of the ministry of propaganda in Rome under Luigi Villari; a group of Italians in London under Camillo Pellizzi, president, and Luigi Gario, secretary, of the Dante Alighieri Society; the Italian embassy in London; the Stefani News Agency; the British Union of Fascists; and private circulation of propaganda material. According to MI5, Villari played an important role in the dissemination of propaganda in Britain, both by post and by English-language broadcasts from Rome. He corresponded regularly with a number of English people who were 'prominent in literary and political circles' and wrote articles in British right-wing periodicals. The Dante Alighieri Society also distributed material in English. MI5 acknowledged that Italian couriers were arriving from Rome at the embassy in London at frequent intervals, carrying 'large suitcases or parcels' which they apparently delivered to Pellizzi.[11] Generally, Villari sent propaganda material from Italy and Gario selected and edited it. If the embassy approved it, the material was printed and dispatched within Britain. Ultimate control was in Grandi's hands.[12]

The anti-British propaganda of the London *Fascio* reflected the contemporary production of massive quantities of anti-British books, pamphlets and newspaper articles in Italy.[13] At the same time, the Fascists in Britain claimed to have a particularly deep knowledge and understanding of the British, since they lived among them. 'Everybody now attacks Britain', *L'Italia Nostra* acknowledged in

July 1935; although it was impossible to expect 'absolutely upright conduct' from Britain, those in Italy who did not know the British well 'used to repeat the usual commonplace which accused the British of hypocrisy'.

> We . . . know well that what appears abroad as hypocrisy and deliberate incomprehension is in fact caused by the peculiar intellectual haziness which is the main aspect of the British mentality . . . The lack of rational . . . coherence means that the Anglo-Saxons, almost in good faith, are not exactly aware of their own political incoherence . . . The lack of sense of criticism and of self-criticism means that they regularly confuse their own convenience with the universal morality, and that they believe themselves to be invested with some pedagogic mission toward the rest of the world, without realising that the rest of the world has had enough of it; and eventually that they carry with fatuous ease the burden of such a fraught conscience which would bend any other people under the load.[14]

L'Italia Nostra became more and more bitterly anti-British toward the end of July and started considering itself as a Fascist newspaper published in an enemy country. It now insisted on the typical themes of Italian anti-British propaganda, attacking the 'cunning financiers of the City' who were at the same time 'greedy arms dealers'. Britain was the *'paese bottegaio'* already described by Napoleon, a country ready to conduct business even with the enemy, because the British, by nature, had no scruples when it came to money. The newspaper also emphasised the alleged racial and cultural inferiority of the Ethiopians. It put forward the typically colonialist argument according to which only the Europeans could civilise Africa, and went on to joke about the absence of hygiene among the native population, arguing that defence of a non-European, non-white country was an indication of the deterioration of the British race as well.[15]

It was exactly this allegedly obsolete British mentality, which was due to Britain's spiritual decadence, that hindered a real understanding of what Fascism was, and therefore prevented any possibility of a friendly Anglo-Italian relationship. That conviction was not simply expounded by the *Fascio* in London but seemed to be shared by Italian diplomats as well. The Italian delegation at Geneva wrote in its report to the Italian foreign ministry during the summer 1935: 'Stationary for thirteen years, this mentality still refers to Mussolini, to the Fascist regime and to Italy as divisions of one of the usual political doctrines, blind in front of the reincarnation of this glorious race into a new civilisation due to the work of the Duce.'[16] According to Grandi, the Foreign Office under-secretary Sir Robert Vansittart was a remarkable example of such a mentality, since he was still linked to pre-fascist conceptions. At this stage Grandi seemed very pessimistic about the state of Anglo-Italian relations. He worried that sanctions against Italy were a trial run for an Anglo-French alliance and would be used in the near future against

Germany if they proved successful against Italy. His words to Mussolini in the summer of 1935 were particularly revealing of his feelings during the months of the Ethiopian War and reflected the way in which anti-British propaganda was describing the military campaign, as a war between Italy and Britain:

> The criminal British policy against us has transformed our African military undertaking into a historical revolutionary conflict between Fascist Italy and the democratic reaction personified by the British imperial despotism . . . You will give Italy an Empire in Africa, but You will first give the Italians something that is as precious as an Empire: the consciousness of their final liberty against the last myth the new Fascist generation had not yet destroyed: . . . the idea that Italy's greatness could not become reality without Britain's permission. You have challenged the dragon, and You are winning. And the world will acknowledge that, before conquering the Ethiopian Empire, You have won and subdued the British Empire.[17]

According to his letters to Mussolini, Grandi was working on the front line of a war that was not only fought on the Tigrai but on the river Thames.[18] The embassy was no longer a headquarters of diplomacy, but *'un ufficio di Stato Maggiore di un esercito in guerra'*.[19] The Italians were besieged by a hostile population, and the embassy was working day and night to contribute to the work done in Rome. In November 1935 Grandi reported in his diary a meeting with Mussolini in Rome, where the Duce gave him the following instructions:

> return to London and consider yourself as if you were in a concentration camp, as the representative of a besieged nation. Avoid contacts. Do not go to the Foreign Office unless requested. You must give the plain impression that at the moment we are not looking for encounters or negotiations.[20]

Grandi continuously received foreign journalists at the embassy, inventing news when he had not received any and relying on help from the British Union of Fascists when he needed to counteract anti-Italian demonstrations.[21] His perception of the Ethiopian War as a war between the Italian and British empires seemed to have influenced his diplomatic work, which, in contrast to his own account in his memoirs,[22] was not focused on finding an agreement with the British establishment but rather on fighting on until Britain was defeated. His attitude was of course dictated from Rome, where the regime had unleashed a fierce anti-British campaign and whence Mussolini supplied him regularly with directives. In particular, during the second week of April 1936 the Duce instructed his embassies in London, Paris and Berlin on how to act at a local level, since the situation had reached crisis point, with a dramatic increase in anti-British feeling among the Italian masses[23] and Italian troops on their triumphal march to Addis Ababa:

A deep hatred against Britain has spread among the masses of the Italian people. The tension is huge . . . The British regime has within itself the solution of the problem: Eden's resignation. We must suggest this way out to our friends . . . Within ten days we shall be at Dessiè: 200 kilometres from Addis Ababa. Our army is untouched: we have exactly 400,000 men available in the heart of Africa . . . Do spread the rumour that we have built submarines and aircraft more than was previously announced. This will give them food for thought. We are now launched and we shall overthrow whoever will attempt to stop us, either by force or diplomacy.[24]

Mussolini likewise ordered the ambassador in Paris, Vittorio Cerruti, to bluff about Italian forces in East Africa: he was to inform the French that the Italian army was untouched, that the air force would become in a few weeks the 'first in Europe' and that Italy possessed 'an impressive fleet of submarines'. However, Mussolini did not seem to consider France as a serious enemy; fundamentally, Cerruti's lies to the French were aimed at convincing Paris to dissociate itself from London.[25]

Mussolini made a last attempt to cow the French a week later, when he informed the Paris embassy that Pompeo Aloisi, head of the *Gabinetto* of the foreign ministry, was leaving for Geneva where he was willing to accept negotiations with the Negus, and even to tolerate a League observer. Yet he added: 'this is for the procedure. As to the facts, I believe that we shall not achieve any result, because no one, and therefore not even the League supporters, is able to square the circle'. After that, Italian troops would arrive at Dessiè, which was clearly 'a stage toward Addis Ababa', another event that was likely to 'exasperate the British'. At that point the British might propose an escalation of sanctions, after which 'Italy will leave the League of Nations and prepare for *any* war, while concluding the Ethiopian one'. The main line of action toward the French was therefore to spread panic about a war allegedly wanted by Britain and of a possible alliance between Italy and Germany, in order to achieve an end to sanctions.[26]

On 13 April a number of telegrams from Mussolini arrived on Grandi's desk at the embassy. No negotiation was requested there and expectations of an imminent war with Britain did not seem far from reality:

For your knowledge for the week starting tomorrow, which will be important:
1) considering the Anglo-French attitude, we shall not sign the pro-Locarno letter nor shall we participate in the [Locarno] staff talks;
2) Aloisi will go to Geneva but the negative chances are 98, the positive ones are 2;
3) to any aggravation of sanctions we shall respond by withdrawing from the League of Nations;
4) we are ready to gamble everything. Accordingly, your activity must intensify to the highest level as indicated in my previous telegram, namely to reassure our conservative friends, to stir up the anti-sanctionists and disseminate alarm against Eden's policy: he has barked too much to give up biting, but to bite means war in the Mediterranean and therefore in Europe.[27]

Although the 'key word' was to 'calm down' nationalist and imperialist elements, Mussolini told Grandi to 'disseminate panic about an imminent Mediterranean war among the *gregge pacifondaio*'. In the meantime, the second telegram concluded, 'we will have arrived at Dessiè, the last stage but one'.[28]

A telegram to the Berlin embassy on the same day also indicated the intention of leaving the League of Nations:

To direct Your Excellency's activity in the next few days:
1) Italy has not sent and will not send the pro-Locarno letter to Belgium and France;
2) Italy will be absent at the conversations between the general staff;
3) Italy will send its delegate to Geneva in relation to the Ethiopian question, without any illusions;
4) once the conciliation attempt has failed . . ., if they vote for any escalation of sanctions, they will provoke Italy's withdrawal from the League of Nations.[29]

Mussolini also intimated to the German embassy that war was likely in the Mediterranean. That step suggested that he was not merely bluffing to divide the French from the British or to create panic among pro-sanctionists: 'to military sanctions – such as the closure of the Suez Canal – Italy will respond with total war, in the air, in the sea and on the ground'. Finally, Mussolini suggested that the League's hostility to Italy was at the same time an attack on the ideological foundations of Nazism as well as those of Fascism: 'During this week I shall study carefully the attitude of German official and non-official spheres, to which it must now be evident that the anti-Italian action is dominated by elements hostile to Fascism as well as to Nazism.'[30]

Ideas of a war against Britain gave rise to dreams of a renewed Roman Empire in Italian publications and in *L'Italia Nostra*, which printed articles on the Roman conquest and colonisation of the British isles, while Italian institutions in London organised lectures on the topic. Ironically, the Mazzini and Garibaldi Society in particular, which had its roots in Anglo-Italian friendship during the Risorgimento, increasingly became a focus for anti-British propaganda. In April 1936 it hosted a lecture by Professor Franzero, who spoke on 'When Britain was a Roman province' at a meeting chaired by the Fascist publisher Edoardo Ercoli. Many young Italians from the youth organisations and the *Piccole Italiane* were present. The orator reminded his audience of the superiority of the Roman Empire over all modern imitators and evoked the 'eternity of ancient Rome while the legions of the new Rome were entering . . . into the towns of the African land', which was to become a new province of Mussolini's Rome.[31] The Dante Alighieri Society likewise became a channel for anti-British propaganda, both as a cover for the 'Centro P. (propaganda)' of the London embassy and for pro-Italian publications in the English language.[32]

The showing of films continued to be a popular aspect of Italian propaganda. From 1935 onward, instead of celebrating the near past, Fascist cinema aimed at building a monument to the present as rooted in the 'millenary history of Italy'. The new mobilisation of intellectuals involved film production as well, and the representation of war became 'the real masterpiece'.[33] From May 1936 Grandi received the new 'movies of Victory': 'Adunata 5 e 9 maggio a Roma', 'Sulle orme dei nostri pionieri', 'Con la colonna Starace a Gondar e al Tana', 'Strade romane in AO', 'Atrocità abissine', 'Tutta la nazione mobilitata', and 'Il cammino degli eroi'. Some of them were in Italian, some in English.[34]

The London 'Trench'

During the Ethiopian War, London was in Grandi's parlance both Italy's most dangerous 'trench' and the headquarters of the enemy. London was also the main centre of Italian resistance to sanctions between 1935 and 1936 and the symbol of Italian power in 1937, when the embassy and the *Fascio* proudly witnessed the emergence of a miniature corporative state in the capital. The resistance was organised at every level of society: from schools to churches, from catering workers to university professors, from the ambassador to the organ-grinders. It fascistised the community and radicalised the *Fasci* in Britain in the way that had been suggested by revolutionary fascists such as Pellizzi and Bastianini, and drew together both revolutionaries and moderates such as Grandi and Parini. It also demonstrated how important the role of summer camps and youth organisations had been, now that the fatherland needed the Italians from abroad. The organisation of volunteers from abroad was the practical realisation of the theory of the *Fasci* Abroad as an aristocracy ready to give their lives for the fatherland when the latter was in danger.

The word 'soldiers' indicated not only the volunteers who went to Ethiopia under the leadership of Parini. According to *Il Legionario*, whose insistence on the revolutionary mission and export of the ideals of the *Fasci* Abroad increased markedly from mid-1935, Italian women who lived abroad were also mobilised for the war. The women's section of the Berlin *Fascio* sent to the newspaper the 'ten commandments of the Italian woman abroad' as a contribution to anti-sanctionist propaganda:

1) . . . a woman who, in public, hearing the hymns of the Fatherland, does not join the men by clapping her hands, may arouse the suspicion that her heart does not beat . . . 6) after two months of war, let us examine our consciences: against the offer of life made by thousands of men, how much have we given? . . . 8) a woman must be an apostle of faith and propaganda, must read the newspapers and be informed about the events in order to challenge false information which could damage the Italian cause . . . 10) any

woman who, in time of war, does nothing for the war, is a deserter, whose guilt is even greater because of the certain impunity.[35]

Teachers in Italian schools were also treated as soldiers; Parini addressed a mobilisation circular to them before his departure for the war. This meant in particular the mobilisation of teachers who lived in the countries which imposed sanctions, and if they did not fulfil their duty they were to be considered traitors and deserters: 'The school must become a *cittadella* of the spiritual resistance of the Italians abroad . . . Teachers . . . are mobilised from today and I shall consider any weakness, negligence or absence as a real treason, which I shall punish in an exemplary way.'[36]

In October 1935 the *Istituto Italiano di Cultura* moved to a luxurious building in one of the richest areas of London, Kensington Park. It was also organised as a school and included a library and a refectory. Classrooms were large and newly furbished; the programmes covered courses from primary-school to high-school level; and buses brought students from home to school and back. Among the first students to register at this school were Franco and Simonetta Grandi, the children of the ambassador.[37] This building, clearly different from the traditional buildings of 'little Italy', soon became one of the symbols of the Italian empire in London. An album of Italian pictures at the National Gallery was displayed in the school, symbolically representing Italian primacy in the greatest of Britain's art collections.[38] According to a British Intelligence report of 1937, the Institute had two main purposes: maintaining the *italianità* of children while 'fitting them to obtain a good position in this country' and preparing them for both Italian and British universities.[39]

Schools thus became centres of imperialist propaganda, as well as of open anti-British agitation. Not only were teachers directed by Parini and books chosen from Rome, but students' homework and other initiatives were also decided by the *Direzione Generale degli Italiani all'Estero*. During the 1936 celebrations of the *Natale di Roma*, students in every Italian school in London participated in a competition, organised again by the *Direzione Generale* in Rome, for the best essay on the topic 'Illustrate the sacrosanct right of Italy to its colonial expansion'. For several weeks the newspaper published the students' essays, carrying the names of the authors as well as their schools. Most essays concentrated on Britain's envy at Italy's civilising mission, a legacy of the Roman Empire, or on the need of the Italian population for land as opposed to Britain's fear of Italian expansion.[40] The idea that 'we are here because there is no space in Italy' led to the expectation that 'many, almost all the Italians abroad will move to East Africa to work there'.[41] Shortly afterwards, another competition asked for a sentence explaining 'Why the territories of the Empire must be loved and defended as those of the Fatherland'. The main reasons the children gave were: (1) they are part of our fatherland; (2) our soldiers are buried there; (3) Italian families will live there.[42]

The expectation that 'many Italians will live there' was probably shared by many working-class emigrants, who envisaged a concrete prospect of returning to their country – to its new colony – in order to live a better life there.[43] This idea probably seemed stronger than the dream of empire itself, although the latter did appear to play a role, at least in Britain, in the creation of a new identity for the Italian community in opposition to the host country. Many articles in the Italian newspaper in Britain claimed that the status of the emigrant was to change because of the empire: from being exploited by other countries to becoming exploiters themselves, directors and supervisors of African workers in their own colony.[44]

Once Italy had conquered Ethiopia, the attitude of the Italians abroad to conquest and to the future enterprises of the regime had to become one of total commitment. Practical help from the emigrants began as early as the end of 1935, when Italians who lived in Madrid started to collect money for the war. The money was raised in pesetas, which could be used to purchase from Spanish sources materials for the war, which Italy might need. Shortly afterwards, the initiative was extended to other countries (although this resulted in difficulties in Britain because it was a country committed to sanctions) thanks to the *Fasci* Abroad, which, starting from Berlin, organised it with the help of Italian embassies.[45]

The Ethiopian War had an impact not only on Italian schools but also on summer camps. During the summers of 1935 and 1936 in particular, the newspaper published articles about the camps and about the war on the same pages. The Italian word *colonia* denoted both: *colonia estiva* and *colonia italiana in Africa*. New summer camps opened in 1935 for the children of Italians abroad: at Tirrenia for the *Piccole Italiane* and at Alpe del Vicerè for the *Balilla*, who also continued to go to the summer camp opened in 1934 at Cattolica, the one most celebrated by the regime. Parini organised the camps in a new 'autarchic' way: all products consumed at Alpe del Vicerè were produced by Italians abroad. For example, emigrants from Brasil provided coffee and those who lived in Argentina provided wheat and jam. A factory near Rome, especially built for the Italian *Fasci* Abroad, provided the furniture for the buildings. At Cattolica, a *casa colonica* behind the buildings of the camp cultivated all the products consumed by the children.[46] Victoria Station in London became the meeting point for the departure both of children to summer camps and of volunteers for Ethiopia.[47]

Finally (at least in theory) these pioneers, who had been practising their duty since the time they were children through summer camps and youth organisations, had the chance to demonstrate their loyalty to the fatherland in a real war. The centralisation Parini had imposed on the *Fasci* since 1928, which seemed to clash with the intransigent and voluntaristic concept of the first *Fasci*, revealed during the Ethiopian War that the original role of the *Fasci* was not over and that their revolutionary aspect in fact had never ceased to exist.[48] Articles by Parini in *L'Italia Nostra* no longer reminded the Italians abroad of their duties toward host countries, as they did at the beginning of the 1930s. The emigrants were now purely Italian citizens, since the 'present times' were characterised by conflict and sacrifice and Italians were gathering everywhere, 'as an aristocracy', with their volunteers. He now told them that Italy was too small, but was becoming larger since Mussolini had restored for them, as an 'immeasurable treasure', 'the greatest pride of the greatest Italy'.[49]

The *Fasci* in Britain insisted during the war on the universal mission of Italian Fascism. They implicitly suggested that if the conquest of an Italian empire meant the beginning of a new European order, Rome was to become the centre of that new order. The article by Parini mentioned above was followed by one by Pellizzi on the universal contribution of Italy to history. A few pages later, an article on Italy in Ethiopia was signed by Guido Piovene, one of the most distinguished Italian intellectuals living in London, who had, significantly, begun writing for *L'Italia Nostra* in 1935.[50]

The primacy of Rome, it was argued, stood in contrast to the inefficiency and corruption of Geneva; among the fifty-two countries that had imposed sanctions, Britain was the most hated. While Italy's colonisation in Africa was due to sentimental reasons of prestige and civilisation, Britain's colonisation was only based on economic motives. A frequent theme in Italian propaganda was that no great men had appeared in British government for a long time; on the contrary, women were increasingly taking part in politics and had begun to dominate a country that had once been dominated by soldiers, adventurers and courageous merchants.[51] At the beginning of 1936 Pellizzi attacked the idea that Geneva, behind which stood London, could claim a role as a new international tribunal:

> Now, it is not possible to create a new universal legal system without Rome, against Rome. Without Rome or against Rome only the happy compromises of the Common Law can be created, which are longlasting and efficient only in their own island. Outside the island, . . . these compromises no longer exist. Even in Scotland the Roman Law triumphs; from Louisiana to Argentina, from the North to the South of Europe, it still remains the most universal existing legal system.[52]

The image of France in the Italian press was generally that of a bourgeois, corrupt and decadent country (this was demonstrated also by the high number of Italian anti-Fascists who found refuge there), neither feared nor admired.[53] On the contrary, the British Empire remained a model to be admired and therefore hated. This created at the same time a sense of inferiority, wounded pride and a desire for revenge.[54] The number of anti-British books published during 1935–6 has no equal in respect to France or to any other country.

L'Italia Nostra concentrated on issues in the life of community, claiming to defend the rights of Italians. The 'traditional friendship', according to *L'Italia*

Nostra, had died forever in October 1935. During that month a group of British waiters gathered in a club in Soho and sent a petition to the Labour Exchange asking for sanctions against Italy to start in London, by giving those jobs that Italian waiters held in restaurants and hotels all over Britain to unemployed British waiters. That hostile act not only confirmed Grandi's impression that London was the most dangerous 'trench', but also indicated the increasing isolation of the Italian community, which risked sanctions although its members lived outside Italy. If in 1936, and even more in 1937, that isolationism was to become the basis for a corporativist community, the Fascist newspaper had already begun to establish the basis of such a stance in 1935, by seeking to create anti-British resentment among the Italians in Britain. When the present crisis ended, *L'Italia Nostra* warned, the British could, if this suited them, rediscover the 'traditional friendship': until then the Italians had to be vigilant and 'keep their nerves under control'. They had to remember that they were hated because they were feared:

> It is fair that we Italians who live in this country . . ., who have refined the habits of these people, by teaching them how to eat decently in decent premises, and have replaced their old, dark and filthy inns with modern hotels provided with the refinements of continental civilisation, it is fair that we . . . express our permanent indifference in front of the foolish show of mean and impotent envy by those who have never been and will never be able to take our place. They hate us because they envy us, they envy us because we are strong, and because we are strong they fear us.[55]

The English waiters who protested were simply a 'gang of unemployed', who deceived themselves by thinking they would 'be able to replace our fellow-countrymen in an activity which requires skills the English have never demonstrated they possess'. For the first time, the newspaper published advertisements such as 'smoke Italian tobacco', 'one glass of Italian wine is worth ten glasses of beer' and 'do prefer Italian tea-shops'.[56]

At the beginning of December the 'collection of gold' (although more money than gold was actually collected) began, apparently assuming a 'totalitarian rhythm' especially from the second week onward. Grandi's wife Antonietta contributed to the creation of the myth of the ambassador as a sort of *duce* of the Italians in London. As the queen had done in Italy, she made an example for Italian women by donating one of her most precious gold possessions to the *Fascio*.[57] Lists of donors with names and surnames were published in the newspaper every week, to celebrate the discipline, loyalty and sense of sacrifice of the community. Offers of gold in every British town were also reported in the newspaper every week. Italians who had apparently integrated into British society and lost contact with Italy appeared to have come back: the newspaper quadrupled its circulation.[58] The number of distinguished contributors also increased, including university professors and well-known intellectuals as well as bankers and scientists.[59] This reflected an increase in support from British Italophiles, some of whom were well known in British society and began contributing to the British version of *L'Italia Nostra*, the *British-Italian Bulletin*. In January 1936 the representatives of the *Fasci* from all over the country met Grandi in London to deliver their communities' gold.[60]

The transformation of the *Club Cooperativo* into a Fascist club, which began in 1932, culminated in 1936, when the massive Italian propaganda effort was followed by successes in the war.[61] At a meeting in April 1936 to change the presidency of the Club, most members present wore black shirts. The same spirit pervaded the Catholic churches; at St Peter in Clerkenwell the Dominican priest Carlo Adelaide, himself the brother of a priest who had fallen as a martyr in Ethiopia, held evening prayers and sermons for the 'liberation' of Ethiopia by Italian troops.[62] The same happened in other societies, which seemed to become societies representing the communities as a whole rather than simply the members. This was evident for example during the '*veglia degli alpini*', described for the first time as a feast day of the whole community, and at the same time as a fascistised day, since the songs most often sung included not only the traditional *Mazzolin di fiori* but also *Giovinezza*.[63] A new song was added, the imperialist *Faccetta nera*, with words and music printed in *L'Italia Nostra*.[64]

From May 1936, the few Italians who had refused to take part in that collective imperialistic dream had a first opportunity, since the time of *Il Comento*, to contribute to a local anti-Fascist newspaper. On 9 May, the day of Mussolini's proclamation of the empire from Piazza Venezia, the first issue of *New Times and Ethiopia News* came to light in London, founded by Silvio Corio, an Italian anarchist who had lived there since 1901, and his companion, the well-known former suffragette Sylvia Pankhurst. However, apart from Corio, who signed his articles under the pseudonyms of 'Crastinus' and 'Luce', no signatures of Italians who lived in London appeared in the newspaper between that year and 1939. Although some articles by Italian *fuorusciti* were published, for example by Giuseppe Emanuele Modigliani and Carlo Rosselli from France, and Gaetano Salvemini from America, the newspaper was an expression of the British Left. The frequent slogans printed next to the title indicated its preoccupation with the growth of Fascism in Europe: 'Remember: everywhere, always, Fascism means war'; 'We stand for international justice'; 'Fascism is the enemy'; 'Maintain the sanctions'. The newspaper interpreted the invasion of Ethiopia by Italy as the first step toward a major war in Europe. Ethiopia was the first victim of Fascism and needed support both during and after Italy's invasion.[65] The newspaper publicised public events in favour of Ethiopia and various pro-Ethiopian societies in London, all of which were British. In August 1936, it informed its readers about a conference organised by the British section of the 'International Committee for the

Relief of the Victims of Italian Fascism', at which representatives from the Italian anti-Fascist parties in exile were speakers. Again, there was no mention of Italians who lived in London.[66]

The Italian empire in London (May 1936–December 1937)

> You . . . have helped me much more than you can imagine. By walking with your head up among the British . . . each of you has been, in his own circle, an ambassador of Italy.

With these emotional words Dino Grandi welcomed the Italian crowd at the embassy assembled to celebrate Italy's victory in the Ethiopian War. He spoke as a Fascist ambassador, as a man who had fought for the fatherland 'one of the most obstinate diplomatic battles in history'.[67] The myth of Grandi as *'duce'* of the Italians in Britain benefited markedly from victory. At the conclusion of a ceremony for the *leva fascista*, organised two weeks afterwards by the youth organisations, he left surrounded by a clapping crowd who followed him as a procession. The newspaper published a photograph of him reviewing the *Piccole Italiane* and called him the 'soldier ambassador' and the 'representative of the Fascist Revolution, prelude to the inevitable formation of the Italian Empire'.[68]

For the proclamation of the empire Grandi was in Rome, where the Duce praised his activity in London and allowed him to stay all night in his company in the *Sala del Mappamondo* at the *Palazzo Venezia*. The bitterness of having been sent to London four years before now seemed alleviated by the belief that his work there had been crucial and that the Duce had acknowledged it: 'No award and no prize could have been more pleasant to my blackshirt heart than Your praise, addressed to me in that great moment, for the work I have done in this London trench.'[69]

In a letter that he never sent, he reminded Mussolini of the war period, a chapter which opened on 14 February 1935 and closed on 18 June 1936, when the House of Commons voted the end of the sanctions. On that occasion, according to Grandi, the British empire confessed 'without reticence and dissimulation' to have been defeated by Fascist Italy: 'To the African victory against Ethiopia, today You have added, Duce, the diplomatic, political and military victory in Africa, in the Mediterranean and in Europe against the British Empire.'

The British decision to end sanctions had allegedly brought to an end a period in Anglo-Italian relations that had stretched from the foundation of the Kingdom of Italy to the foundation of the Fascist empire. Fascist empire and British Empire were now facing each other, in a completely new balance of power, in a relationship that Grandi described as one of military and political equality, *'nemici potenziali che si sorvegliano e si misurano in Europa, nel Mediterraneo e in Africa'*. The *pax Britannica* had ceased to exist in the Mediterranean as well as in

Africa. A state of peace could only exist between a strong nation and a weak one. Between two strong nations, Grandi claimed, there could be no peace, but rather an armistice. He wanted to remind Mussolini of his efforts and of all the dangers he had faced in dealing with British politicians and journalists:

> You knew perfectly well that, during the toughest and most difficult days, the British, while seeking to scare me and to defeat me, had always largely utilised material provided to them by . . . the *caporettismo* of *pseudo-fascisti* in Italy, among whom the Intelligence Service used to work. During those eighteen months . . . the number of communications on the Ethiopian question sent from London to Rome was 5151. About 30,000 pages written by myself and by my collaborators. About 3,000 night hours . . . At day and at night, without timetables, without breaks or rest, in an atmosphere which was effectively the atmosphere of a trench.

At the beginning of the conflict, Grandi continued, the British had believed they could trust him, but they suddenly realised they had been wrong: 'I was nothing but the enemy ambassador of an enemy country'.[70] The fact that Grandi decided not to send this letter may show his uncertainty, not simply about how to deal with Mussolini, but also about how to deal with the British. On the one hand, he almost certainly believed he had worked as an internal enemy in Britain; on the other hand, he worried about the consequences of a perpetuation of this state of affairs after the war.

That relations with Britain were not returning to normal became more evident at the outbreak of the Spanish Civil War, which followed almost immediately on Mussolini's success in Ethiopia, and led to swift Italian – and German – intervention. The Non-intervention Committee was, according to the *Fasci* in Britain, typical of the democracies, which at every crisis started founding international committees, usually in London, where they could waste time 'with avalanches of words without concluding anything'. Conversely, Fascism proclaimed that 'silence was golden' and that only deeds mattered. While democracy was paralysing government action, Italy continued its 'upright conduct'.[71]

At the end of 1936 the *Fasci* in Britain refused to consider the Spanish Civil War as an ideological European civil war. Europe's problem was not the Spanish War itself but the attempt made by France and Britain to see the war as one between ideologies, fascism and democracy, instead of a simple civil war within Spain.[72] The *Fasci* insisted that the democracies had attempted to transform the conflict into an ideological war between themselves and authoritarian states and did not realise that the Soviet Union was trying to found in the Mediterranean a centre of 'subversive infection'.[73] It was evident to Grandi that those British politicians who were not aware of the communist danger had at the same time an anti-Nazi attitude and were working for an isolation of Nazi Germany. He was clearly worried by the idea that France and Britain might support a democratic

Spain, 'barbarian and anarchist', rather than a 'civil and ordered' Spain under Franco.[74] That this international situation might lead to an Italo-German alliance against the democracies and the Soviet Union became increasingly plausible in the following months.

However, the main ploy of the Italian Fascist newspaper in Britain was to pretend that Mussolini was still showing the way to peace in Europe: his quasi-alliance with Hitler represented another attempt to reconstitute the Four-Power Pact, waiting now for France and Britain to join the Fascist countries against the Soviet Union. Rome was again leading the way.[75] Only at the end of November 1936 did the newspaper begin to admit the European dimension of the Spanish Civil War, in which two opposed political conceptions were fighting. Russia and France were sending every military and financial help to the 'reds', and this suggested that France was going to be excluded from the Four-Power Pact proposed by Mussolini.[76] Italy and Germany stood for the cause of European civilisation, and hoped that Britain would join them, since Italo-German agreement was never meant, the newspaper insisted between the end of 1936 and the beginning of 1937, to obscure the new attempts to reconstitute an Anglo-Italian friendship as the basis of a European peace.[77] Articles in favour of Anglo-Italian friendship now reappeared, and Anglo-Italian events, such as Pellizzi's lectures at the Friends of Italy society, were once again advertised.[78]

This situation changed from March 1937 onward, when the London *Fascio* reorganised in a way more suited to both the new 'imperial' aspect of the community and the needs of Italian foreign policy. Indeed, according to MI5, the political situation in Europe had 'undergone considerable changes' since 1936:

> Mussolini has conquered Ethiopia and sent Italian troops to fight in Spain. He has engaged in propaganda among Moslem peoples which is calculated to create difficulties to the British authorities in countries bordering on the Mediterranean and the Red Sea. In brief, the circumstances are such that the possibility might not in the far distant future consider the moment suitable to adopt an aggressive policy towards this country cannot be ruled out.

Furthermore, British Intelligence believed, on the basis of reliable information, that Parini was organising the *Fasci* Abroad 'in such a way as to enable the Italian government to employ them for sabotage purposes'.[79] It was alleged that a close relationship existed between the secretaries of the *Fasci* in Britain, Italian consulates and Italian intelligence, and that Italian firms in Britain were engaged in espionage.

The change in the organisation of the London *Fascio* came with a change in personnel. According to Parini, Camagna seemed more occupied with the newspaper and with his own social life than with the affairs of the *Fascio*. At the beginning of March 1937 he received peremptory instructions to go to Rome for an interview with Mussolini. While he was in Rome, Thaon de Revel, one of Parini's principal assistants and a member of the Fascist Grand Council, paid a visit to London apparently to investigate the affairs of the *Fascio* in Camagna's absence. Consequently, Parini replaced Camagna with a *commissario straordinario* whose duty was to reorganise the London *Fascio*. He chose Guglielmo Della Morte, who was also secretary of the Berlin *Fascio*. MI5 considered Parini's choice, together with other exchanges between the Italian foreign ministry and Germany, as proof that the *Fascio* was being reorganised on German lines. Further evidence of this, according to MI5, was an increase in the pro-German and anti-Communist propaganda of the *Fascio*: 'this would seem to indicate that Parini is to some extent imitating Hitler's campaign against world communism'.[80]

The general secretary of the *Fasci* Abroad, and consequently *L'Italia Nostra*, presented the change at the secretariat of the *Fascio* as a choice made by Camagna himself. In a public letter to Camagna, Parini accepted his resignation and praised him for his activity in the fascistisation of the community in the crucial years from 1932 to 1937. Yet if fascistisation had been the main imperative in 1932, something else now seemed necessary. Grandi's attempt to regenerate the spirit of the community with a new Fascist imperial perspective needed the help of a *Fascio* organised in ways appropriate to Italy's new international position. That this was the main reason for the change of secretary is shown also by the fact that Parini had called in a *commissario straordinario*. Della Morte's *curriculum vitae* was not simply that of a Fascist of the 'first hour', but also showed his suitability for the major new task, since he had been living and working in Germany for the Berlin *Fascio*.[81]

MI5's supposition that the new anti-Bolshevik stance of *L'Italia Nostra* was due to the reorganisation – and germanisation – of the *Fascio* is probably an over-interpretation of the evidence. The anti-Bolshevik articles were a consequence of the Spanish Civil War rather than of a 'germanisation' of the *Fascio*, and they had begun to appear before Della Morte's arrival. Their increase after that may have occurred simply because of the continuation of the Spanish Civil War and of the realisation of its European and ideological dimension. Nevertheless, two significant changes followed Della Morte's arrival in London: the recent attempts toward Anglo-Italian friendship abruptly died within three days of his becoming director of the newspaper, and new organisations controlled by the party attempted to give a totalitarian, corporativist direction to the Italian community.

In an article signed '*L'Italia Nostra*', Della Morte launched the first call for the propaganda war against Britain that was to continue until the outbreak of the Second World War. His attack on Britain expressed neither a sense of inferiority, nor a demand for revenge. Nor did it put forward Grandi's notion of Italian and British empires facing one another. It was rather a reaction against any criticism from Britain whatsoever – criticism Italians now had to reject as anti-Fascist, and see as a prelude to war between democracy and Fascism:

> The clarifying, firm and unequivocal word of the Duce reaches us in a particularly delicate moment, due to a repeated, furious anti-Fascist attack against imperial Italy. It thus comes after the extremism which has characterised the anti-Italian attacks of these last days; it comes after the tendentious, defamatory and false claims which in Parliament, from the press, and even from the churches London launched against Italy . . . How far do they want to go, in Great Britain, with this shifty and treacherous policy?[82]

Under the supervision of Della Morte, the *Fascio* organised not in a 'germanised' way, but along corporativist lines. He founded a new Fascist group strictly dependent on the *Fascio*, the *Fascio Giovanile*, also named *Giovani Fascisti*, which organised Italians between 18 and 21 years old. This institution was meant to complete the education of the Italians of the youth organisations in a pre-military manner. He then appointed E. Toti Lombardozzi to supervise the new group. The latter was a young Fascist, although his 'Fascist seniority' preceded the March on Rome.[83] MI5 defined the *Giovani Fascisti* as a senior 'pre-military corps' and warned the Home Office that most of these young Italians were British-born and therefore British subjects. In case of war they were likely to give their loyalty to Italy; yet they 'would not be liable to deportation and such other restrictions as would normally be placed on Italian subjects'.[84]

Parini claimed that it was no longer relevant if Italians had to work far from the fatherland for other countries: 'today the ancient sense of injustice and humiliation which oppressed the heart of every emigrant has disappeared'. The 'vexed spirits of the Italian masses who in the last fifty years have broken their hands and lost their lives in the hardest jobs under the greediest foreign capitalists, are now pacified'. The new pride now shared by many Italians in the world had made foreigners less favourable. This situation could be overcome only if the Italians expressed total solidarity among themselves by establishing separate communities of pure Italian 'race':

> We must close our ranks and help each other with absolute honesty . . . We must gather in the Italian communities abroad and keep them alive. The Italians must know each other and must favour marriages among Italians as much as possible. A mixed marriage is always an attack on the *italianità* of the family. Most of the time, children will not speak the Italian language and will have lost part of their own soul . . . by confusing blood, languages, habits and ideas.[85]

The greatest symbol of the new community and of the Italian empire in London was the new building of the *Casa d'Italia*. The *Fascio* bought it in November 1936 and opened it officially one year later. In the meantime, many articles described it, photographs appeared in the newspaper and it became a central topic in the correspondence between Rome and the embassy. It was a huge building on Charing Cross Road, named *Casa del Littorio*, with a main salon and three galleries named the *Sala dell'Impero* for the community's gatherings. The basement contained a restaurant, recreation rooms and a *circolo dopolavoristico* organised like those in Italy. The latter was in fact the old *Club Cooperativo*, centre of Italian life in London since before Fascism. The *Fascio* was to be the first organisation to move there, followed by the Veterans Association and the Alpini, and finally, when the upper floors were ready, by the semi-official organisations of the Italian community.[86] Parini understood the importance of such a change in the image of the Italian community in London, which, for its position in the new international order, needed proof of the interest of the Italian government. He therefore approved the requests for more funds from the consul in London, Giuseppe Biondelli, and even planned to be present at the opening.[87]

In July 1937 Parini considered that Della Morte's 'mission had been completed' and therefore the time had come to nominate a permanent secretary. Della Morte was to return to Berlin, not merely as secretary of the *Fascio* but also as inspector of the *Fasci* of Germany.[88] The new secretary, as Grandi proclaimed in a letter published two weeks later in *L'Italia Nostra*, was to be Giovanni Telesio, the London correspondent of *Il Resto del Carlino*, not only a 'blackshirt of the Revolution', but also a *legionario* of the African war, who, significantly, had volunteered from the London *Fascio* for service in Ethiopia.[89]

The reorganisation of the *Fascio* and the new direction given by Della Morte remained visible in the newspaper. The language itself made the newspaper very similar to Fascist newspapers in Italy particularly in the attitude to Britain, which it now attacked recklessly and even with contempt. From June 1937 onward the alliance with Germany became an exclusive alliance, without any consideration of overture to the democracies. The Rome-Berlin Axis was mentioned for the first time in June 1937, and its basis was now explained not in terms of diplomacy but in terms of the spiritual values of two 'new peoples'. The two Axis ambassadors, Grandi and Joachim von Ribbentrop, were fighting for European civilisation in the Non-Intervention Committee in London, and the readers of *L'Italia Nostra* suddenly discovered that Italy's mission in Europe was now to be an Italo-German one, led by two leaders, Hitler and Mussolini, and in Britain by both the Italian and the German ambassadors.[90]

The climax came with Mussolini's visit to Hitler in Berlin in September 1937. Parini requested the active participation of the *Fasci* in Germany organised by Della Morte, and addressed to them a message in which he emphasised that Italo-German friendship was not 'an accidental event', but constituted 'a formidable garantee for the future'. He then reminded the Italians that the imminent journey of the Duce to Germany . . . represents the highest and proudest emotion to the Italians who live and work there. They have the opportunity to see, outside the borders of Italy, in the historical and political climate of a country linked to Fascist Italy by an intimate solidarity of faith and deeds, the Man toward whom the Italians abroad, more than anyone else, feel the most ardent love and passionate devotion.[91]

Italians who lived in the British Empire were not as lucky as those living in Germany:

a foreigner who has lived there, who had to toil hard to earn daily bread under British laws, moving under the shadow of the Union Jack, becomes either mad because of desperation or consumed with anger. No people know the art of humiliating peoples of other origins as well as the British.[92]

These humiliations no longer (allegedly) offended the Italians, who could now measure the abyss that separated them and the Germans from the democracies. Germany and Italy stood as examples of success and continuous improvement for many years (although Germany had in fact appeared in the newspaper only recently). 'They are not so unlucky', admitted *L'Italia Nostra*, 'as to enumerate Anglican archbishops or hysterical suffragettes among the figures of their political life'. However, even if this happened, 'no one in Germany and in Italy would hesitate in finding immediately a suitable place for their disturbing activity'.[93] The remilitarisation of the Rhineland, which the London *Fascio* had viewed with anxiety two years before, it now compared to the Italian victory in Ethiopia, and the Berlin crowds now became 'Italo-German multitudes'.[94]

The change in Italian foreign policy was also visible in the organisation of summer camps. MI5 had recognised a change in the propaganda at the summer camps due to the conquest of Ethiopia in 1936. From that summer, the object was also to 'remind Italians that they now have an Empire of which they must be worthy'. Even more than before, it became necessary that children had some knowledge of the Italian language since it was no longer acceptable that the Italian public hear 'a strange language spoken among Italian children from abroad'. In selecting the children, the *Fasci* in Britain gave preference to sons and daughters of volunteers or those either killed or wounded in the Ethiopian campaign. According to MI5, summer camps were the most dangerous institution of the *Fasci* Abroad and it was important to keep record of all the names of the children from Britain, 'so that these may be available in case in the event of war it should be necessary to take action regarding persons of dual nationality (who had then become of military age)'.[95] For the first time, in the summer of 1937 foreign children, especially from Nazi Germany, were also invited to participate in the camps; children came from Spain too, where they were allegedly hoping to bring forward their own fascist revolution and to enjoy similar holidays in their own country once Franco had won the civil war.[96]

The Italians who lived in Britain therefore witnessed notable changes in Italian propaganda in the course of 1936–7. It was no longer simply anti-British as during the Ethiopian War, but rather noticeably more proud and aggressive, and based on the concept of a joint Italo-German struggle against the Western democracies. The reorganisation of the *Fascio* and the new *Casa d'Italia* also meant to convince them that the regime now looked at them under a different light and expected more from them. Corporativism was particularly encouraged. Every Italian profession in Britain was praised as patriotic for its resistance during the war, and the *Fascio* sought to encourage the creation of corporative organisations. Every sector began to be described as a corporation with a particular mission.[97] The most successful example of corporativism was the foundation at the end of November, in the presence of the secretary of the *Fascio* Telesio, of an *Associazione dei caffettieri*.[98] According to MI5 records, it included the owners of about 150 out of the 700 Italian cafés in inner London, and those principally responsible for setting it up were prominent members of the London *Fascio*. At the foundation ceremony, the authorities of the *Fascio* proposed that Italian Fascists in Britain use their profits to purchase land in Italy and return to their country as landowners. They also insisted that owners of Italian coffee shops buy their supplies only from Italian stores in Britain, or directly from Italy, rather than from British suppliers.[99]

In 1937 the membership of the London *Fascio* stood at approximately 900 adults, or 1,000 including the *Fascio femminile*. MI5 considered this to be a very low number, given the community of 10,942 Italians then living in London. Yet the number of those affiliated to other Fascist institutions in London might have made the figure much higher. MI5 calculated that by adding the members of the *Fascio* to those affiliated to the Youth Organisations, the total came to 2,092, although according to the newspaper the figure was 2,379. To this the newspaper added those who had recently applied to the *Fascio*, the members of the *dopolavoro*, of the *dopolavoro sportivo* and of the *sezione dopolavoristica Mazzini e Garibaldi*, bringing the total to 3,479. As the newspaper emphasised, this number represented the organisations directly dependent on the *Fascio*. Adding all the other Italian veterans', patriotic and corporativist organisations, brought the total to over 6,000.[100]

At the end of 1937, Dino Grandi's image among the Italians seemed to have reached its zenith as well. Hero of the Ethiopian War, he was both a charismatic and revolutionary leader and a father who loved all common Italians as his own family. During the Ethiopian War he had praised those Italians who helped keep his morale high, including the poorest organ players who played patriotic songs. In October 1937 he published in the newspaper a letter of gratitude to an old woman who had played her organ outside the embassy during the war: 'The small humble woman who, during sanctions, used to come every day and play *Marcia Reale* and *Giovinezza* with her organ under the windows of the Italian embassy, encouraging my fight and my work, is in my eyes worth more than one hundred duchesses.' When she fell ill at the beginning of October, Grandi paid her a visit at the hospital. She had emigrated from Naples when she was a young girl, and she spoke to Grandi with a mixture of English and Neapolitan. Among a crowd of Italians and of surprised English nurses, everyone was moved, according to *L'Italia Nostra*, by such an emotional meeting.[101]

The final turning point in the transformation of the Italian community came with Italy's withdrawal from Geneva and was anticipated by a dramatic speech by Grandi at the opening of the new *Casa d'Italia*. The radically Fascist style of his speech well represented the ideals supported by Pellizzi of a revolutionary community led by a revolutionary *Fascio* and embassy:

> *Camerati*,
> tonight's gathering is not a meeting, nor a reunion just to listen to speeches: it is a report, a great typically military and spiritually Fascist report, and, I would like to add, a *squadrista* report.

He then reminded the audience of the help he had received from his fellow-countrymen during the most difficult battle of his life:

> The Italians in London have helped me, every time I had a doubt, a weakness, I used to go and look for them all over London, to see their proud and firm smile and to find my faith again and restart the struggle.

Subsequently, he thanked the consul Biondelli for coordinating the transformation of the *Club Cooperativo* into the *Dopolavoro Fascista*, and underlined how deep and meaningful this change had been:

> Someone said that this was not necessary, that nothing has changed, that everything is like it used to be. No! My dear *camerati*, it is no longer the same! Until recently, we were still in the nineteenth century, we were in the pre-Fascist period. People were philo-Fascist rather than Fascist.

The spirit of the Empire must now transform the attitude of Italians toward their fatherland:

> To accept a revolution and a regime is no longer enough: we must have the courage and the sense of responsibility to bind our personal destiny, however great or small, to this revolution and to this regime.

He reminded them of his first visit to the old headquarters of the *Fascio* in London: 'that first time I felt my heart wringing'; the new *Casa d'Italia* was not simply a new and more beautiful headquarters, it was the very symbol of a community, which, from that very moment ceased once and for all to be Little Italy, and became an Italian empire in the heart of London:

> This *Casa* is not in Greek street . . . This *Casa* is not in Soho, an area which, thank God, will disappear, just as the tradition of Little Italy will be buried: although it had the great joy to see a great Italian, Giuseppe Mazzini, walking in its little streets, still it will remain a 'little Italy', far away from our spirit,

and, dramatically, he concluded: 'we want to see it buried for ever'.[102]

A week later the community gathered again in the *Sala dell'Impero* at the *Casa d'Italia*, this time to listen by radio to Mussolini's words, as he proclaimed to the entire world Italy's withdrawal from the League of Nations.[103]

Conclusion

In his memoirs, Grandi criticised the way Mussolini conducted the Ethiopian War and accused him of having intended to defeat the League of Nations through the Ethiopian War.[104] However, his own activity in Britain as well as his correspondence with the Italian foreign ministry in 1935 and 1936 show that his point of view at the time was not very different. In his letters to Mussolini, he repeatedly claimed that the Ethiopian War was a war against Britain and the League, and played the part of Fascist revolutionary ambassador in the Italian community in London.

Collaboration between the embassy, the *Fascio* and other Italian institutions was very efficient, and the policies of the *Fasci* obviously reflected those of the embassy. The Italian *Fasci* in Britain adopted an anti-British propaganda line from 1935 onward, although only in 1937 did they also become pro-German. These shifts reflected the development of Italian foreign policy during the Ethiopian War and subsequently during the Spanish Civil War. The policies of the London *Fascio* toward the Italian community were clearly decided in Rome by Parini, whose organisation was part of the Italian foreign ministry. Centralised control made the *Fasci* most efficient both in organising the resistance to sanctions and in creating new organisations for the community. Their revolutionary mission of transforming the Italian colonies abroad into Fascist corporate communities reached a high degree of apparent success after the conquest of the empire, and in particular through the reorganisation of the London *Fascio* in 1937. And while *Fasci* and embassy disseminated anti-British propaganda among the Italians living in Britain, they also made use of pro-Italian propaganda among British fascists and conservatives. As the next chapter will outline, Grandi's relationship with British Italophiles was another vital aspect of his fight from the 'London trench'.

Notes

1. 'Appunti', November 1935, ASMAE, *Gab* 243 ('Corrispondenza relativa al conflitto italo-etiopico'), 1935, II.
2. Fortunato Minniti, 'Il "nemico vero". Gli obiettivi dei piani di operazione contro la Gran Bretagna nel contesto etiopico (maggio 1935-maggio 1936)', *Storia Contemporanea*, XXVI (August 1995), 4, p. 592, stated that plans for a war against Britain concentrated especially in August 1935. After that date, Mussolini's intention was to create a political conflict with Britain rather than a direct military conflict (pp. 601–2). In *Fino alla guerra. Strategie e conflitto nella politica di potenza di Mussolini 1923–1940* (Naples: Edizioni Scientifiche Italiane, 2000), Minniti took this thesis further to suggest that Mussolini's policy toward war was not constant, and apart from some periods (1935 and 1940 in particular) the Duce had no interest for war.
3. Renzo De Felice, *Mussolini il duce*. I. *Gli anni del consenso (1929–1936)* (Turin: Einaudi, 1974), p. 602, claimed that after the conquest of Ethiopia Mussolini's policy was pro-British and anti-German. He also wrote that until 1940 Mussolini did not make a decisive choice between France and Germany (p. 340). Rosaria Quartararo, *Roma tra Londra e Berlino. La politica estera fascista dal 1930 al 1940* (Rome: Bonacci, 1980), p. 35, argued that until 1940 Britain remained Italy's only constant reference point. Richard Lamb, *Mussolini and the British* (London: Murray, 1997), p. 15, accused the British, and in particular Foreign Secretary Anthony Eden, of having rejected Mussolini's friendship and of having thrown him into Hitler's arms.
4. 'La lingua di Dante bandita da Malta', *L'Italia Nostra*, 9 November 1934, n. 300, p. 2.
5. 'Dopo il convegno di Londra – Le tre tappe', ibid., 8 February 1935, n. 313, p. 1.
6. Grandi to Mussolini, 28 March 1935, ASMAE, *DeF*, *CG*, b. 39, f. 93, sf. 1, ins. 1.
7. 'Stresa', *L'Italia Nostra*, 12 April 1935, n. 322, p. 1.
8. 'Mussolini costruttore della pace dei popoli', *Il Legionario*, 20 April 1935, n. 16, p. 4.

9. 'Il viaggio di Eden', *L'Italia Nostra*, 28 June 1935, n. 333, p. 1; 'I volontari del Negus', *Il Legionario*, 6 July 1935, n. 27, p. 3.

10. Grandi to Suvich, 5 June 1935, ASMAE, *Gab* 248.

11. 'Italian Propaganda in the U.K.', MI5 to Home Office,7 November 1935, PRO, *HO* 144/21079, 699617/5. However, MI5 reports must be taken cautiously. For example, according to them, 'Ezio Garibaldi was in England for about a week from 20th to 26th October, when in Grandi's opinion he did excellent work in connection with propaganda among the English, who venerate the memory of the great Garibaldi. Grandi has urged the Duce to approve of his returning to continue this propaganda until the Election takes place' (ibid). On the contrary, after Garibaldi's visit, Grandi wrote to Mussolini begging him to keep Garibaldi in Italy because he was only causing troubles to the embassy (Grandi to Mussolini, 28 October 1935, ASMAE, *DeF*, *CG*, b. 39, f. 93, sf. 1, ins. 1.

12. 'Italian Fascism in U. K. – Forward note on the organisations', MI5 to Home Office, 19 May 1936, PRO, *HO* 144/21079, 699617/7.

13. See Denis Mack Smith, 'Anti-British Propaganda in Fascist Italy', in *Italia e Inghilterra nel 900* (Florence: La Nuova Italia, 1973); Luigi Goglia, 'La propaganda italiana a sostegno della guerra contro l'Etiopia svolta in Gran Bretagna nel 1935–36', *Storia Contemporanea*, XV (1984), 5, pp. 845–908.

14. 'A proposito dell'Abissinia – Il "Leghismo" britannico', *L'Italia Nostra*, 12 July 1935, n. 335, p. 1.

15. 'La questione abissina – I mercanti all'arrembaggio', ibid., 26 July 1935, n. 337, p. 1.

16. Aloisi to Mussolini, 2 August 1935, *DDI*, 8, I, 654, p. 671.

17. Grandi to Mussolini, 17 August 1935, ibid., 8, I, 765, p. 782.

18. Grandi to Mussolini, 5 October 1935, ibid., 8, II, p. 240.

19. Grandi to Mussolini, 28 October 1935, ibid., 8, II, p. 469.

20. Grandi, *Diario di Londra*, entry for 20 November 1935, ASMAE, *DeF*, *CG*, b. 151, f. 199, sf. 2, ins. 2.

21. Grandi to Mussolini, 7 October 1935, ibid., b. 39, f. 93, sf. 1, ins. 1.

22. Dino Grandi, *Il mio paese. Ricordi autobiografici* (Bologna: Il Mulino, 1985), p. 397. The original version, *I sette anni a Londra*, which Grandi wrote in Lisbon after 1943, is now in ASMAE, *DeF*, *CG*, b. 153, sf. 1, ins. 3.

23. Evidence of anti-British feelings in Italy had started worrying the British Foreign Office as early as October 1935 (see PRO, *FO* 371/19555, R6168/ 4276/22, R6183/4376/22, and *FO* 371/19553, J7559/1/1, R6651/4376/22).

24. Mussolini to Grandi, 6 April 1936, *DDI*, 8, III, p. 660.

25. Mussolini to Cerruti, 6 April 1936, ibid., 8, III, p. 661.

26. Mussolini to Cerruti, 13 April 1936, ibid., 8, III, p. 701. Italic in the original.

27. Mussolini to Grandi, 13 April 1936, ibid., 8, III, p. 702.

28. Mussolini to Grandi, 13 April 1936, ibid., 8, III, p. 707.

29. Mussolini to Attolico, 13 April 1936, ibid., 8, III, p. 703.

30. Ibid.

31. '"Quando la Britannia era provincia di Roma" alla Mazzini e Garibaldi', *L'Italia Nostra*, 24 April 1936, n. 377, p. 4.

32. Grandi to Mussolini, 28 April 1936, ASMAE, *DeF*, *CG*, b. 39, f. 93, sf. 1, ins. 2. See also Luigi Villari, *Italy, Ethiopia and the League* (Rome: Dante Alighieri Society, 1936).

33. Gian Piero Brunetta, *Cent'anni di cinema italiano* (Rome and Bari: Laterza, 1991), pp. 220–1.

34. Grandi to ministry of press and propaganda, 15 May 1936, ACS, *MinCulPop*, *DGSP*, *AG*, b. 121, f. 2.

35. 'Il "decalogo" della donna italiana all'estero', *Il Legionario*, 47, 10 December 1935, p. 10.

36. ASMAE, *AS* (1929–1935), b. 1024, f. 'Affari generali, 1934–35'. Parini to the directors and teachers of Italian primary schools abroad, no date but autumn 1935.

37. 'Un'affermazione nobilissima della cultura italiana all'estero – L'Istituto italiano di Londra', *L'Italia Nostra*, 11 October 1935, n. 348, p. 3.

38. 'Sabato prossimo al Westminster Hall la premiazione alle Scuole Italiane', ibid., 21 June 1935, n 332, p. 1.

39. 'Italian Fascism in U. K. – Forward note on the organisations', MI5 to Newsam (Home Office), 19 May 1936, PRO, *HO* 144/21079, 699617/7.

40. 'OGIE – Gara d'onore XX1 aprile fra gli alunni delle scuole italiane di Londra', *L'Italia Nostra*, 24 April 1936, n. 377, p. 5.

41. Giovanna Servini and Anita Dichiara, school of King's Cross, *ibid.*, 8 May 1936, n. 379, pp. 5–6.

42. 'I bambini e l'impero', ibid., 7 May 1936, n. 431, p. 3.

43. See also Simona Colarizi, *L'opinione degli italiani sotto il regime*, 1929–1943 (Rome and Bari: Laterza, 1991), p. 188–9.

44. See for example the letters of Nicola Gattari, former emigrant who volunteered to serve in Ethiopia as a lorry driver, *La strada per Addis Abeba. Lettere di un camionista dall'impero (1936–1941)*, edited by Sergio Luzzatto (Turin: Paravia, 2000). See also Angelo Del Boca, *Gli italiani in Africa Orientale. La caduta dell'impero* (Rome and Bari: Laterza, 1982), p. 185.

45. 'Appunto per l'ufficio', note of the foreign ministry, 26 November 1935, ASMAE, *Gab* 243, 'Corrispondenza relativa al conflitto italo-etiopico', 1935, II. Sent as a telegram to all principal embassies.

46. 'Il re soldato inaugura a Tirrenia una nuova colonia marina dei fasci italiani all'estero', *L'Italia Nostra*, 12 July 1935, n. 335, p. 1 (also Parini and Ciano participated in the event); 'Aria e sole per i piccoli italiani all'estero. Dopo la

colonia di Tirrenia s'inaugura quella di Alpe del Vicerè', ibid., 19 July, n. 336, p. 1.

47. 'Duce siam pronti!', ibid., 13 September 1935, n. 344, p. 1.

48. When Parini brought them under the control of the foreign ministry, they became more efficient and successful within the communities, but they never gave up their main revolutionary mission, as Luca De Caprariis argued, on the contrary, in 'Fascism for export? The Rise and Eclipse of the Fasci Italiani all'Estero', *Journal of Contemporary History*, XXXV, 2 (April 2000), pp. 151–83.

49. Parini, 'Gli italiani all'estero', *L'Italia Nostra*, 27 December 1935, n. 359 ('40° giorno dell'assedio economico'), p. 1.

50. Pellizzi, 'La lingua italiana in Gran Bretagna', ibid., p. 2; Piovene, 'Le materie prime', p. 6. On Piovene see Renato Camurri, *Il 'lungo viaggio' di Guido Piovene nell'Italia fascista*, in *Guido Piovene tra ideali e ragione*, edited by Stefano Strazzabosco (Venice: Marsilio, 1996). See also Piovene's works *Italy* (London: 1956) and *In Search of Europe* (New York: St Martin's Press, 1975).

51. Emilio Canevari, *La conquista inglese dell'Africa* (Rome: Istituto Grafico Tiberino, 1935), p. 307; p. 59.

52. Pellizzi, 'Esperimenti e compromessi ginevrini', *L'Italia Nostra*, 3 January 1936, p. 1.

53. Enrico Serra, *Appunti sull'immagine della Francia nella propaganda fascista*, in *Il vincolo culturale tra Italia e Francia negli anni Trenta e Quaranta*, edited by J. B. Duroselle and E. Serra (Milan: Angeli, 1986), pp. 21–7; Gilles Martinet and Sergio Romano, with Michele Canonica, *Un'amicizia difficile. Conversazioni su due secoli di relazioni italo-francesi* (Florence: Ponte alle Grazie, 2001). See also Virginio Gayda, *Italia e Francia* (Rome: Stabilimento Tipografico del Giornale d'Italia, 1939), pp. 131–50; Maurizio Claremoris, *Noi e la Francia*, foreword by Roberto Farinacci (Cremona: Cremona Nuova, 1939).

54. Mack Smith, *Anti-British Propaganda*, pp. 87–117, insisted on the salience of decadence and pacifism in the Fascist image of Britain. But until the conquest of Ethiopia, these aspects could not conceal Fascist admiration of the British Empire and consequently hatred and envy. See also Mario Borsa, *Gli inglesi e noi* (Milano: Fasani, 1945), p. 71.

55. 'I camerieri all'arrembaggio', *L'Italia Nostra*, 11 October 1935, n. 348, p. 1.

56. 'I camerieri all'arrembaggio', ibid., 18 October 1935, n. 349, p. 4.

57. 'Date oro alla Patria', ibid., 6 December 1935, n. 357, p. 1.

58. 'Le contro-sanzioni degli italiani a Londra – La raccolta dell'oro ha raggiunto le 10,000 sterline – ininterrotta prova di fede italiana alla sede del *Fascio*', ibid., 3 January 1936, n. 361, p. 1.

59. Their names were published in *L'Italia Nostra*, 10 January 1936, n. 362, p. 1.

60. 'La nostra risposta alle sanzioni: 18,480', ibid., 17 January 1936, n. 363, p. 1.

61. See for example 'La marcia fantastica nel cuore dell'Etiopia – L'avanzata trionfante'; 'Le ali vittoriose d'Italia'; 'Il tricolore ed il fascismo in marcia', ibid., 3 April 1936, n. 374, p. 1.

62. 'Chiesa italiana di San Pietro in Clerkenwell', ibid., 3 April 1936, n. 374, p. 5.

63. 'Quel mazzolin di fiori . . .', ibid., 27 March 1936, n. 373, p. 4.

64. Ibid., 24 January 1936, n. 364, p. 1.

65. The interpretation of the Ethiopian War as prelude to the Second World War was later explained by Gaetano Salvemini, *Prelude to World War II* (London: Gollancz, 1953).

66. *New Times and Ethiopia News*, 15 August 1936, p. 8.

67. Ibid., 8 May 1936, n. 379, p. 1.

68. 'La sagra della gioventù', ibid., 29 May 1936, n. 382, p. 1.

69. Grandi to Mussolini, 22 May 1936, ASMAE, *DeF*, *CG*, b. 39, f. 93, sf. 1, ins. 2.

70. Grandi to Mussolini, 25 June 1936, ibid., b. 41, f. 102 ('Documenti non spediti').

71. 'Falsa premessa', *L'Italia Nostra*, 11 September 1936, n. 397.

72. 'Falsa premessa', ibid., 11 September 1936, n. 397.

73. 'I rapporti anglo-italiani', ibid., 27 November 1936, n. 408, p. 1.

74. Grandi to Affari Esteri, letter written but never sent, 14 November 1936, entitled 'Spagna – Comitato di non intervento', ASMAE, *DeF, CG*, b. 41, f. 102 ('Documenti non spediti').

75. 'Mussolini per la pace', and 'Roma Caput Mundi', *L'Italia Nostra*, 23 October 1936, n. 403, p. 1.

76. 'Precisazione', ibid., 27 November 1936, n. 408, p. 3.

77. 'Goering dal duce', ibid., 15 January 1937, n. 415, p. 1; 'Il pensiero del Duce nell'intervista di un giornale tedesco', ibid., 22 January 1937, n. 416, p. 2.

78. See for example 'Per l'amicizia anglo-italiana' and 'L'amaro in bocca', ibid., 8 January 1937, n. 414, p. 3.

79. 'Italian Fascist Organisation Activities in U.K. Dominions and Colonies' – 'Secret. Additional Notes on the Organisation and Activities of the Italian Fascist Party in the United Kingdom, the Dominions and Colonies', MI5 to Home Office, 28 June 1937, PRO, *HO* 144/21079, 699617/22.

80. '*Fascio* di Londra – internal affairs', MI5 to Newsam, 11 March 1937, ibid., 699617/16A.

81. *L'Italia Nostra*, 12 March 1937, n. 423, p. 1. Della Morte already had London experience, since he had worked there for the Banca Commerciale Italiana in 1931–32. Born in Milan in 1902, member of the *Fasci* di Combattimento since May 1919, *legionario fiumano* and *squadrista*, organiser of the *Fasci* in Valtellina in 1920, from 1934 he was secretary of the *Fascio* of Berlin, to which he returned after the few months at the London *Fascio*.

82. 'XVIII Annuale dei *Fasci* – Ricordare e prepararsi questo è il monito dell'odierna celebrazione', *L'Italia Nostra*, 26 March 1937, n. 425, p. 1.

83. '*Fasci* giovanili', ibid., 2 April 1937, n. 426, p. 1.

84. 'Italian Fascist Organisation Activities in U.K. Dominions and Colonies', MI5 to Home Office, June 1937, PRO, *HO* 144/21079, 699617/22.

85. Parini, 'Italianità integrale', *L'Italia Nostra*, 26 March 1937, n. 425, pp. 1–2.

86. 'La Casa del Littorio', ibid., 20 November 1936, n. 407, p. 1.

87. Parini to Grandi, 10 April 1937, ASMAE, *DeF*, *CG*, b. 48, f. 121; Grandi to Parini, 4 May 1937, ibid.

88. 'La vibrante assemblea del *fascio* "Arnaldo Mussolini"', *L'Italia Nostra*, 16 July 1937, n. 441, p. 1.

89. 'Una lettera di S. E. Dino Grandi al segretario del *Fascio*', ibid., 30 July 1937, n. 443, p. 1.

90. 'Il perché', ibid., 14 May 1937, n. 432, p. 1; 'L'asse Roma-Berlino', ibid., 4 June 1937, n. 435, p. 1; 'Punti fermi', ibid., 16 July 1937, n. 441, p. 1.

91. 'Gli sguardi del mondo su Berlino per l'incontro tra Mussolini e Hitler – Le Camicie Nere di Germania chiamante (*sic*) a raccolta da un appello di Piero Parini', ibid., 24 September 1937, n. 451, p. 1.

92. 'Italiani in terra d'Albione – Sensazioni identiche sotto cieli diversi', ibid., 24 Sept 1937, n. 451, p. 3.

93. 'Rinnovo di patente', ibid., 8 October 1937, n. 453, p. 1.

94. 'La Russia e il Comitern – Il patto anticomunista', ibid., 19 November 1937, n. 459, p. 3.

95. 'Italian Summer Camps', MI5 report, 18 August 1937, PRO, *HO* 144/21079, 699617/20.

96. 'Verso il sole, il mare, le montagne', *L'Italia Nostra*, 6 August 1937, n. 444, p. 1; 'Al campo Mussolini di Roma', ibid., 3 September 1937, n. 448, p. 1; 'Ventimila giovani fascisti all'estero acclamano il Duce in Roma eterna', ibid., 10 September 1937, n. 449, p. 2.

97. See for example the appeals to hotel keepers and to chefs in *L'Italia Nostra* of 7 May 1937, n. 431, p. 1 ('Benemeriti') and of 21 May 1937, n. 433, p. 1 (again 'Benemeriti').

98. 'I proprietari di caffè si uniscono in associazione', ibid., 26 November 1937, n. 460, p. 4.

99. 'Association of Italian Cafè Keepers in London – Formation', Metropolitan Police, Special Branch, Scotland House, 18 December 1937, PRO, *HO* 144/21079, 669617/26.

100. 'Italian Fascism in U. K. – Forward note on the organisations', MI5 to Newsam, ibid., 699617/7; 'L'assemblea generale alla casa del *Fascio* – Le camicie nere di Londra salutano l'anno XVI col grido: viva il Duce!', *L'Italia Nostra*, 5 November 1937, n. 457, p. 1.

101. Dino Grandi, 'L'ambasciatore da Teresa Papa', ibid., 8 October 1937, n. 453, p. 1.
102. 'L'ambasciatore Grandi e l'on. Cianetti nel nome del Duce inaugurano la Casa del Littorio', ibid., 3 December 1937, n. 461, p. 1.
103. 'L'Italia ha lasciato la SdN – Fuori? Sì!', ibid., 17 December 1937, n. 463, p. 1.
104. Which rather contradicts De Felice's version of Mussolini's intentions. See also Goglia, 'La propaganda italiana a sostegno della guerra contro l'Etiopia svolta in Gran Bretagna nel 1935–36', p. 847.

–4–

A 'Wonderful Colonisation': Italian Fascism and the British Italophiles during the Ethiopian War

As explained in Chapter 2, until 1935 Grandi had been interested in establishing some degree of collaboration with the BUF. He had often praised Mosley to Mussolini, and had convinced the Duce that he should finance the British movement. At a local level, the Italian *Fasci* in Britain established many contacts with the BUF, and similar contacts between British and Italian fascism existed in Italy thanks to the creation of BUF offices in several Italian towns. During the Ethiopian War Mosley did his best to support the Italian cause, and in the conflict between the British and the Italian governments he had chosen the latter, a position that appeared notably inconsistent with his movement's claim that its main principle was 'Britain first'.

However, from 1935 onward Grandi's relationship with the BUF cooled, and Anglo-Italian fascist solidarity became limited to mutual support on issues such as Ethiopia. Although the BUF's pro-Italian campaign was useful to Grandi in his battle against sanctions, Grandi stalled requests from Mussolini for help for the BUF, declaring the movement almost dead: he no longer had hopes for their possible success in Britain.[1] Moreover, Grandi needed to work with the British establishment and could no longer risk association with a British fascist movement, especially during the crucial months of the Ethiopian War, and he was also increasingly aware of the BUF's closeness to Germany. That in turn raises a further issue: to what extent did the German threat and the continued British-Italian confrontation compromise Grandi's expectations for closer Italian-British relations?

After an investigation of the causes of the shift in Anglo-Italian fascist relations, this chapter will focus on the contacts between Grandi and British right-wing Conservatives during the Ethiopian War. Indeed Grandi thought that British Conservative Italophiles, integrated in their society, could be more effective in spreading pro-fascist propaganda than the BUF, which was advocating a 'revolution' and therefore had little impact on the centres of power. Not only have these people not been studied (only a few biographies exist, generally by authors who were close friends of the subjects), but they have never been seen as a group since they did not give birth to a political party.[2] However, they belonged to the same organisations and clubs, they wrote in the same periodicals, and, unlike the BUF members, they contributed to the Italian embassy's paper *The British-Italian Bulletin*, which appeared in 1935 and 1936, at first as an appendix to *L'Italia Nostra*, and subsequently on its own. This chapter will therefore treat them as a group and will try to analyse their relationship with Italian Fascism and assess its influence on Anglo-Italian relations. As demonstrated in the previous chapter, Grandi's activity in Britain during the East African campaign was obviously anti-British, and in line with Mussolini's directives from Rome. However, the ambassador's relationship with British Italophiles was one of friendship, which involved close collaboration, including attempts to improve Anglo-Italian relations once the war was over.

Mussolini considered Grandi's activity among the Italophiles, which intensified from the beginning of 1935 onwards, to be a crucial aspect of the ambassador's work in Britain. Yet secondary works have always focused on Grandi's contacts with the Foreign Office and have neglected this aspect. It can therefore contribute, along with Grandi's activity in the Italian community, to an understanding of Fascist foreign policy and propaganda during probably the most crucial years in Anglo-Italian relations before the Second World War.[3] This chapter will distinguish between the work of Italophile 'intellectuals', who wrote for Grandi's paper and helped the embassy in disseminating pro-Italian propaganda among British society, and of Italophile 'politicians', who were members of Parliament and regularly met with the Italian ambassador during the period of the Ethiopian War.

Grandi and the BUF during the Ethiopian War

Grandi reported on pro-Italian BUF activities mainly from the spring of 1936 onward, often at Mussolini's request.[4] He seemed to be impressed by the choreography of Mosley's speeches: fascist hymns, a vast display of flags and guidons, the use of drums, and the sudden appearance of the leader surrounded by a group of stewards, walking amid rows of blackshirts demonstrating their reverence with the Roman salute.[5] During the meetings, BUF officers handed out leaflets, some of which had been provided by the Italian embassy, in defence of the Italian campaign in Ethiopia. Although according to one historian of British fascism Mosley's 'Mind Britain's Business' campaign 'raised natural suspicions that Mosley, at the very least, had more than ideological ties with the dictators',[6] BUF meetings were never simply pro-Italian. Their banners explained the reasons why the BUF supported the Ethiopian campaign: 'sanctions and unemployment' and 'seven million pounds wasted': for Britain rather than for Italy. Additional banners demanded 'peace with Germany'.[7] The main BUF theme was the sacrifices imposed on British workers by sanctions, rather than the rights of Italy in Ethiopia.[8]

However, Mosley supported Italy's right not to be 'suffocated in the Mediterranean'. Furthermore, Italian and British interests in the Mediterranean were deemed not to clash; on the contrary, if the two countries did not collaborate, a universal catastrophe, namely the triumph of Bolshevism, might follow.[9] A BUF member, Richard Bellamy, wrote in his memoirs that Eden 'was prepared to risk a war in the Mediterranean' not only on behalf of 'the most backward corners of the globe', but also of a League of Nations whose leader was the Russian Jewish Bolshevik Maxim Litvinov.[10] At a public meeting in Huddersfield at the end of 1936 Mosley announced that Mussolini, during a speech in Milan, had 'offered his hand to Britain'. Consequently, Mosley claimed, the people of Britain, despite the intentions of their politicians, were offering their hands to Italy.[11]

Grandi sent Mussolini several articles that had appeared in either *Action* or *The Blackshirt* denouncing sanctions. The articles carried violent criticism of the British government, which was described as 'the mad people who are governing us', together with illustrations of atrocities by the Ethiopians. They also relayed information received from Grandi himself. The BUF regularly asked the embassy for Italian news, not only regarding Ethiopia, but also welfare and other Fascist programmes such as the corporations and town planning in Italy, in order to contradict anti-Italian articles in the press.[12] The BUF press also reported on Italian books, periodicals and articles written by Italians.[13] Grandi in turn reported on disturbances and political violence between fascists and communists, which regularly took place at BUF meetings. He believed that these events usually helped the fascist cause, because they ensured press coverage of the BUF.[14]

Grandi was also aware of the strongly anti-Semitic policy of the BUF. He shared Mosley's opinion that the Jews in England were linked to the communists and were therefore an enemy. He even shared Mosley's language, calling the East End anti-fascists 'the Jewish-Communist thugs'.[15] He had informed Mussolini of Mosley's assumption, as early as spring 1935, that the principal enemy of fascism was 'international Jewish finance'.[16] Grandi also received information on the BUF from Italian consuls in other British cities. The consul in Liverpool, for instance, wrote to the ambassador in 1936 that British fascism was successful in cities such as Manchester and Leeds, because many Jews allegedly lived in those cities. There they purportedly used their capital to open big department stores and thus forced smaller non-Jewish shop owners into bankruptcy. The shop owners consequently could be influenced by BUF propaganda. The consul shared the common opinion that the Jews were also moneylenders who charged high rates of interest.[17]

Although Grandi was publicly grateful for the BUF's attitude toward Italy and the Italian embassy, his private perception of Mosley's movement was more pessimistic, as was evident from a report he wrote as early as the end of 1935, although he never sent it to Rome:

Since last year, the British Union of Fascists has continued to decline. The main reasons for this are the British reaction to the events of 30 June 1934 in Germany, the murder of Dollfuss, and Nazi policies. At first Mosley sought to dissociate himself from Nazism, emphasising the differences between Fascism and Nazism, but then he came closer to Hitler and imposed an anti-Semitic line on the BUF. It has been a huge mistake, not only because racism has no support among the British people, but also because it has disfigured the character of British fascism, moving away from its real bases, namely criticism of parliamentary democracy and of socialism, and the attempt to reform the British State according to the corporativist system. In this way Mosley has become isolated and has lost contact with political currents that had previously been interested in fascism.[18]

The relationship between the BUF and Italy was thus complicated and ambiguous; the Italian government and the BUF shared Grandi's doubts. It is therefore difficult to interpret the BUF decision in October 1935 to shut down its offices in Italy. The Italian ministry of the interior informed the Italian foreign ministry that according to the prefect of Florence the orders had come from the BUF headquarters in London. The Florence group, some members of which had been born in Italy, protested against the new anti-Italian attitude of the BUF. The prefect reported that one BUF member had reacted by applying for Italian citizenship, and had asked to be sent as a volunteer to East Africa.[19]

Mussolini himself regarded Mosley's activities in Britain favourably, as an element in pro-Italian propaganda in that country. He was also proud of the existence of foreign fascist movements, which he believed to be one more proof of his genius.[20] Yet at the same time, he sought to discourage too direct a collaboration with the BUF, perhaps because of Grandi's continuous warnings about British government and Labour Party enquiries into the origins of the BUF's funds, which they assumed came from either Rome or Berlin, or both. The Italians became cautious as a result of Sir John Simon's declaration in November 1936 that the BUF was receiving money from abroad and because of the subsequent decision, after a debate in the Commons, to ban the public use of uniforms in Britain.[21] Grandi also reported Mosley's November 1936 visit to Goebbels in Germany, in addition to frequent journeys to Germany undertaken by other BUF members.[22] Grandi was particularly annoyed by Ian Hope Dundas's association with a radio station in Rome, from which he had been allowed to broadcast weekly commentaries. This was particularly the case in the summer of 1936, during one of the most difficult periods for Grandi's London embassy, when Dundas began broadcasting open propaganda for the BUF, praising Mosley, describing BUF demonstrations in the East End with hugely exaggerated numbers, and announcing that the present British government was going to fall in the forthcoming elections. All this was of course likely to appear in Britain as an Italian attempt to interfere in British internal politics.[23]

In July 1936 Mosley fell ill and the Italian Foreign Secretary Galeazzo Ciano immediately ordered Vitetti to convey to him his best wishes;[24] yet in October a request from Mosley to the Duce to grant an audience to the BUF officer William Allen was denied simply on the grounds that 'for the moment' it was not possible.[25] A similar Italian reticence now characterised contacts between Italian and British fascists in Britain, particularly for Italian consuls. When Mosley held speeches in provincial British cities, Italian consuls were often invited to BUF luncheons and festive occasions. The embassy decided that they should no longer participate, and should plead prior appointments.[26]

This shift in the Italian relationship with British fascism corresponded with a growth in Italian Fascists' fears about German ideas of a new European order. While Mussolini continued to favour the expansion of fascism in other countries, he made clear that the new European civilisation was Mediterranean, since it had developed from Rome and was made universal again by Rome. The entry on *Fascismo nel mondo* in the *Encyclopaedia Treccani* of 1938 stated that differences existed between Italian Fascism and German Nazism due to individual traditions, geographical conditions, social structure and mentality, of which the main example was the German identification of nation with race.[27] However, it became clear that for the BUF European fascism was no longer a Roman form of fascism but rather a Teutonic one, led by Germany and Britain.

BUF support for the Ethiopian campaign was thus politically and culturally a pro-British fight rather than a pro-Italian one. It was, according to Daniel Waley, an 'extreme form of the conventional right-wing mixture of imperialism and isolationism'.[28] The BUF believed that a threat to British prestige in Africa from Italian ambitions was less serious than the threat posed by the possibility of African success over Europeans. At a deeper level the Italian cause was also a British cause, the Ethiopian was not.[29] In fact Mosley continued to see African colonisation as a necessary policy for the Europeans even after the Second World War, when he claimed that Africa was the 'way out from the dole'. Since 'the Black' in his opinion was 'not nearly fit for self-government', the British 'economic problem could be solved by negro labour under white direction in Africa', instead of importing foreign labour into Britain.[30]

Italy, the 'Necessary Ally'

With the decline of the BUF and of Anglo-Italian fascist solidarity as it had developed between 1932 and 1935, Grandi focused his attention on another section of British society, the pro-Fascist intellectuals (mainly writers and journalists) and right-wing Conservative politicians who worked together in various ways and shared common views. Conservative MPs such as George Ambrose Lloyd, Leo

Amery and John Edward Bernard Mottistone, journalists such as Francis Yeats-Brown, Douglas Jerrold, Charles Petrie, Harold Goad and Muriel Currey, and military men such as John Frederick Charles Fuller and Edward William Polson Newman were all strongly pro-Italian. An obvious difference existed between politicians and intellectuals: the former had contact mainly with Grandi and did not expose themselves by writing in Italian newspapers; the latter also worked with Grandi, but their influence was effective mainly in the press. Not only did they share political views, but also personal friendship. For example, Yeats-Brown was in close contact with Douglas Jerrold and was a close friend of Harold Goad and Muriel Currey; the latter also helped him with research and the typing of his books.[31] Petrie, Currey and Goad were also close friends of Luigi Villari. Petrie was constantly in contact with Grandi and remained so even after the Second World War.

The British Italophiles were convinced imperialists who bitterly criticised the attitude of the British government for neglecting the Empire and pursuing an allegedly feeble policy in India.[32] They believed the parliamentary system could not continue to work as it was: while not in favour of a dictatorship in Britain, they wanted a stronger executive and the creation of a corporativist system like the Italian, but adapted to the British constitution.[33] They were strongly anti-Bolshevik and saw the Russian threat expanding in Europe, particularly in Spain and France. They were genuinely pro-Italian and fervent admirers of Mussolini, an admiration different from the typical sympathy which most British Conservatives felt for Fascism as a regime suitable for Mediterranean peoples, and for Mussolini as a man able to discipline the Italians, to end the strikes and to make the trains run on time.[34] On the contrary, the Italophiles had no sense of superiority over the Italians, whose country they genuinely loved; indeed, some of them chose to live there for long periods, others to travel there often. Some of them were Catholics rather than Anglicans, which was also an important distinction between them and the members of the BUF. Some were strongly anti-Nazi; others were worried by Germany but did not completely reject Hitler, mainly because of their anti-Bolshevism. In their view, and unlike Nazi Germany, Fascist Italy was not only the state of the Fascist movement (of *squadrismo* and of corporativism), but also a state with a compromise between these forms of Fascist radicalism and conservative forces (crown, church and industrialists).[35] They believed British foreign policy had to be pro-Italian and favour the building of an Italian empire, which had to work with the British Empire, with both eventually organised along corporativist lines. However, their support for Fascism was not simply based on foreign policy; it was spiritual and cultural; they had studied Fascism and were personal friends of many members of the PNF and of the Fascist Grand Council. They played a role in the dissemination of Fascism outside Italy and often developed their own interpretations of Fascism.

Italy was a model because they saw it as a rising nation, as opposed to a declining Britain. In this sense they were patriotic as well as pro-Italian, since their focus was always Britain. Their perception of the decline of Britain indeed reinforced their belief in Fascism. Britain's slums and mass unemployment indicated that Baldwin's and MacDonald's methods were half-hearted compared with the myth of Mussolini 'pulling down derelict areas in Rome, draining the Pontine marshes, and establishing new and healthy colonies in the Campagna [Romana]'.[36] Dissatisfied by the present, the pro-Fascists looked to a recent past in which Britain still shared Victorian ideals. They believed themselves to be the bearers of a Victorian legacy, building 'a brave and better world'.[37] Although they were proud of the recent past, they thought Britain lacked something Italy had, namely real leadership:

> we were the most powerful people in Europe. We had a victorious army, a large and undefeated fleet and the largest airforce in existence. But we were without leaders, without a policy . . . The more powerful the ship, the greater the risk of disaster.[38]

The fascination the Duce exercised on them was not due simply to his policies; the pro-Fascists appeared to be as influenced by his myth as Italian followers of the Duce. To the writer John Squire, who met Mussolini in 1933, the Duce was 'at heart a poet'.[39] Following this meeting, Squire became one of the founders of the January Club, formed by figures from different political groups, but all in favour of fascism. The Club was an occasion for meetings between BUF members and British Italophiles who did not belong to Mosley's party.[40] For example, it organised a debate on 'Roads to fascism', chaired by Squire, at which Mosley and Petrie were speakers. In general, members of the January Club believed that the existing democratic system of government in Britain had to change, and although the change was unlikely to come about suddenly, as it had in Italy and in Germany, they regarded it as inevitable.

Jerrold fought on the Nationalist side in the Spanish Civil War in the conviction that he was fighting for the freedom of the Catholic religion, which Franco allegedly sought to save from the atheism of the Republicans. The secularisation of education, confiscation of clerical properties and legalisation of divorce all meant for him that the Spanish republic was persecuting religion.[41] Yeats-Brown, besides frequent travels to Italy, went to Spain, met Franco, 'and returned home an even stronger partisan of the Caudillo'.[42] In 1937 he attended the annual Nazi Party rally at Nuremberg and met Hitler, with whom he became disillusioned only after the March 1939 invasion of Czechoslovakia. However, he continued to trust Mussolini and admire the affection he believed the Italian people had for the Duce.[43] The role of the crown in Italy, according to Petrie, distinguished Fascism from Nazism. An ardent monarchist, Petrie believed that Fascists regarded the crown as the 'incarnation of the national idea'.[44] The corporative state could be 'more success-fully worked under a monarchy', especially in Britain, where according to Jerrold, all that was left of national pride was 'centred on Windsor not on Westminster'.[45]

One of the major Fascist myths, which transformed Italy into a sort of a Mecca for foreign sympathisers, was that of the classless society. Mussolini's propaganda had not invented this image of Italy; it had already been present in Anglo-Saxon literature during the nineteenth century.[46] Another myth was the influence of the Roman Empire, which the Italophiles thought fundamental in the understanding of Fascism. Italy's determination to be a great power could 'only be understood if allowance be made for the part which the Roman Empire, and the republics of Venice and Genoa, played in the Mediterranean in the past'; Italy had recently revived the tradition of Venice and Genoa, and had again become a formidable naval power.[47] Yet perhaps the principal myth was that of the Duce. Whether or not the Italophiles truly believed that in Italy classes did not exist, that Right and Left had disappeared and that even the Mafia had been finally defeated, the power of fascination Mussolini exercised over them is evident. He was not, like Napoleon, the 'child of a revolution', he was rather 'the revolution itself; for he has gone through the same spiritual exercises as the Italian people, and he has consequently been able to produce both the crisis and its solution'.[48] He was also a master in foreign policy and might, '*mutatis mutandis*, be compared with Augustus'.[49] Italy had not simply provided an experiment worthy of study, but represented the true spirit of the twentieth century, which was

> pre-eminently an age of monarchy, in the etymological sense of the term, and some of the most convincing proofs of this are to be found on the shores of the great inland sea. First and probably foremost there is Mussolini, the greatest figure of the present age, and perhaps one of the most notable of all time.[50]

Yeats-Brown, the son of a British consul in Liguria, frequently sojourned in Portofino and considered Italy as his second country: 'the longer I live the more I thank God that I'm an Englishman. But after that I think I'd rather be a Florentine or a Venetian, for they have great traditions too'.[51] In June 1933 he went to visit Predappio, to see the room where Mussolini was born and the Duce's parental house. Fascism was not for Yeats-Brown simply an economic solution; it was a whole system of moral values. He felt that he understood the true spirit of Fascism thanks to his visits to the *Mostra della Rivoluzione Fascista*, a pilgrimage 'to the core of the nation',[52] an exhibition that helped in the dissemination of the myth abroad:

> But it is the Sacrario, The Hall of the Martyrs, which no visitor will ever forget. I think it is a room that only New Italy could have conceived, in its combination of strength and simplicity, with a particular note that no Nordic race would have conceived. You enter

it with a mind full of the terror and tragedy of the formative years of Fascism: you are in the semi-dark and see a colossal cube in the centre of the room, leading the eye upwards to a metallic cross . . . Round the walls the word 'Presente' is written, and you remember that that was the answer of the arditi in memory of their fallen. You think at first there is silence in this darkened room, but as you walk round it, (and here is the touch that no Nordic race would have added), faint and far away comes the lilt of Giovanezza [*sic*]: it is played on a muted gramophone and comes to you as the very voice of all these young men who gave their lives for the cause. Ever after, when you hear Giovanezza [*sic*], as you will throughout the length and breadth of Italy, you will remember the Sacrario.[53]

Like other Italophiles and right-wing conservatives, Yeats-Brown had been a keen supporter of Mosley, and had admired him until the Olympia rally of 1934. The connection of British fascism with Nazi Germany may also have influenced the Italophiles' attitude, since they continued to believe that Italian Fascism was fundamentally different from German Nazism and to hope that Mussolini would not ally himself to Germany.

A discrepancy was increasingly evident between the pro-Italian and anti-German stance of the Italophiles and the pro-German and anti-British stance of Italian propaganda. Two aspects sometimes worried the Italophiles: Italian anti-British propaganda and activities in the Mediterranean and, even more, Italy's rapprochement with Germany. The two aspects were often related, since Italy's disputes with Britain in the Mediterranean might lead Italy to seek German support. In that case, Britain needed to be prepared against naval and land attacks in the Mediterranean theatre. The most crucial area, according to vice-admiral Henry C. Usborne, was 'between Gibraltar and Malta, Malta and Port Said, and Malta and the Dardanelles' and now that Italy was 'building two fast 35,000-ton battleships', 'battle-cruisers or some new type of battleship' also had to 'be called into play'. It was particularly necessary to strengthen overseas bases and Malta was 'the key-stone of everything'. However, as a friend of Italy, he claimed to hope that Britain and Italy would always remain friends and that Italy could feel certain, now that she had 'joined the ranks of 'satisfied nations', that peace-loving Britain will never provoke her'.[54] Charles Petrie wrote several anti-German articles in *The English Review* well before the Ethiopian War. As early as summer 1934, he had made clear his opposition to an Italo-German alliance.[55] His support for Italy on the Ethiopian question was thus partially linked to fear of Germany. In March 1935 he warned that Austria was 'more important than Ethiopia', and that Europe could not 'spare the guardians of the Brenner for a campaign in Africa'. He indicated that Germany was responsible for many of the present international troubles: it was seeking to distract Italian attention from Central Europe and to make 'bad blood between Italy, France, and ourselves'.[56] Muriel Currey agreed with him and stressed the importance of Carinthia, due to its geographical position between Italy, Yugoslavia and Austria. Because of economic depression and poverty, it was an easy target for the Nazis and some of its inhabitants were allegedly awaiting the Germans and *Anschluss*, which was a danger for Yugoslavia, Italy and the whole of Europe. She concluded on a note that sounded like an advertisement from a travel agency: 'a pleasant and practical way of helping Austria is that everyone who is able to do so, should spend their holidays in that country'. At the same time, they could help to defeat 'a cruel and unscrupulous plot against a small and helpless country'.[57]

British Italophiles were also active members of the Royal Institute of International Affairs. They organised meetings and conferences, published several of the Institute pamphlets and wrote in the *Bulletin of International News*. The latter was less openly pro-Fascist than *The English Review* and most of its articles were not signed; yet it favoured a pro-Italian and anti-German foreign policy. Since 1934 the *Bulletin* had blamed Hitler for his methods, had supported the independence of Austria and had distinguished between Fascism and Nazism.[58] Several articles in the *Bulletin* propagated the myth that Mussolini was a master of foreign policy. They congratulated him for the January 1935 agreement with France, which had allegedly weakened Germany's position, and especially for the April 1935 Stresa conference. They believed Italy and Britain had to continue their role as guarantors of the Locarno treaty.[59] At the beginning of the Ethiopian dispute, the *Bulletin* remained neutral and proposed an investigation of the various aspects of Italy's grievances.[60] However, shortly after, it explained that Italy was a country with an over-large population and an 'exceptional lack of essential raw materials'. This was in fact the major point of pro-Italian propaganda in Britain, as it was possible to see from the embassy's publications.[61] Among them was the *British-Italian Bulletin*, which was indeed written by Italophiles who were also members of the Royal Institute.[62] In September 1935, the *Bulletin* of the Royal Institute began to report Mussolini's and other Fascists' views. It considered very seriously Mussolini's contention that the measures he intended to take in Ethiopia were purely colonial in character and that the question, therefore, did 'not come within the province of the League'. Ethiopia, the Duce declared, had 'forfeited her right to membership of the League, by her failure to carry out her undertakings, especially as regards the abolition of slavery' and it was therefore 'impossible for Italy to deal with her on terms of equality'. The *Bulletin* accepted the assumption that Ethiopia was incapable of governing itself and consequently found 'Italy's claims to a major share in the task of working a mandatory system' plausible.[63]

The *British-Italian Bulletin* and the Italophiles in Ethiopia

On 8 November 1935 *L'Italia Nostra* advertised 'the English pages', a supplement entitled *The British-Italian Bulletin*. Rather than serving as a propaganda instrument, the latter was meant to explain facts in their 'truthfulness' and to clear up some misunderstandings originated by the British press.[64] As Grandi explained to Mussolini, the newspaper was an emanation of the embassy and he regarded it as his own.[65] It carried few articles in Italian; most articles were in English and the authors were British Italophiles. This demonstrates the extent to which Grandi not only had personal contacts with these Italophiles, but unlike his relationship with the BUF, also cooperated with them publicly. The newspaper was obviously created because of the Ethiopian War: the first issue, only two pages long, was dedicated to the Italian conquest and intended to explain the Italian case. Only from August 1936 did the journal begin to discuss topics other than the Ethiopian War. However, a deeper reason existed behind this publication, which helps to clarify the relationship between Italians and British Italophiles, and also the extent to which these Italophiles were actually fascists. The usual Italian pretext for invading Ethiopia, namely the overpopulation and poverty of Italy, was obviously a major topic, but this was always linked with deeper reasons which were entirely British and not simply a clone of Italian propaganda. One important aspect was the recognition of Britain's 'immemorial' spiritual debt to Italy. This was not simply a British debt but a world debt 'for spiritual services whereby in law and letters, as in art and half the sciences, she has ever led the way to civilisation and enlighten-ment'.[66] This feeling was shared mainly by those who, like Harold Goad, lived or had lived and worked in Italy, especially in some cultural capacity. Figures of this kind looked upon themselves as a 'distinctive class of cultured English people who knew Italy and had a clear idea of what she stood for in her relations with England'.[67] The former secretary of the British Academy of Arts in Rome, L. D. Cosgrove, wrote that

> no one who is in any way interested in the arts can be other than horrified at the thought of a possible conflict between England and Italy. The cultural and social relations between the two countries have been for five hundred years stronger than those between any two other nations in history. Geoffrey Chaucer, the father of modern English poetry, owed a great deal to Boccaccio.

He went on to mention Keats, Byron and Shelley, Rossetti and the pre-Raphaelites, and Browning's love for Italy. He also reminded his readers how the English had always gone to Italy for the climate, and how so many painters, sculptors and artists had found a 'welcome and a temporary home' in Italy. Only since 1870 had the Italian people begun to think and act in the same imperial manner which for three hundred years was typical of the British: 'let us not treat them as hereditary enemies'.[68] The most recent demonstration of this 'past comradeship', which the BUF had also emphasised at times, was participation in the Great War.[69]

Grandi found this special relationship with Italy very beneficial. He received many letters from both British politicians and common people describing their feelings of love and of guilt for their country's alleged injustice to Italy.[70] The insistence on this theme, which has more recently inspired both literature and cinema,[71] was able to attract part of British society to Italy's side and was paralleled by the work that some right-wing politicians such as Lloyd, Mottistone and Amery carried out in Parliament. If serving MPs did not commit themselves so far as to sign articles in Grandi's paper, former Conservative MPs did, as well as well-known military men and right-wing journalists. H. K. Hales (former Conservative member for Stoke-on-Trent), Major E. W. Polson Newman, General Fuller, Robert Hield (journalist and political writer) and Robert Machray (novelist and journalist) were among the contributors. The most regular reporters, who were for the most part already associated with Italian fascism, were Douglas Jerrold, Muriel Currey, Harold Goad and the famous poet Ezra Pound. The latter wrote a number of anti-League articles in which he explained Italy's position in terms of a new civilisation and a new challenge. Italy's major contribution to the present world was in his opinion the substitution of the concept of freedom with that of responsibility. Freedom of the press, for example, meant simply that third-rate journalists were allowed to write, and the same principle applied to every other section of society. He realised that 'the founders of the USA did not state that all men are equal', but rather that they were *born* equal. This was perfectly understood only in Italy: Italians were allegedly equal in front of the law, but differed 'in the grade of responsibility', a Fascist ideal 'vastly higher than the ideal of liberty', which was the major cause of degradation of Western society.[72] He advocated a strong Italy because he believed Italy represented the keystone in world civilisation.[73]

The myth of the rebirth of the Roman Empire,[74] far from being considered a threat to Britain in the Mediterranean, strongly impressed the Italophiles since they believed Rome to be the 'mother' of all Europe. To make war on Italy, 'a country which has had two great periods of civilisation where other European countries are fortunate if they have had one', would have been like 'murdering our own mother': war against Italy was 'a form of spiritual matricide'.[75] Like the British Union of Fascists and many Conservative politicians, these Italophiles shared the perception that in defending Ethiopia the British government was standing against the cause of European civilisation. The latter was in this case defended by Italy, as it had been at other points in history: 'the war is not between Rome and Ethiopia', wrote G. K. Chesterton, 'it is between Rome and Carthago [*sic*]'.[76] As he wrote to Villari in 1936, Chesterton believed Italy was 'doing what everybody else has done' and was consequently taking part in the wider European colonisation of Africa.[77] Politically this implied that Ethiopia was an agent of non-civilisation, anti-European and therefore also anti-French and anti-British. It was obvious, wrote General Polson Newman, 'that Ethiopia must gradually become brought into line with the methods of modern civilisation for her own benefit and that of her neighbours'.[78] Although some Conservative Italophiles had once been members of the League of Nations Union, they suspended their collaboration with the League, and bitterly attacked Lord Cecil of Chelmwood and the Archbishop of Canterbury over their allegations about the Italian use of poison gas in Ethiopia.[79]

Unlike Mosley, who was publicly pro-German, the Italophiles believed that a policy of friendship with Italy in Ethiopia was necessary in order to restrain Germany. In March 1936 the *British-Italian Bulletin* condemned Germany's violation of Locarno when it remilitarised the Rhineland, and insisted on the importance of keeping Italy separated from Germany.[80] The *Bulletin* closed publication when Italy conquered Ethiopia. The last issue, reflecting both the general policy of *L'Italia Nostra* at that stage and also Grandi's own hopes, expressed its wishes for a better future in Anglo-Italian relations and celebrated Italy as 'the necessary friend' of Britain.[81]

Some Italophiles did not confine themselves to writing for the *British-Italian Bulletin*, but showed their solidarity in a more vigorous way: they decided to follow the Italian troops to Ethiopia. In this way they believed they could inform British society about what was 'really' happening there. General Polson Newman, General Fuller (who was both an Italophile and a BUF member) and Muriel Currey wrote diaries during their travels in Ethiopia, which they published immediately after their return to England.[82] Thanks to Lord Rothermere, Fuller followed the Italian forces as a *Daily Mail* special correspondent. He included extracts from some of his despatches in his book. He felt a deep obligation to Douglas Jerrold for his book on the future of the League of Nations, *They that Take the Sword*,[83] and was also one of the organisers of the BUF's 'Mind Britain's Business' campaign, together with Joyce, Dundas and Beckett.[84] Fuller joined the BUF after the Olympia meeting of 1934, having become convinced that the Western political system needed to be remade, even by war if necessary, and that fascism had 'come to stay'. When Mussolini asked him an explanation for the anti-Italian attitude of the British press, Fuller replied that 'Jewish influence was the reason'.[85] According to Fuller, the Ethiopian War was a turning point in history, it was 'a stupendous historical event and a most significant political and military undertaking'.[86]

Italian colonisation reminded Muriel Currey of the British colonisation of India, which her friend Yeats-Brown and Rudyard Kipling had described.[87] She had admired films of 'Italian cavalry officers riding down the sides of precipices', and some of her narration of the Ethiopian War was indeed imaginative and idealised. She reported Italian soldiers leaving for Africa and singing the songs of the Revolution, of Italian soldiers in Asmara building roads and cleaning up the town, of Italian soldiers resting and talking about their own regions and the different ways of making macaroni. She recalled that at night, 'outside in the darkness the soldiers were singing the traditional songs of the Tuscan countryside to the accompaniment of a mandoline'.[88] Fuller's account described the same happy and relaxed atmosphere that existed among the Italian troops. In the Italian General

Headquarters, 'there was never any fuss or flurry' and 'every officer could afford to take a by no means short siesta after his midday meal'.[89] The leading idea behind the army organisation 'was not tactics but politics'. The political enthusiasm, the presence of war veterans, blackshirts, regular troops and native troops were altogether the 'symbol of a united Fascist Italy'.[90] The Italian army was 'a huge melodramatic troupe; a Fascist demonstration; a gathering of armed men in which each group possessed a discipline or lack of discipline of its own'. The blackshirts were strangely picturesque: they considered themselves to be 'the salt of the earth' and sang most of the time. It was an 'Army of the Exodus which crossed the Red Sea in search of the Promised Land'.[91] Their leaders were not always selected because of their military skill, but because they were 'poets, orators, or futurist artists'. They were also 'the most generous and kindly men in the world' and 'the more unmilitary their actions' the more they were pleased. 'In spite of their glitter and glamour, their terrifying badges and knives', they were not soldiers: 'they may be good sub-machine-gunmen, street fighters and town sackers, but they are not soldiers'; yet 'as collectors of glory they stand unrivalled – these men of the Army of the old Adelphy'. They were 'the war chorus of the Duce, and the troubadours of his cult'.[92] Although he admitted that one of the reasons for the Italian victory in the war was that the enemy was much weaker, Fuller emphasised that Italy won also thanks to the peculiarly Fascist organisation of the war. It was a new idea of war, unknown to British colonial practice:

> had a British General been in Badoglio's place . . ., how many Staff Officers, Experts and Advisers would he have required? Probably several hundreds. What would the result have been? Not only a cautious but a routine war, the very weight of advice complicating every problem and slowing down every decision. With us it is always a matter of too many cooks spoil the broth, but with the Italians there were so few that, when the order 'Annihilate your enemy' was received, Marshal Badoglio, being a man of decision, was in no way impeded by his Staff from striking immediately. It was decision and not consideration, action and not the perfection of routine, which won him the war and established for ever his reputation as the most successful of colonial war generals.[93]

The Italians allegedly 'fought like Crusaders', they were 'a revolutionary army imbued with the spirit of the army of Huss and those who fought in the religious wars of the sixteenth century'.[94]

Fuller believed that the Italians had 'transformed tracks into negotiable roads as if by the wave of a magician's wand'.[95] Bellamy of the BUF considered that poison gas, bombs 'and other civilised refinements, contributed to the Italian victory; but the war was won mostly by the amazing speed with which roads were made and bridges built in appallingly difficult terrain'.[96] Currey wrote that Italians were teaching the natives to transform their country into a modern agricultural and industrial society, by introducing them to machinery and new methods. They also liberated slaves, provided women and children with medicines and introduced education, for which the natives were supposed to be very grateful. In some villages the natives welcomed the Italians as liberators. Unfortunately for the Italians, the Negus and local 'brigands' who had always exploited and enslaved the populations did not want to accept these developments. Currey did occasionally mention that this 'wonderful colonisation' also involved a war: 'I knew that they were happy and contented, but I thought, too, of all that war costs in human lives and suffering, of its glory and its misery'. War was 'both good and bad' and 'as a woman one must hate and dread it, while one's heart is with the men who fight'.[97] The myth of the Italian soldier who goes to war even though he dislikes it, and when at war plays the mandolin, is nice to the natives and talks about macaroni, seems to have remained in English literature until recent times, together with the belief that these Italian characteristics marked an overwhelming difference between themselves and the Germans, between Fascism and Nazism.[98] Muriel Currey shared this view. She reported that she never heard one word glorifying war for its own sake, and added: 'let those who profess to see no difference between National-Socialism and Fascism ponder this fact'.[99]

The myth of the 'good Italian'[100] also included Mussolini. During a broadcast addressed to the English people from a Rome radio station, Currey described her recent meeting with the Duce, in which she 'found that the only thing in which he was particularly interested was the native population in the province of Tigrai'.[101] Despite sanctions and the fact that she was English, Currey recalled that Italians always welcomed her, as if international relations and anti-British propaganda had never really influenced them. She wondered 'if there were any other nation in the world at once so civilized and so chivalrous'.[102] She left Ethiopia with these thoughts: 'because I was a woman, the thing that I desired was that the war should end . . . I wanted to see these horrors put an end to . . . It was a war against ignorance, dirt, disease, and apathy'. She felt sure the Italians would win the war because in the conquered territories the native populations were happy, while in the areas still to be 'liberated' misery triumphed.[103]

After the conquest, Major Polson Newman described a three months' journey with his wife in the East African territories under Italian rule. Before leaving, he met Mussolini at the Palazzo Venezia. They talked about the prospects for Anglo-Italian agreement in the Mediterranean and Mussolini suggested that he go to Ethiopia. This confirms that Mussolini continued to receive British Italophiles and to be in contact with them after the conclusion of the war.[104] Polson Newman's book continued Currey's account, illustrating the progress of Italian civilisation in Ethiopia after the conclusion of the war. He wrote about attractively built tennis clubs and the 'incessant traffic of lorries, cars, and motor-cycles'; in Asmara every evening the restaurants were packed, and people were queuing outside cinemas. When he left Asmara, 'the road surface was admirable and the speed of the car fast.

Where possible cactus and aloes were planted along the roadside, and everything connected with the road had a brand-new appearance'.[105] On the roads Italians, Amharas and liberated slaves were always working together. It seemed as if Italy's alleged classless society had now arrived in Ethiopia; the natives were always happy and saluted cheerfully as the British couple passed by.[106] He met Marshal Graziani and described him as a heroic figure: 'great personal charm, besides being tall and distinguished-looking. Strength of character was written on every feature and line of his face. His hands also were those of a man of action.' Graziani was also 'positively loved by the army . . . and he has done a great deal to win the affection of the native population by his sympathy and understanding'.[107]

Like Currey two years before, Polson Newman and his wife 'met nothing of the strong hostility to Britain about which we had heard so much'. Yet Italians could not understand 'British ways and methods, just as in England there is a corresponding want of knowledge about the Italian system and way of looking at things'.[108] He concluded that the problem was the inclination of both British and Italians to 'lose sight of the many important differences between the two races':

> Britain is a northern country, with a cold, damp, and depressing climate; her people are Anglo-Saxon in race, chiefly Protestant in religion, and the majority are occupied in industry. Italy, on the other hand, is a southern country, enjoying a pleasant, sunny, drier climate; her people are Latin in race, almost entirely Catholic in religion, and the majority are occupied in agriculture. With these fundamental differences there cannot possibly be the same outlook towards many aspects of life.

Italy, too, had unified recently and had become an empire only lately, which reflected the psychological differences between youth and maturity: 'while youth regards maturity as slow, out of date, and obstructionist, maturity regards youth as impetuous and unreasonable'.[109] Fuller found that the same problem characterised Italian warfare. There was a deep psychological reason why bloodless wars were 'repugnant to young nations, namely, that a war without a battle is like an unconsummated marriage, it is a sterile event'.[110]

'The Traditional Friendship Never Existed': the Invention of an Anti-British Tradition in Italy

While the Italophiles and Grandi were seeking to make the Italian cause popular in Britain, Italy's anti-British propaganda was making the 'necessary friendship' difficult to realise. In fact, Italian propaganda was denying the very principles in which the British Italophiles believed. Despite the latter's wide literature on the 'traditional friendship', Italian propaganda from 1935 onward concentrated on describing Britain as a 'traditional enemy'.[111] Furthermore, the image of the Italian soldier described by the Italophiles who went to Ethiopia appeared completely opposed to Mussolini's conception of the new Italian. At the beginning of the war, Mussolini stressed that Britain had failed to realise that 'we are no longer the nation we used to be'. The 'British had always seen the Italians as happy, picturesque and nice people'; Italy had always represented 'an important part of the pleasure of their lives'. Yet now the Italian people were radically different. The Great War had educated them to bear privations and had created 'on our soil grave and austere men'. However, the real secret of the Italian metamorphosis was that Fascism had concentrated all its efforts on educating and preparing Italians from childhood.[112] Unlike the Italophiles, British supporters of sanctions in London had clearly understood the importance of Mussolini's 'secret' and discussed it during a particularly dramatic meeting at the League of Nations Union in 1936: 'with Mussolini training the youth of Italy to war from the cradle upwards, the risk of war would be far greater in the future'.[113]

In 1936, the Italian writer Giovanni Saracino proclaimed that 'after 15 centuries the Roman Empire has been reborn. The solemn event brings us back to Caesar and to the military and civil feats of our Roman fathers'.[114] His book on the Italian empire and Britain was one of several examples of the link now being made between the myth of the new Roman Empire and rivalry with Britain. The Italian people, who were said to have fallen asleep on the 'ancient traditional friendship', were still unaware of several aspects of British history and mentality.[115] Like other books written in the years that followed, the most important point was to convince the Italians that British support in the *Risorgimento* had never really existed and that self-interest and cynicism, never friendship, had always characterised British actions.[116] This became evident at the time of the Italian attack on Corfu in 1923, which had underlined once and for all the new Italian attitude – a Fascist attitude – toward Britain.[117] Italian irredentist activities in Malta from the late 1920s onward represented another example of the cultural aspects of anti-British propaganda and of the invention of an anti-British tradition in Italy. According to MI5, at the beginning of the Italo-Ethiopian dispute a large number of Italians living in Malta gathered information and spread subversive propaganda. A similar situation existed in Egypt, where as a result of the Ethiopian campaign Fascism spread among the Italian community there. The *Fascio* received a number of new recruits, including some Egyptians, and Fascist centres were established at Alexandria and Cairo.[118]

Another myth created in 1936 was that of British decadence as opposed to Italian military strength; it was now assumed that Italy would win a war against Britain.[119] Ciano reported in his diary that, shortly before the Ethiopian campaign, Mussolini had studied the composition of the British people and had divided it according to age. He had found that 22 million men and 24 million women lived in Britain, and that 12 million citizens were more than 50 years old, the 'age limit of belligerence'. This meant a 'predominance of the static masses against the dynamic masses of youth'.[120] Britain's alleged military decadence was due to a general decadence, which the Italians also examined from an economic point of view. The most detailed study, published in 1940 but written before the outbreak of the Second World War, explained the reasons for British decadence in the economic rise of other countries during the nineteenth century. However, it was Italy, by the invasion of Ethiopia and the defeat of sanctions, that demonstrated for the first time that Britain could no longer dictate European politics. Germany, it was said, followed the Italian example.[121] At the same time, demographic decrease meant that the quality of the British race worsened. It was therefore clear that 'today England no longer retains the requirements and the material and moral strength which are necessary to maintain a predominant position'. It was also evident that Britain 'had to clash with younger and more dynamic countries with a high demographic potential, which is the main factor in a steady imperial activity and in a legitimate and natural hegemony'.[122] Mussolini had already publicly praised Germany, where the population had increased and had shown the healthy state of the German race, a development that foretold major changes in Europe.[123]

Another Italian writer, Colonel Emilio Canevari, claimed that the British appeared pacifist not because they loved peace but because they knew that 'the Empire is exhausted and would collapse in case of a new conflict'.[124] Yet it was not simply a question of military strength; nations decayed when they lacked courage. While courageous men such as Graziani had characterised Italy's conquest of Africa,[125] new men had not appeared in Britain for a long time: 'the feminine element dominates this country, which once was the fatherland of the harshest sailors, soldiers, adventurers and merchants who wanted to conquer the world'; moreover, the 'intimate decadence' was also due to Jewish influence.[126] According to Ciano, Mussolini announced privately in 1937 that he planned to write a book on 'Europe in 2000': the races that were going to play an important role, the Duce told Ciano, were the Italians, the Germans, the Russians and the Japanese. 'The other peoples will be destroyed by the acid of Jewish corruption. They even refuse to have children because it involves pain. They do not realise that pain is the only creative element in the life of nations'.[127]

The Italian way of colonisation, allegedly based on justice and the export of the Fascist ideal, was a new concept to the British, whose colonisation had always been based on exploitation and injustice: the Italian challenge was thus principally a moral challenge. That meant that the confrontation was a clash of two opposed types of civilisation, and could lead only to war:

> The Anglo-Italian contest . . . is a deadly contest, because our Empire, based on Roman peace and justice rather than on the exploitation of subordinates, is for the British a serious danger, not only because of its weight but also because of the comparison which it imposes.[128]

The main difference between Italian and British domination in Africa was thus that the latter was due only to economic motivations: 'any sentimental reason, of prestige, of civilisation etc. is unknown to it'.[129] Another myth, which persisted until the Second World War, was that Britain had been responsible for the outbreak of the First World War: '1914–1935: two dates, two facts which reproduce themselves along the same tradition'.[130] The invention of an anti-British tradition sometimes unleashed pure hatred:

> God, who is wiser than all politicians, had chosen that England was an *island*. He has thus indicated to us the attitude we have to adopt toward the inhabitants of that island: ISOLATE THEM. For everybody's sake, it is necessary to transform the English Channel into an immeasurable abyss, and the island into a quarantine zone of the selfish, to be avoided like the lepers.[131]

Mario Borsa, former correspondent of *Il Corriere della Sera*, reported a 'prayer' the regime wanted the Italians to say during the months of the Ethiopian War. It emphasised once more the image of the British as pirates, but went further by wishing for the fall – forever – of the British Empire, leaving Italy – again forever – its place in the sun, while Britain paid back to Italy the debts accumulated since the Great War. It was a twisted parody of the Lord's Prayer, beginning 'Our Pirate, who art an Englishman / Cursed be Thy name':

> Pirata nostro che sei inglese/ sia maledetto il nome tuo,/ venga a crollare per sempre il regno e l'impero tuo./ Sia sanzionata la bestiale volontà tua/ siccome in terra così in mare./ Lascia per oggi e per sempre le tue mire sul nostro posto al sole/ e rimborsaci i nostri crediti dal 1915 al 1918/ siccome il Negus, nostro debitore,/ ci rimborserà a noi/ Così sia.[132]

Anti-British propaganda alarmed the British Foreign Office and complicated Grandi's work in London. Vansittart was also worried by alarming reports from the British ambassador to Rome, Eric Drummond.[133] Grandi's difficulties increased when Eden became foreign secretary after Hoare's fall in December 1936. Grandi thought that Eden had always propagated the idea that the Ethiopian question was merely a part of wider Italian aims in the Mediterranean that included Egypt, Malta and Cyprus.[134] And although he did not advocate a clash with Britain, Grandi also contributed to creating the belief that Britain was not ready to fight Italy. He reported optimistically on the military balance to Mussolini, probably because he felt he needed to show confidence in Italy's victory. His optimism and enthusiasm clearly increased toward the end of the Ethiopian War.[135] However, Fascist propaganda continued to associate Eden's name with the 'crime of sanctions' well into the Second World War. Luigi Villari, writing in 1943, believed the origins of the war were to be found 'on the Ethiopian mountains'.[136]

Grandi and the Italophiles

The role of the embassy in supporting British sympathisers was crucial; the creation of the *Bulletin* harnessed them to the Italian cause. Italians who worked for the embassy, including Luigi Villari, contributed to *The English Review*, which propagated the views of the Italophiles both on Italy and on international politics. Grandi met regularly with some of them, especially Charles Petrie, but also figures such as Viscountess Georgina Milner, pro-fascist director of the *National Review*, another extreme right-wing conservative periodical which during the Ethiopian War was particularly useful to Italian propaganda. She believed that the pacifists were 'traitors to England' and that the League was 'a son of Satan'.[137]

As with Grandi's relations with the BUF, the aggressive anti-British campaign in Italy and Mussolini's increasingly pro-German foreign policy also created problems for Grandi in dealing with Conservative Italophiles. In 1935 Mussolini banned some British newspapers, including Conservative papers that had never been particularly anti-Italian, because of their attitude toward the Ethiopian War. One example was the *Sunday Express*, owned by the pro-Italian Lord Beaverbrook, whose friendship with Grandi never ceased and in fact continued into the post-1945 period. Beaverbrook was obviously astonished by Mussolini's decision and complained to Grandi: 'I would like to know why we are banned. These papers are not hostile to Italy. These papers are not criticising Italian policy in Africa'.[138] In 1935, Austen Chamberlain had warned Grandi that the Italian campaign in Ethiopia was going to complicate both Anglo-Italian relations and European politics in general. According to Chamberlain, Grandi himself was aware of this but 'had no hope that Mussolini could now be deflected from his purpose'.[139] The British political figures most helpful to Grandi during the Ethiopian War were Sir George Ambrose Lloyd, John Edward Bernard Seely Mottistone and L. S. Amery.[140] As long as Italy did not openly side with Germany, they thought its anti-British reaction justified, and believed that they were working for an improvement in Anglo-Italian relations. However, unlike Vansittart, they were not simply 'appeasing' Mussolini because they feared Nazi Germany, but were wholehearted supporters of Italy's cause. For them Mussolini was not simply a 'lesser dictator', but rather a completely different phenomenon from Hitler. Their activity in the British Parliament and among the upper classes was parallel to that of the Italophiles who wrote in the *English Review* and in the *British-Italian Bulletin*.

Grandi worked in close contact with Lord Lloyd, who followed his advice and discussed several issues with him before preparing speeches in favour of Italy in the House of Lords. Lloyd believed that if Britain sought to counter Fascism, that would open the doors of the West to Bolshevism. Mussolini was also friendly with Lloyd and invited him to Rome several times.[141] When he met Lloyd, Grandi stressed in particular the 'dangerous alliance' between Eden and Litvinov. He despised Vansittart as 'one of the deceitful authors' of the situation that had developed between Italy and Britain during the previous few months.[142]

Grandi considered Amery together with the bankers of the City of London as the most important figures in his efforts to win Conservative support. In 1935 Amery published a book in which he expressed immense admiration for the Duce.[143] He described post-war Italy as a country on the verge of Bolshevism until Mussolini had saved it. The latter possessed 'that all-round *virtù*, that talent for creation and reorganisation, which marked his two greatest fellow-Italians, Julius Caesar and Napoleon Bonaparte'. Mussolini's feelings toward Italy were comparable to those expressed by Dante, Petrarch and Leopardi. His regard for the dignity of both king and papacy demonstrated the historical continuity of Fascism with Italian traditions.[144] The weight of tradition was important to a right-wing Conservative, and Amery saw it as the main difference between Fascist Italy and Nazi Germany. The essence of Fascism was the corporative state, while the dictatorship simply 'an incident, indispensable for the immediate purpose'; Hitler, by contrast, came from the Prussian ruling tradition, and was anti-Semitic and anti-Catholic. His racial theories, Amery thought, were 'fanatic nonsense'.[145] In 1936, Amery dedicated a smaller book to the German question, in which he explained that Germany did not really need colonies, while Italy's need for space and raw materials justified its claims.[146] He sent *The Forward View* to Grandi, asking the ambassador to give it to the Duce in the hope that the latter might read at least the chapter about Fascism. Grandi asked Mussolini to write a short letter of appreciation to Amery as soon as possible, together with his opinion of the book. He believed that Amery, after a letter from the Duce, would do anything Grandi asked him.[147]

Although the Italophiles always showed admiration for and faith in Mussolini, Italian anti-British activity in Africa or the possibility of an Italo-German agreement caused them increasing anxiety. As early as October 1935, Lord Lloyd told Grandi that he had noticed a growing belief in England that Mussolini's real aims were directed against British interests in Egypt and against the British naval position in the Mediterranean. He mentioned 'Italy's enormous and ever-increasing cultural propaganda in Egypt', to which Grandi had little answer. Lloyd also touched upon several articles by Virginio Gayda about the *mare nostrum*, part of a larger propaganda campaign that questioned England's rights in the Mediterranean, and reported to Grandi that he had heard rumours among British Conservatives about a 'working arrangement between Italy and Germany to that end – not to be realised quite immediately perhaps, but in the next three or four years'. The Ethiopian adventure allegedly represented only one part of the plan.[148] Whenever he received letters of that kind, Grandi organised meetings in which he sought to deny all allegations. He was evidently able to convince the Italophiles, since they continued their pro-Italian activity. He found their attitude typical of imperialist Conservatives, but typical too of a more general British psychology, and reminded Mussolini of the difficulties in dealing with 'these stubborn, ignorant and heavy people': 'they are like fishes, which dart away from your hand at the very moment when you feel you have caught them'. That Grandi was not fully aware of the extent of Italy's growing contacts with Germany seemed evident from his letter to Mussolini in regard to Lloyd's letter: 'I draw your attention to the part of the letter regarding alleged Italo-German agreements'.[149]

Lord Mottistone likewise contributed to Fascist propaganda in the House of Lords. He challenged anti-Fascist positions and prepared his speeches in collaboration with Grandi. He was accustomed to asking the ambassador for information and material to help him prepare his speeches, and to sending drafts to Grandi to look over before addressing Parliament. Sometimes he asked Grandi to supply falsified documents to use as evidence, which Grandi provided only after Mussolini had read and approved them.[150] On one occasion, Grandi and Mussolini decided to write a bogus letter from De Bono to Mottistone in which De Bono explained the present situation at Asmara, denying allegations of ill-treatment and bombing in Ethiopia, and describing the help the Italians were giving to the local population. Both De Bono and Mottistone were aware of the fake letter, which Mottistone needed for one of his speeches.[151] Mottistone was convinced that he was working for a better understanding between Britain and Italy. He considered Italy 'a great country', and felt a deep admiration for Mussolini and Rome.[152]

At the end of the Ethiopian War, the Italophiles expressed their admiration for Mussolini to Grandi. However, it was evident from their letters that their main feeling was relief. Now that the Italian adventure in Africa was over, they hoped that the Anglo-Italian relationship could once more improve. They were willing to travel to Italy even more and to increase the number of Anglo-Italian events in London right-wing clubs. According to Charles Petrie, who was also one of the organisers of the '1900 Club', invitations to well-known Italians such as Marconi served 'a most useful purpose'.[153] Lloyd was optimistic that the end of the Ethiopian War marked a new era in international politics. He believed that public emotions would diminish 'with the *fait accompli*'. Grandi's letters to him were very affectionate and conveyed the sense that they had fought a battle together, although with more challenges to come: 'not only the spirit of friendship is to be restored but an "entente" established between our two countries. They have the same problems to face and hold the same solutions for the future of Europe'.[154] Amery shared the feelings of admiration for Mussolini (who had sent Amery a signed picture of himself via Grandi) and of optimism for the future: 'I think things are steadily moving our way and that Germany can be persuaded in the end to guarantee the peace of all the frontiers of Europe – providing it is clearly understood that Russia is not Europe'.[155]

Austen Chamberlain took a more cautious line and warned Grandi that the future was 'still in the balance'. He wondered if Mussolini was really great enough to be 'moderate and wise in victory', which was 'the sharpest test of states-manship'. In his view, Mussolini should have been content with placing Ethiopia under a mandate.[156] Grandi acknowledged that many difficulties still existed, but considered Austen Chamberlain's speeches in the Lords as 'the new start, the rebuilding, after this momentous year, and, I hope, the beginning of a new real friendship between our two countries' and thanked him not only as an Italian but also as a European.[157]

The most pro-Italian figures in the House of Lords were Lloyd and Mottistone, although they were increasingly joined by Sir John Lawrence Stonehaven and Lord David Malcom Mansfield, who belonged to an organisation called the Imperial Policy Group and strongly opposed sanctions. The division within Britain over sanctions, according to Grandi, was no longer bound to the issue of sanctions itself but extended to the future orientation of British foreign policy. Those who opposed sanctions believed that Germany was Britain's chief potential enemy and that Britain consequently needed an agreement with Italy in Europe, in the Medi-terranean and in Africa. From being a minority, they were increasing remarkably thanks to Italian victories in Ethiopia. Those who supported sanctions on the contrary believed that a historic conflict had already begun between Britain and Italy.[158] It was evident from some letters from Italophiles to Grandi that they perceived their campaign in both the House of Commons and the House of Lords as a battle for the future of Britain and not only for the Italian cause. That was clear especially in spring 1936, when Italian victories in Ethiopia helped the Italophiles' pro-Italian struggle. In March 1936 Lord Phillmore met Grandi, informed him of the Italophiles' vigorous activity, and took the occasion to 'express once again his admiration and loyal cordiality to the Duce'.[159]

Conclusion

Unlike most British Conservative imperialists, the Italophiles supported the Italian cause during the Ethiopian War because they were genuinely, and even roman-tically, pro-Italian and pro-Fascist. Their fight to preserve Anglo-Italian friendship was not simply dictated by fear of Hitler, although Hitler's shadow seemed to be always present as a threat to the European order. Grandi's letters to Mussolini, in which the ambassador explained his activity among the Italophiles, showed the continuous conflict between the good relations he established with them and Italy's deliberate creation of an Anglo-Italian rivalry in Italy. The next chapter on Italian Fascism and British society will investigate the consequences of that campaign. With Italian and German intervention in the Spanish Civil War, Grandi's work in London in sustaining an effective Anglo-Italian relationship once more became very difficult.[160]

Notes

1. Mike Cronin, *The Failure of British Fascism: The Far Right and the Fight for Political Recognition* (London and Basingstoke: MacMillan, 1996); Richard Thurlow, 'The Failure of British Fascism, 1932–1940', in Andrew Thorpe (ed), *The Failure of Political Extremism in Inter-War Britain* (Exeter: Exeter University Press, 1989); Thurlow, 'The Return of Jeremiah: the Rejected Knowledge of Sir Oswald Mosley in the 1930s', in Kenneth Lunn and Richard Thurlow (eds), *British Fascism: Essays on the Radical Right in inter-War Britain* (London: Croom Helm, 1980).

2. For example, Quartararo and Nello, who defined their activity as typical of British conservative policy, along the lines of Vansittart's, have almost ignored them (Rosaria Quartararo, *Roma tra Londra e Berlino. La politica estera fascista dal 1930 al 1940*, Rome: Bonacci, 1980, p. 89; Paolo Nello, *Un fedele disubbidiente. Dino Grandi da Palazzo Chigi al 25 luglio*, Bologna: Il Mulino, 1993, p. 253). Richard Griffiths has however recognised their peculiarity in an interesting book dedicated to British pro-Nazis (*Fellow Travellers of the Right: British Enthusiasts for Nazi Germany, 1933–39*, London: Constable, 1980, p. 15).

3. David N. Dilks, 'British Reactions to Italian Empire-Building, 1936–1939', in Enrico Serra and Christopher Seton-Watson (eds.), *Italia e Inghilterra nell'età dell'imperialismo* (Milan: Angeli, 1990), pp. 165–94; Aaron L. Goldman, 'Sir Robert Vansittart's Search for Italian Cooperation against Hitler', *Journal of Contemporary History*, 1974, 13, pp. 93–130; Ken Ishida, 'Mussolini and Diplomats in the Ethiopian War. The Foreign Policy Decision-Making Process in Fascist Italy', *Journal of Law and Politics of Osaka City University*, 42, 4 (1996), pp. 1–11.

4. Suvich to Grandi, 21 March 1936, ASMAE, *AL*, b. 912, f. 1, sf. 1.

5. 'Comizio fascisti britannici all'Albert Hall', Grandi to foreign ministry, 23 March 1936, ibid.

6. Thurlow, *The Failure*, p. 73.

7. 'Comizio fascisti britannici all'Albert Hall', Grandi to foreign ministry, 23 March 1936, ASMAE, *AL*, b. 912, f. 1, sf. 1.

8. 'Settimanale "Action" – campagna anti-sanzionista', Grandi to foreign ministry, 2 May 1936, ibid.

9. 'British Youth Refuse to Fight for the League of Nations', *The Saturday Review*, 14 March 1936.

10. Richard Reynell Bellamy, *We Marched with Mosley* (Holt, Norfolk: 1968), 4 vols, typescript, SUL, *Special Collections and Archives, BU Collection, Memoirs of Members of the BUF*, 5/6, p. 424.

11. Grandi to foreign ministry, 5 November 1936, ASMAE, *AL*, b. 912, f. 1, sf. 2.

12. Anne Brock Griggs, BUF Women's Propaganda Officer, to Italian embassy, ASMAE, *AL*, b. 912, f. 1, sf. 1.

13. See for example the review of a book by Mario Pigli, *Italian Civilisation in Ethiopia* (Rome: Dante Alighieri, 1936) in *Action*, 21 May 1936; Virginio Gayda, 'Italy and Empire', *The Fascist Quarterly*, II, 3, July 1936, pp. 353–60.

14. 'Campagna anticomunista e antisemita fascisti britannici', Grandi to foreign ministry, 14 October 1936, ASMAE, *AP*, *GB*, b. 12, f. 2.

15. Grandi to foreign ministry, 15 October 1936, ASMAE, *AL*, b. 912, f. 1, sf. 2; 'Manifestazioni fascismo britannico', Grandi to foreign ministry, 16 October 1936, ASMAE, *AP*, *GB*, b. 12, f. 2.

16. Grandi to foreign ministry, 25 March 1935, ASMAE, *AL*, b. 912, f. 1, sf. 1.

17. Italian consulate in Liverpool to London embassy and to foreign ministry, 29 September 1936, ibid., sf. 2.

18. ASMAE, *DeF*, *CG*, b. 41, f. 102 ('Documenti non spediti, 1934–37'). No date, probaby end of 1935.

19. Italian ministry of interior to foreign ministry, 4 October 1935, ASMAE, *AP*, *GB*, b. 12, f. 2.

20. On Mussolini's definition of Fascism as universal in 1932, and on his commitment to international fascism even before 1932, see Roger Griffin (ed.), *International Fascism: Theories, Causes and the New Consensus* (London: Arnold, 1998).

21. Grandi to foreign ministry, 13 November 1936, ASMAE, *AL*, b. 912, f. 1, sf. 2. On BUF violence and the question of uniforms, see Thurlow, 'British Fascism and State Surveillance, 1934–45', *Intelligence and National Security*, 1988, 3 (1), pp. 77–99; Stephen M. Cullen, 'Political Violence: the Case of the British Union of Fascists', *Journal of Contemporary History*, 1993, 28 (2), pp. 245–67; Robert Benewick, *Political Violence and Public Order: A Study of British Fascism* (London: Penguin, 1969).

22. 'Fascismo e comunismo in Gran Bretagna. Eventuali provvedimenti legislativi', Grandi to foreign ministry, 6 novembre 1936, ASMAE, *AP*, *GB*, b. 12, f. 2.

23. Grandi to foreign ministry, 15 giugno 36, ASMAE, *AL*, b. 912, f. 1, sf. 1.

24. 'Personale per Vitetti', De Peppo a Vitetti, 31 July 1936, ibid.

25. 'Fascismo inglese – William Allen – Domanda di udienza con S. E. il Capo del Governo', Grandi to foreign ministry, 23 October 1936, ASMAE, *AL*, b. 912, f. 1, sf. 2; De Peppo to Grandi, 3 November 1936, ibid.

26. See for example the Italian consul in Cardiff Renato Citarelli to Grandi, 13 October 1936, ibid., and embassy to Citarelli, 14 October 1936, ibid.

27. Guido Bartolotto, *Il fascismo nel mondo* (1938), in *Il fascismo nella Treccani*, edited by Giorgio Galli (Milan: Terziaria, 1997), p. 218; p. 228.

28. Daniel Waley, *British Public Opinion and the Ethiopian War, 1935–6* (London: Temple Smith, 1975), p. 25.
29. Ibid., p. 76.
30. Oswald Mosley, *A Policy for Britain* (Ramsbury: Mosley Publications, 1947), pp. 7–8.
31. John Evelyn Wrench, *Francis Yeats-Brown, 1886–1944* (London: Eyre and Spottiswoode, 1948), p. 243; after 8 September 1943 none of them could remain in or travel to Italy safely, since they were suspected of being fascists (p. 255).
32. G. C. Webber, *The Ideology of the British Right, 1918–1939* (London and Sidney: Croom Helm, 1986), pp. 37–8.
33. Charles Petrie, *The British Problem* (London: Ivor Nicholson and Watson, 1934), pp. 19–20; L. P. Carpenter, 'Corporatism in Britain, 1930–45', *Journal of Contemporary History*, 11 (1976), p. 8.
34. Gianni Silei, 'I conservatori britannici e il fascismo (1929–1935). La parabola discendente di una "storica amicizia"', *Il Politico*, LVII, 1992, 3, pp. 527–8.
35. Martin Blinkhorn (ed.), *Fascists and Conservatives: The Radical Right and the Establishment in Twentieth-Century Europe* (London: Unwin Hyman, 1990), p. 7.
36. Wrench, *Francis Yeats-Brown*, p. 120.
37. Douglas Jerrold, *Georgian Adventure* (London: Collins, 1937), p. 8.
38. Jerrold, *Britain and Europe, 1900–1940* (London: Collins, 1941), p. 84.
39. Patrick Howarth, *Squire: Most Generous of Men* (London: Hutchinson, 1963), p. 223. See also Squire's literary autobiography, John Squire, *Reflections and Memoires* (London: William Heinemann, 1935).
40. Another conservative club, the Carlton Club, played a similar role. See Charles Petrie, *The Carlton Club* (London: Eyre and Spottiswoode, 1955); Nick Smart, *The National Government, 1931–40* (London and Basingstoke: MacMillan, 1999), p. 102.
41. Jerrold, *Britain and Europe*, pp. 132–3. See also Id., *Georgian Adventure*, p. 27: 'I have lived, thank God, to see the beginning of a Catholic revival in England'.
42. Wrench, *Francis Yeats-Brown*, p. 224.
43. Ibid., p. 228.
44. Charles Petrie, *Mussolini* (London: The Holme Press, 1931), p. 77. The book was part of a series on 'Makers of the Modern Age', edited by Osbert Burdett. Petrie, *Monarchy in the Twentieth Century* (London: Dakers, 1952); id., *The Modern British Monarchy* (London: Eyre and Spottiswoode, 1955).
45. Petrie, 'Foreign Affairs', *The English Review*, XXIX, vol. 60, February 1935, p. 230; Jerrold, 'The King's Jubilee', ibid., XXIX, vol. 60, May 1935, p. 522.

46. See Maura O'Connor, *The Romance of Italy and the English Political Imagination* (New York: St Martin's Press, 1998). See also Wrench, *Francis Yeats-Brown*, p. 166, and the proliferation of pamphlets on the classless society during the 1930s: Harold Goad, *The Making of the Corporate State: A Study of Fascist Development* (London: Christophers, 1932); Goad and Currey, *The Working of a Corporate State: A Study of National Co-operation*, (London: Nicholson & Watson, 1933); Currey, *Insurance and Social Welfare in Italy* (London: 1938); Karl Walter, *The Class Conflict in Italy* (London: P. S. King & Son, 1938); Harold Goad and Michele Catalano, *Education in Italy* (Rome: Laboremus, 1939).

47. Petrie, *Lords of the Inland Sea: A Study of the Mediterranean Powers* (London: Lovat Dickson Limited, 1937), p. 6.

48. Petrie, *Mussolini*, p. 37.

49. Ibid., p. 171.

50. Petrie, *Lords of the Inland Sea*, p. x.

51. Wrench, *Francis Yeats-Brown*, p. 179.

52. Marla Susan Stone, *The Patron State: Culture and Politics in Fascist Italy* (Princeton: Princeton University Press, 1998), p. 165.

53. Wrench, *Francis Yeats-Brown*, p. 168.

54. Henry C. Usborne, 'The New Mediterranean Problem and its Solution', *The English Review*, December 1936, vol. 63, pp. 565–7.

55. Charles Petrie, 'Foreign Affairs', ibid., XXVIII, vol. 59, August 1934, pp. 224–31; Id., 'Foreign Affairs', ibid., XXVIII, vol. 59, July 1934, pp. 93–100.

56. Charles Petrie, 'Foreign Affairs', ibid., XXIX, vol. 60, March 1935, p. 353.

57. Muriel Currey, 'Where Three Frontiers Meet', ibid., XXIX, vol. 61, November 1935, p. 590.

58. 'Germany's Second Revolution', *The Bulletin of International News*, XI, 1, 5 July 1934, p. 11; 'The Independence of Austria', ibid., XI, 4, 16 August 1934, p. 4.

59. 'The Agreements between France and Italy', ibid., XI, 14, 10 January 1935, p. 3; 'The Stresa Conference', ibid., XI, 21, 18 April 1935, p. 3. On the feeling of optimism after the Stresa conference in Britain, see R. J. Q. Adams, *British Politics and Foreign Policy in the Age of Appeasement, 1935–39* (London and Basingstoke: MacMillan, 1993), pp. 20–1.

60. See for example 'Italy and Ethiopia', *The Bulletin of International News*, XII, 2, 27 July 1935.

61. See Luigi Goglia, 'La propaganda italiana a sostegno della guerra contro l'Etiopia svolta in Gran Bretagna nel 1935–36', *Storia Contemporanea*, XV (1984), 5, pp. 845–908.

62. 'Italy's Economic Position', *The Bulletin of International News*, XII, 4, 31 August 1935, p. 5.

63. 'Italy, Ethiopia, and the League Committee's Report', ibid., XII, 6, 28 September 1935, p. 5.

64. 'La nuova "Italia Nostra" – Le pagine inglesi', *L'Italia Nostra*, 8 November 1935, n. 352, p. 1.

65. Grandi to Mussolini, 5 November 1935, ASMAE, *DeF*, *CG*, b. 39, f. 93, sf. 1, ins. 1.

66. Harold Goad, 'Italy's proud poverty', *The British-Italian Bulletin*, 8 November 1935, n. 352, pp. 1/2.

67. Helen Rossetti Angeli, 'Peoples' Short Memory', ibid., 2 May 1936, p. 3.

68. L. D. Cosgrove, 'World's debt to Italian culture – The new Italy', ibid., 13 December 1935, p. 2. See also Charles Peter Brand, *Italy and the English Romantics: The Italianate Fashion in Early Nineteenth-Century England* (Cambridge: Cambridge University Press, 1957).

69. 'A record of past comradeship', 5 June 1936, *The British-Italian Bulletin*, p. 1.

70. See especially ASMAE, *DeF*, *CG*, b. 39, f. 93, sf. 1, ins. 1.

71. See for example the novel by Muriel Spark, *The Prime of Miss Jean Brodie* (London: Penguin, 1961) also transformed into a movie, and Zeffirelli's recent movie *Tea with Mussolini* (1999).

72. Ezra Pound, 'The Fascist Ideal', *The British-Italian Bulletin*, 18 April 1936, n. 16, p. 2.

73. Ezra Pound 'A keystone of Europe', ibid., 27 December 1935, p. 1.

74. 'Ancient Roman Spirit Reborn', ibid., 25 April 1936, n. 17, p. 4.

75. Osbert Sitwell, 'Alma Mater', ibid., 3 January 1936, p. 1.

76. G. K. Chesterton, 'Rome v Carthago', article from *La Revue Catholique des Idees et des Faits*, edited in Brussels, quoted in *The British-Italian Bulletin*, 18 January 1936, n. 3, p. 1.

77. G. K. Chesterton to Villari, 12 February 1936, British Library, *Manuscript Collection*, Add. 73240, f. 139. Chesterton also provided Villari with his own pro-Italian articles allowing him to quote them in several newspapers.

78. Polson Newman, 'A nuisance to civilisation', *The British-Italian Bulletin*, 7 March 1936, n. 10, p. 1.

79. 'Ethiopia as a model!', ibid., 4 April 1936, n. 14, p. 1; 'Public ignorance exploited', ibid., 2 May 1936, n. 18, p. 1.

80. 'Italy's part', ibid., 14 March 1936, n. 11, p. 1; Arnold H. Richmond, 'A partner indispensable', ibid., 21 March 1936, n. 12, p. 1.

81. 'To a brighter future', ibid., 4 July n. 27, p. 1.

82. John Frederick Charles Fuller, *The First of the League Wars: Its Lessons and Omens* (London: Eyre and Spottiswoode, 1936); Muriel Currey, *A Woman at the Abyssinian War* (London: Hutchinson & Co, 1936); E. W. Polson Newman, *The New Ethiopia* (London: Rich and Cowan, 1938).

83. Jerrold, *They That Take the Sword: The Future of the League of Nations* (London: John Lane, 1936).

84. John Beckett, *After My Fashion: Twenty Post-War Years* (London: 1940), typescript, SUL, *Special Collections and Archives, BU Collection, Memoirs of Members of the BUF*, 5/1, p. 363.

85. Anthony John Trythall, *'Boney' Fuller: the Intellectual General, 1878–1966* (London: Cassell, 1977), p. 181; p. 188.

86. Fuller, *The First of the League Wars*, p. 1.

87. Francis Yeats-Brown, *Bengal Lancer* (London: Victor Gollancz, 1930).

88. Currey, *A Woman at the Ethiopian War*, p. 76.

89. Fuller, *The First of the League Wars*, p. 55.

90. Ibid., p. 57.

91. Ibid., p. 58; p. 60.

92. Ibid., p. 61; p. 62.

93. Ibid., p. 56.

94. Ibid., p. 63.

95. Ibid., p. 63.

96. Bellamy, *We Marched with Mosley*, p. 439.

97. Currey, *A Woman at the Ethiopian War*, p. 70.

98. The most recent example is the worldwide success obtained by the London writer Louis de Bernières with the novel *Captain Corelli's Mandolin* (London: Martin Secker & Warburg, 1994, first edition), on the Italian and German occupation of Greece, in which the Germans were fanatical and cruel soldiers, while the hero, an Italian officer, only aimed to have a 'peaceful war', was civilised, had a sense of humour, played the mandolin and fell passionately in love with a young Greek woman.

99. Currey, *A Woman at the Ethiopian War*, p. 24.

100. See David Bidussa, *Il mito del bravo italiano* (Milan: Il Saggiatore, 1994).

101. Currey, *An Englishwoman's Impressions of Tigrai under Italian Rule: A Broadcast* (Rome: 1936), typescript, p. 1, BLPES, *Pamphlets Collection*.

102. Currey, *A Woman at the Ethiopian War*, p. 146.

103. Ibid., p. 249.

104. As early as 1936 Mussolini publicly praised the British Italophiles, 'journalists, writers and politicians who in the middle of the tempest never lost the exact vision of history' (Benito Mussolini, 'Verso Addis Abeba', *Il Popolo d'Italia*, 124, 3 May 1936, also in *Opera Omnia*, ed. by Edoardo and Duilio Susmel, vol. XXVII, Florence: La Fenice, 1959, p. 260).

105. Polson Newman, *The New Ethiopia*, pp. 25–6.

106. Ibid., p. 74.

107. Ibid., p. 142. In fact Graziani was known in Ethiopia mainly for being vindictive and ferocious in repressing the local resistance. See Giorgio

Rochat, *Guerre italiane in Libia e in Etiopia. Studi militari* (Treviso: Pagus, 1991), pp. 177–214.

108. Polson Newman, *The New Ethiopia*, p. 216.
109. Ibid., pp. 217–18.
110. Fuller, *The First of the League Wars*, p. 51.
111. See Enrico Serra, 'Diplomazia italiana, propaganda fascista e immagine della Gran Bretagna, *Rivista di storia contemporanea*, XV, 3 (1986), especially pp. 461–4.
112. Mussolini, 'La necessità di espansione dell'Italia in Africa', *Il Popolo d'Italia*, 241, 8 October 1935, also in *Opera Omnia*, p. 161.
113. Session on 'Italy and Ethiopia', 20 June 1936, BLPES Archive, *League of Nations Union*, 1/3, MF 416.
114. Giovanni Saracino, *L'impero italiano e l'Inghilterra* (Milan: Impresa Editoriale Italiana, 1936), p. 7.
115. Ibid., p. 7.
116. Alfredo Signoretti, *Italia e Inghilterra durante il Risorgimento* (Milan: Istituto di studi di politica internazionale, 1940).
117. Saracino, *L'impero italiano e l'Inghilterra*, p. 21.
118. 'Italian Fascist Organisation Activities in U.K. Dominions and Colonies', MI5 to Home Office, 8 June 1937, PRO, *HO* 144/21079, 699617/22. The propaganda against the British in Malta continued after the conclusion of the Ethiopian War. See Luigi Preti, *Gli inglesi a Malta. Una politica errata, la cui fine contribuirebbe a migliorare i rapporti anglo-italiani* (Milan: Bocca, 1938).
119. England was a great nation, 'but only on the map' (Saracino, *L'impero italiano e l'Inghilterra*, p. 22). In fact 'war with Britain would reduce Italy to a "Balkan level". But Mussolini had by then committed over 200,000 troops and the regime's prestige to war in Africa' (MacGregor Knox, *Hitler's Italian Allies: Royal Armed Forces, Fascist Regime, and the War of 1940–1943*, Cambridge: Cambridge University Press, 2000, pp. 10–11).
120. Galeazzo Ciano, *Diario 1937–1943* (Milan: Rizzoli, 1980; first ed. 1946), pp. 32–3.
121. Aldo Fiaccadori, *La supremazia economica inglese e le origini della sua decadenza* (Milan: Hoepli, 1940), p. 380.
122. Ibid., p. 388.
123. Mussolini, 'Riscossa demografica . . . in Germania', *Il Popolo d'Italia*, 49, 26 February 1935, also in *Opera Omnia*, p. 36.
124. Emilio Canevari, *La conquista inglese dell'Africa* (Rome: Istituto grafico tiberino, 1935), p. 59. Canevari later blamed the British for the origins of the Second World War in his *La guerra italiana. Retroscena della disfatta*, 2 vols (Rome: Tosi, 1948), accusing them of having been false friends of Italy ever since the First World War.

125. Canevari, *Graziani mi ha detto* (Rome: Magi-Spinetti, 1947), p. 26.

126. Canevari, *La conquista inglese*, p. 59.

127. Ciano, *Diario*, entry for 6 September 1937, p. 34.

128. Saracino, *L'impero italiano e l'Inghilterra*, p. 8.

129. Canevari, *La conquista inglese*, p. 307.

130. Saracino, *L'impero italiano e l'Inghilterra*, p. 32.

131. Ibid., pp. 113–14 (capital letters and italic in the original).

132. Mario Borsa, *Gli inglesi e noi* (Milano: Fasani, 1945), p. 71.

133. Grandi to Mussolini, 8 August 1935, *DDI*, 8, I, 691, p. 706.

134. Grandi to Mussolini, 26 December 1935, ibid., 8, II, 919, pp. 910–11.

135. Grandi to Mussolini, 14 August 1935, ibid., 8, I, 731, pp. 738–9; Grandi to Mussolini, 15 August 1935, ibid., 8, I, 746, pp. 755–6; Grandi to Mussolini, 23 April 1936, ibid., 8, III, 735, p. 783.

136. Luigi Villari, *Storia diplomatica del conflitto italo-etiopico* (Bologna: Zanichelli, 1943), p. 11.

137. Lady Milner to Grandi, 29 August 1935, ASMAE, *DeF*, *CG*, b. 39, f. 93, sf. 1, ins. 1; Grandi to Mussolini, 31 August 1935, ibid.

138. Beaverbrook to Grandi, 9 June 1935, HLRO, *Lord Beaverbrook Papers, Correspondence with Dino Grandi 1935–1964*, Ref: C/145.

139. Austen to Hilda Chamberlain, 18 May 1935, *The Austen Chamberlain Diary Letters: The Correspondence of Sir Austen Chamberlain with his Sisters Hilda and Ida, 1916–1937*, edited by Robert C. Self, Camden Fifth Series, Vol. 5 (Cambridge: Cambridge University Press, 1995), p. 482.

140. Grandi to Mussolini, 25 February 1936, *DDI*, 8, III, 297, p. 362.

141. Mussolini to Grandi, 19 October 1935, ASMAE, *Gab 248*, 1935.

142. Grandi to Mussolini, 17 October 1935, ASMAE, *DeF*, *CG*, b. 39, f. 93, sf. 1, ins. 1.

143. Leopold Stennet Amery, *The Forward View* (London: Jeoffrey Bles, 1935).

144. Ibid., pp. 134–5.

145. Ibid., pp. 141–3.

146. Amery, *Hitler's Claims for Colonies* (London: Trustees for Freedom, 1936), p. 3.

147. Grandi to Mussolini, 19 October 1935, ASMAE, *DeF*, *CG*, b. 39, f. 93, sf. 1, ins. 1.

148. Lord Lloyd to Grandi, 21 October 1935, ibid.

149. Grandi to Mussolini, 23 October 1935, ASMAE, ibid. In the same letter he also revealed that his work among the Conservatives had began ten months before.

150. 'Discorso Lord Mottistone', Grandi to Mussolini, 19 October 1935, ASMAE, *Gab 248*, 1935.

151. Mussolini to De Bono, 21 October 1935, ibid.

152. Mottistone to Grandi, 8 November 1935, sent from Grandi to Mussolini on 10 November, ibid.
153. Petrie to Grandi, 9 April 1936, ASMAE, *DeF*, *CG*, b. 43, f. 105; see also Lloyd to Grandi, 24 May 1936, ibid.
154. Lloyd to Grandi, 18 May 1936; Grandi to Lloyd, 23 May 1936, ibid.
155. Amery to Grandi, 25 October 1936, ibid.
156. Austen Chamberlain to Grandi, 7 May 1936, ibid.
157. Grandi to Austen Chamberlain, 8 May 1936, ibid.
158. Grandi to Mussolini, 22 May 1936, ASMAE, *DeF*, *CG*, b. 39, f. 93, sf. 1, ins. 2.
159. Grandi to Mussolini, 9 March 1936, ASMAE, *Gab 257* (1936), f. 3; see also Grandi to Mussolini, 6 March 1936, *DDI*, 8, III, 371, pp. 435–6.
160. Goldman, 'Sir Robert Vansittart's Search for Italian Cooperation against Hitler', p. 129; William C. Mills, 'The Chamberlain-Grandi Conversations of July-August 1937 and the Appeasement of Italy', *International History Review*, 19, 3 (1997), pp. 594–619; MacGregor Knox, *Common Destiny: Dictatorship, Foreign Policy, and War in Fascist Italy and Nazi Germany* (Cambridge: Cambridge University Press, 2000), p. 97.

–5–

Resistance and Decline: the *Fasci Italiani all'Estero* in Britain, 1938–39

When I think about the destiny of Italy, when I think about the destiny of Rome, when I think about all our historical events, I am brought to see in all this development the infallible hand of Providence, the infallible sign of the Divinity.[1]

The transformation of the Italian community of London into a corporative and imperial community, begun in the course of the Ethiopian War and solemnly announced by Dino Grandi at the end of 1937, continued until the end of the Grandi era. In fact, only Italy's declaration of war on Britain brought Fascist activities in London to an end. After the conquest of Ethiopia, and especially after British recognition of the Italian empire in April 1938, the attempt to improve Anglo-Italian relations was continuously interrupted by Italy's pro-German foreign policy, and was also complicated by the continued intervention in Spain. The crisis reached a climax with the racial laws of 1938. While the next chapter analyses Grandi's activity among the British right and his attempt to balance the pro-Italian policy of the right-wing Conservatives with the Rome-Berlin Axis, the present chapter focuses on the activity of the *Fasci* among Italian communities in Britain during the last two years of Grandi's era.

At the end of 1937 the foreign secretary, Galeazzo Ciano, suddenly decided to dismiss Piero Parini, the zealous organiser of the *Fasci* Abroad since 1928. Beyond the formal explanation, namely a question of financial mismanagement, it is important to understand whether the change at the general secretariat also involved substantial changes in policy, and whether this had an impact on the activity of the *Fasci* in Britain, and consequently on Anglo-Italian relations. At the same time, Italian foreign policy secured greater coverage in the Fascist newspaper published for Italians in Britain, and also in the teaching programmes of Italian schools. From the end of 1937 onward, the *Fasci* also organised the communities outside London into corporations; the fascistisation of small communities met a number of difficulties and proved less successful than it had first appeared at the end of the Ethiopian War.

Until May 1940 the organisation of schools, summer camps, *dopolavoro* and other assistance institutions in London continued as if Italy were not going to enter a war that the London *Fascio*, the consulate and the embassy regarded as solely

– 129 –

British: the moral and financial efforts of the Italian government for the education of Italians abroad had to continue, in theory until the conflict was over. This raises the question of the role of the *Fasci* Abroad within Italian foreign policy at the end of the 1930s: the chapter analyses the part that the spiritual preparation of the Italians abroad played in the preparation of the country for the war fought against Britain from June 1940 onward.

The Italian *Fasci* Abroad after Parini

The news of his own dismissal, after ten years of dedicated and enthusiastic work for the Italians abroad, came quite unexpectedly to Parini. His letters to Mussolini and to Grandi show shock and desperation; he sought at the same time to prove his innocence and to regain his position. Ciano informed Parini that the reason given for his dismissal was that he had been responsible for excessive expenses in the organisation of the *Fasci*. In response he not only justified his financial administration by reporting all expenses (and reminding the Duce that they had always been agreed by the foreign ministry) but also presented his personal crisis as a moral drama. Above all, Parini did not want the Duce to believe that he had been dishonest:

> If I am expelled so suddenly, in Italy and abroad major misconduct will be attributed to me, which will ruin my name with distrust and suspicion. I therefore appeal to your heart as a Leader for an act of generosity and leniency that may avoid a moral contamination of my past as a Fascist, as a fighter and as a soldier of Mussolini's Revolution. Whichever Your decision, Duce, I wish to reaffirm my untouched faithfulness as a soldier, as in all battles I fought following Your orders.[2]

When he provided data about his administration, he admitted that he had invested considerable sums of money in the building of schools and summer camps for the Italians abroad; not only were these buildings necessary, he argued, but also all the expenses of the general secretary had been audited annually by the Italian financial administration. In the tones that disappointed Fascists always used in writing to Mussolini,[3] he expressed his regret, in terms of the deepest pain mixed with flattery and unconditional love: 'The bitter pain that wrings my heart in these days, especially knowing that I have made You sad, is, I swear, the harshest punishment . . . You, as Caesar, do not condemn without having listened and I dare to ask you the privilege to be admitted to Your presence.'[4]

However, Mussolini did not seem interested in Parini's fate. He showed a peculiar lack of sympathy for and gratitude toward a man who so successfully dedicated his life to Fascism abroad.[5] It was indeed likely that, if Parini had made mistakes, it was as he claimed because of 'passion and faith, never from scepticism or carelessness'. The seven million lire of mortgages he had undertaken on buildings worth an estimated 30 million lire were 'worth the age in which the Italian empire had been born'. Yet his major successes were not simply financial: 130,000 children of Italians abroad had had the opportunity to get to know their fatherland; Italian schools, *Fasci, Case d'Italia* and *dopolavoro* organisations had appeared all over the world; between 1928 and 1938 the number of Italian teachers abroad had increased from 700 to 2,000; and 8,000 wives of Italians abroad had given birth to their children in Italy, thus avoiding their naturalisation outside Italy. When the Ethiopian War broke out and the League's sanctions were applied, the emigrants had sent about 160,000,000 lire to Italy. Over 4,000 emigrants volunteered to serve in Ethiopia, out of the more than 12,000 Italians who applied for service there: 'If we compare this data to that of the Italians who volunteered from 1915 to 1918, we shall have a sure sign of the incredible progress of patriotism of Italy's sons, the majority of whom had been born abroad.'[6] The children who came back from summer camps were filled with enthusiasm, new ideas, faith and health: any mistake that had been made, Parini swore, had been made for these children, 'and they have never betrayed us'.[7]

Parini also wrote to Grandi informing him about his personal situation. Yet these were clearly letters to a friend, from whom he did not appear to expect any practical help. Toward the end of 1938, he finally seemed to have accepted his fate, although he still remained fearful that his personal situation had not been clarified to Mussolini.[8] One aspect was clear by then: neither Mussolini nor Ciano made any precise accusation against Parini, whose letters remained simply unanswered. As had happened in 1932 to Grandi, and repeatedly to other members of the Fascist party, Mussolini's decision to dismiss someone did not need justification. The most likely reason for Parini's dismissal may therefore be found in Ciano's diary, in which the foreign secretary recorded his indignation that in September 1937 Parini had sent a proclamation to the Italians in Germany without informing the foreign ministry: 'he has lost any sense of proportion'.[9] Ciano immediately decided that Parini should be removed, a solution Mussolini ordered anyway in January 1938 because of the alleged waste of money in the management of the *Fasci*.[10] According to Ciano's diary, Parini might have spent too much money, but the principal problem was that Parini had claimed too much independence from the foreign ministry. His replacement by Attilio De Cicco, who was already a functionary of that ministry, was thus meant to strengthen the links between the *Fasci* Abroad and the ministry.[11] The change occurred at the point at which Italy left the League of Nations and strengthened its alliance with Germany, and may be considered as part of a general attempt from 1938 onward to strengthen Italian totalitarianism and Mussolini's personal dictatorship.[12] The fact that the summer camp organisation continued to expand – financially as well – in 1938,[13] suggested that Parini's removal was not due to financial reasons but to a shift in policy. For example,

L'Italia Nostra never mentioned the new chief of the *Fasci* Abroad; while it had always presented Parini as the father of the Italian children abroad and as leader and organiser of the *Fasci* throughout the world, De Cicco's personality never emerged.[14] It was now Ciano himself who became the organiser of the *Fasci*, even of summer camps, the 'direct *gerarca* of the Italians abroad'.[15]

Some changes in the organisation of the Italian *Fasci* Abroad did occur at the beginning of 1938. In February the foreign ministry ordered the *Fasci* to adopt a new measure of subscription. Instead of asking Italian communities to subscribe for every new initiative, the *Fasci* were ordered to ask for annual subscriptions, which were then distributed among the various activities. This was intended to alleviate the financial strain on Italian emigrants, who were experiencing economic difficulties in most countries, but most importantly had the advantage of marking a distinction between 'good' and 'bad' Italians. Indeed, never before 1938 had the control on Italians abroad had been so strict. According to Bastianini,

> the single subscription . . . will serve to indicate the *roles* of the good Italians, who must consider the registration of their names in the *albo d'onore* of the subscription as the accomplishment of an absolute duty to the Fatherland. The names of the absentees must be signalled and presented as evidence. Today all Italians must feel proud to march on the new path of imperial Italy.[16]

In June, De Cicco announced that the statute of the *Fasci* had been modified according to the new statute of the *Partito Nazionale Fascista*. Symbolism also underlined the change: the banners of the Legions of the *Fasci* Abroad that went to fight in East Africa became the new ensign of the *Fasci*.[17] After a long period in which the general secretariat had directly supervised the activity of the *Fasci*, it was now decided to decentralise the organisation in order to make it more efficient. Four delegations were created at the general secretariat: one for Europe; one for America and Australia; one for Asia, Africa and the Mediterranean; and one for the youth organisation abroad, the *Gioventù Italiana del Littorio all'Estero* (GILE). New positions were also created at the periphery: the *ispettorato di zona*, which had to control the *Fasci* of a national, or multinational, area; the *segretario di zona*, who controlled the *Fasci* of a consular area (a region within a country); the secretary of the *Fascio* and the *fiduciario di sezione*. The system became therefore more hierarchical than it had been. The secretaries of the *Fasci* no longer needed to communicate directly with the general secretary, but rather with the *segretari di zona* and the latter with the *ispettori di zona*, who then corresponded with the general secretary. The new statute also established that, since embassies and consulates were the highest authorities of the regime abroad, the *Fasci* had to be subordinated to them, although they were administratively independent. In particular, the *ispettore di zona* had to be in tune with the embassies and consulates in order to avoid having the *Fasci*'s activities clash with local politics. In fact, this supposed decentralisation resulted in a greater control of the centre over the periphery. Such a hierarchical organisation likewise favoured greater control by the *Fasci* over the Italian communities, and ultimately served the building of the totalitarian system: the joint work of the *Fascio* with the consulate meant that both were working for a common cause, since 'in a totalitarian regime such as Fascism the State is the party and the party is the State'.[18] The adaptation of the new statute of the *Fasci* to that of the PNF did not however mean that the *Fasci* Abroad moved under the jurisdiction of the Party. On the contrary, their activities remained under the supervision of the embassies, and ultimately of the foreign ministry, of which the general secretary remained part. Rather than the *Fasci* becoming influenced by the PNF, it was the PNF that lost independence.[19] The area most under the influence of the Party was the *Gioventù Italiana del Littorio all'Estero*, since the *Gioventù Italiana del Littorio* (GIL) was controlled by the PNF. However, although the GILE was organised along the lines of the GIL, it was still controlled by a delegation of the general secretariat of the *Fasci* Abroad, and therefore, from a practical point of view, by the foreign ministry, and only from an organisational point of view by the Party.

New rules likewise applied to membership of the *Fasci*. Whenever ascertaining the suitability of an applicant, secretaries had to check his 'military position in time of peace and especially in time of war', and his or her 'political and moral conduct'. The subscription fee was reduced to a fixed sum of 12 lire per year, which all Italians could supposedly afford to pay. The general secretary had to be informed of those who offered more: in this way, a form of Fascist solidarity was established, 'which honours the wealthy *camerata* and does not humiliate the *camerata* temporarily in need'. The main duty of women remained to help the *Fasci* in assisting the Italians in need. To the usual official Fascist celebrations, namely the foundation of the *Fasci di Combattimento* (23 March), the *Natale di Roma* (21 April), the March on Rome and the First World War victory (celebrated together between 28 October and 4 November), a new one was added, the Found-ation of the Empire on 9 May.

The GILE was ordered to expand as much as possible: its leaders, together with ambassadors and consuls, had to begin 'effective work to increase youth member-ship'.[20] The mission of the GILE was, even more than previously, one of military training, since the war office called for a voluntary recruitment of 4,000 pupils of the GILE, which also included youths living abroad.[21] Another major area of action concerned the *dopolavoro*, which played a fundamental role in the attempt to organise the communities into corporations.[22] The principal duty of Fascists abroad was above all to send their own children to Italian schools: 'on this aspect the secretaries of the *Fasci* must be intransigent by proposing adequate disciplinary measures against those who – without any justification – refuse to send their children to our schools'.[23]

The decline of a 'wonderful community'

When Giovanni Telesio handed over the secretaryship of the London *Fascio* to Bernardo Patrizi on 18 January 1938, the *Fascio* had almost 1,000 members.[24] The GILE numbered 1,371; and 140 children from London (200 from the whole of Britain) had been to the camps in Italy in the summer of 1937. The *dopolavoro* had been created in the previous few months, and was divided into three groups: the *Circolo del Littorio*, with 940 members; the *Mazzini e Garibaldi* in the Clerkenwell area with 210 members; and the sport section at Edgware with 236 members and four different sections (tennis, bowls, football and athletics). Apart from the usual organisations (the *Alpini*, the *Mutuo Soccorso Mazzini e Garibaldi*, the Ex-Servicemen), the new ones were created as corporations, such as the *Associazione esercenti di ristoranti e caffè* and the *Associazione tra gli importatori ortofrutticoli ed agrumari*.[25] During the previous year, the *Ambulatorio* of the *Fascio* had visited 2,123 children and had paid for 27 children to be cured in the Italian hospital. During the same year, the legal office of the *Fascio* had given free advice to more than 250 Italians. At the time 766 Italians were subscribing to *L'Italia Nostra*.[26] In March 1938 the newspaper described the London community as the finest Italian community in the world:

> It is not an exaggeration to describe the Italian community of London as wonderful. We do not believe it is possible to find in any other country on earth, even in places where Italians exemplify every magnificent civic and patriotic virtue, such a compact, enthusiastic, harmonious and Fascist community.[27]

The corporative direction of the community continued under Patrizi. In May 1938 the *Fascio* instituted a new workers' organisation, the *Associazione Nazionale Fascista dei Lavoratori*. Patrizi was very pleased about the response the new organisation received from the community, since within a few days 200 Italians had already subscribed to it. Yet the major reason for satisfaction, he reported to Grandi, was the attitude of the community toward Fascism: in his speech to the community at the end of 1937, the ambassador had encouraged the participation of Italians, and they now seemed to be more active than ever before, and showed themselves increasingly willing to accept responsibilities. Those who were most active were to be found among the members of the ex-servicemen's organisations and of the *Associazione Caffettieri*, which was an outstanding example of a Fascist corporation abroad. Although the financial situation of the *Fascio* was improving at the time, the *Fascio* had not been able to keep the restaurant in the *Casa d'Italia* open during weekdays. A group of about 60 Fascists, most of whom were members of the *Alpini* and of the *Associazione Caffettieri*, decided to rescue the restaurant by submitting a tender and by offering £500 as annual rent.[28] They constituted the 'Italian Catering Association Limited', later officially approved by the consulate.[29]

Corporativism and autarchy became part of the same effort toward organising the community in totalitarian fashion. The slogans that had frequently appeared during the period of sanctions, asking Italians to buy only Italian products, continued into 1938. The products advertised were generally those sold by the new corporations: for example in February, shortly after the foundation of the organisation of citrus-fruit sellers, new slogans appeared such as 'Italian housewives do use Italian lemons' and 'Italian chefs do prefer Italian lemons'.[30] In April, *L'Italia Nostra* calculated that if all 40,000 Italians who lived in Britain bought only Italian fruit and vegetables, they would give Italy about £1,000 per day. The *Fascio* presented autarchy abroad as part of the regime's permanent state of war:

> The regime entrusts your consciousness with such activity, and no one could ever control your consciousness. It will be an unknown and unacknowledged effort, comparable to the effort of a soldier in a trench. But is was exactly the unknown soldier who won both the war of 1918 and the Ethiopian War.[31]

Linked with autarchy and with the new empire was the myth of repatriation. Italy, it was claimed, no longer needed other countries' help, either in terms of imports or of emigration. That did not mean that Italy intended to withdraw from its project of world expansion: emigrants who were successful abroad because of their skills were required to remain abroad and continue their economic (and possibly political) activity. But poor emigrants had to return to Italy, where, thanks to the empire and Fascist economic policy, jobs were now supposed to be available to everybody. Together with the African colonies, the foundation of new 'autarchic' towns in the Italian countryside was intended as a replacement for emigration abroad. Both the Pontine Marshes (where Mussolini founded five new towns between 1932 and 1938) and the colonies in East Africa had to be considered as new lands of Italy. One of the main aspects of the new towns was their 'autarchic economy', since each of them was responsible for one particular type of production.[32] The regime's propaganda thus reflected two major dreams of the 1920s and 1930s: the Fascist dream that the Italian abroad would no longer be a working-class emigrant, and the emigrant's eternal dream to return to his or her own country.[33]

From the correspondence between the London *Fascio*, the London embassy and the Italian foreign ministry, it is evident that the control of the *Fascio* over the Italians increased considerably from 1938 onward. That confirmed MI5's belief that Italian Fascists were working as spies in the community and reporting information about the non-Fascists to the embassy. However, the increase in control also served to identify those Italians who were facing economic problems and needed help. The *Fascio* began reporting about almost everybody in the community, be they members who needed help or letters of recommendation or anti-Fascists who needed to be threatened. The general secretary's renewed insistence on strict application of the rules for admission to the *Fasci* was also a reason for investigating more fully the backgrounds of those who asked to become members. According to the statute, rules 'did not need commentary', which meant the authorities of the *Fasci* had to respect them without discussion. Yet cases occurred in which the secretary of the London *Fascio* asked to be allowed to make exceptions, particularly in the case of rich, influential employers who could be useful members. Two Italian brothers, Giovanni and Ernesto Quaglino, offer one such example: they had previously asked for British citizenship, but later withdrew their applications, choosing instead to apply for *Fascio* membership. To have asked to become British was of course enough to prevent the *Fascio* from accepting them, since that was considered a most anti-patriotic gesture. Yet as Patrizi explained to the general secretary, the Quaglino brothers represented 'English interests worth millions of pounds', and it clearly did make a difference if they presented themselves to the British as Italians and Fascists. Secondly, the two brothers represented one of the top hotel groups in London, which was not only a sign of prestige for Italy in a foreign country, but also meant that they employed hundreds of their compatriots. Hence if they were part of the *Fascio*, it 'would facilitate the work of assistance and penetration among Italian employees, which would not happen if the Quaglino were not part of the *Fascio*'.[34]

Arturo Magnocavallo, who replaced Patrizi as secretary of the *Fascio* in September 1938, continued to strengthen control over Italians in London. They were divided into good Italians – to be defended and recommended – and bad Italians – to be identified and reported to Rome. The consul also acted as a defender and mediator with the British authorities on behalf of the rights of Italians who needed, for example, permanent work permits and were part of the *Sindacato Lavoratori Italiani*. The reason given by the consul for doing so was that they were 'wonderful and hard-working fellow-countrymen who during their long residence in London had always maintained irreproachable conduct'.[35] Recommendations to help Italians find good jobs or become part of the *Fascio* depended on their being *ottimi italiani*, a status that could only be verified by establishing if the rest of the community held them in high esteem as hard workers and patriots. Patriotism needed to be proven. For example, emigrants who, despite financial difficulties, sent their children to Italy because they wanted them to receive a complete Fascist education were cited as models. So, too, were those emigrants with the almost mandatory large family.[36]

However, control over Italians abroad also took the form of calumny and denunciation, typical means of Fascist control in Italy since the very beginning of Mussolini's government.[37] The surveillance of Italian communities was based on the creation of feelings of generalised suspicion. Italians who had no open political views were suspected of being subversive. Whenever they travelled to Italy, the police stopped them at the Italian border and searched them. Rather than the OVRA (the *Organizzazione per la Vigilanza e la Repressione dell'Antifascismo* – the Fascist secret police), it was the activity of the *Fasci* that served as a means of control, a function that facilitated the emigrants' integration into the regime.[38]

The spy system also acted within Fascist institutions. At the beginning of January 1939, the President of the *Circolo del Littorio*, Enrico Andrea Abbiati, organised a vigilance commission, whose members had to check that no one in the *Circolo* acted in opposition to any of the rules of the statute.[39] From several letters between the secretary of the *Fascio* and the consul it is possible to see that many Italians had been watched regularly in earlier years; yet between 1938 and 1939 the consulate required the *Fascio* to provide an update about them. Information usually came to the secretary of the *Fascio* from anonymous 'voices', which meant from someone within the community. The 'voices', for example, provided information for a number of years that the owner of an Italian restaurant in the West End, Abele Giandolini, who employed Italian staff, secretly held anti-Fascist views. Although no one ever found proof – and for the previous three or four years nothing was ever reported about his political opinions – in 1939 the consulate asked for information about him. Someone promptly reported to the secretary of the *Fascio* that not only was Giandolini no longer suspected of anti-Fascism, but that he even contributed financially to several Fascist assistance institutions. The *Fascio* also knew about his earnings and investments both in Britain and in Italy.[40] Another case was that of anti-Fascists who had converted to Fascism, which in most cases occurred during the Ethiopian War, but who were still watched in 1939: the *Fascio* continued to check on them and to report on their affiliations and on their private life.[41] It was enough to fail to be part of the *Fascio* to be the subject of enquiries, even in the case of 'good Italians' who simply showed no public political attitude.[42]

One form of control openly employed was the interrogation of Italians who appeared to be informed about other Italians' anti-Fascism. Rome sometimes requested information on particular individuals in London. In January 1939, the general secretary of the *Fasci* Abroad ordered the London *Fascio* to interrogate the Fascist Abbiati, himself a member of the *Direttorio* of the *Fascio*, because he knew from Emilio Sala, a fellow-countryman who was also member of the *Fascio*, about the anti-Fascist behaviour of an Italian emigrant, Angelo Tosetti. Both Sala and Tosetti were employed by the same English industrialist. During a journey to London, talking with both the English employer and Sala, Tosetti apparently expressed 'shameful' opinions about the regime and the Duce. However, interrogation of Abbiati and Sala did not produce a 'concrete version', because the latter refused to collaborate. The secretary of the *Fascio* thus decided that they should confront each other. When this happened, Sala again refused to give information and claimed he did not want anyone to be accused on his evidence. He concluded by saying that if he ever told anything to Abbiati, he was ready to bear the consequences himself. This case showed the difficult position of Italians who were members of the *Fascio* and at the same time worked for a British firm. For Sala, to denounce anyone else employed in the same firm meant the risk that the employer would find out about it and possibly sack him.[43] Work relationships with the British, the denunciation of anti-Fascists and fear of being interrogated by the *Fascio*, all contributed to creating an atmosphere of mutual suspicion throughout the community, even – and perhaps especially – among the Fascists themselves.

Control over Italians increased even more when the regime inaugurated the census of the Jewish race in September 1938, following Mussolini's proclamation of the racial laws. The census also applied to Italian communities abroad,[44] and in November 1938 the embassy sent the following demand to its consulates throughout Britain: 'Please urgently communicate the names of the consular employees who appear to be of Jewish religion or of Jewish descent by listing also the uncertain cases. Enquires must be extended also to these employees' wives.'[45]

Anti-Semitism in Italy was not simply a result of the alliance with Germany, but part of the regime's propaganda about the improvement of the Italian race, based, especially after the Ethiopian War, on the concept of 'superiority of the Italian blood'.[46] Like Hitler, Mussolini began claiming that international Jewry was responsible for anti-Fascism; yet his anti-Semitism was above all a consequence of his totalitarian experiment toward the creation of an ethnically homogeneous Italian race.[47] Throughout the 1930s, he insisted that Fascism was transforming the Italians, both in their character and in their physical aspect, and racism was the necessary 'tool'.[48]

Persecution of the Jews nevertheless came quite unexpectedly to the Italian communities in Britain. *L'Italia Nostra* had always emphasised an extreme nationalism and the improvement of the race through the education of children, especially when promoting the summer camps and the activities of youth organisations. Yet in this case, as with the Italo-German Alliance two years earlier, Italian anti-Semitism appeared in the newspaper very suddenly. The racial laws were not preceded by any explanation, nor had the newspaper ever mentioned Jews or even German anti-Semitism before. At the beginning of 1938 *L'Italia Nostra* had for the first time put forward the view that some countries needed to reduce Jewish influence.[49] The first article on the question of race in Italy appeared in August and included a quotation from a speech by Mussolini during a visit to a summer camp of *Avanguardisti*: 'You must know, and everybody must know, that on the question of race we shall also shoot straight. To say that Fascism has imitated someone or something is simply absurd.'[50]

The explanation came only a week later. The newspaper claimed that it was hardly surprising that Italy felt the need to deal with the racial problem, and rejected the accusation that Italy had only copied the German example. Like most Fascist newspapers abroad,[51] *L'Italia Nostra* chose to downplay the Jewish question and to focus on the strengthening of the Italian race in general. Reporting an article previously published in *Il Legionario*, *L'Italia Nostra* claimed that the racial laws had emerged through the autonomous processes of Italian history. Moreover, the Italian theory of race was different from the German one: Italy, it was alleged, never saw the matter as a question of supremacy of one race over the others, but only of distinctions between races. As the newspaper emphasised, one great event had caused the racial problem to become an urgent one: the conquest of the empire, from which arose the question of the relationship between Italians and Africans. Yet independently of the colonial question, the defence of the race was something the regime had been building upon since its very beginning; the summer camps were vital in this:

> How can we define this wonderful performance, which renews itself every year, of thousands and thousands of young Italians, Italians by name and by blood, who come to our summer camps to the sea and to the mountains from all over the world, in order to draw more deeply the consciousness of their origins from the native soil? How can we define it if not the expression of the defence of the race?

It was thus evident that, even on this issue, Mussolini's Italy had not been imitating, but rather anticipating other countries.[52] Italian racism, according to *L'Italia Nostra*, started as early as 1919; Mussolini underlined the importance of the defence of the race during a party congress in 1921, and continued to express the same views after the March on Rome.[53] The press made evident the beneficial results of the regime's policy over race: in 1938 *L'Italia Nostra* proclaimed that the average height of Italians was 'in progressive increase', and *Il Legionario* published a list of Mussolini's speeches about the question of race from 1920 onward.[54]

Certainly a solution to the problem had become urgent when Mussolini founded the empire in Ethiopia. As Italian families began moving to Africa it was crucial, from the Fascist point of view, that they not mix with the local population and remained racially pure. *Il Legionario* explained that racial laws and the Jewish question were a consequence of the empire: 'history has taught us that empires are conquered through weapons, but are maintained through prestige'.[55] *L'Italia Nostra*, although less openly, hinted that anti-African racism was linked with anti-Semitism: 'to discriminate does not mean to persecute. This must be told to the all too many Jews of Italy and of other countries', in order that they refrain from 'panic', 'haughtiness' and 'useless lamentations'. The census was necessary in order to make Jewish participation in the nation's life proportional to the number of Jews living in Italy. Moreover, *L'Italia Nostra* continued, the Jews had always been racist themselves by claiming to be the chosen people; the 'equation' between

Semitism, Bolshevism and Freemasonry had been 'historically accepted' all over Europe in the last twenty years.[56] However, unlike *Il Legionario*, which insisted on the Jewish question and attacked the Jews on several issues, *L'Italia Nostra* tended to describe the racial question as part of a more general defence of the Italian race.[57] The racial question itself soon disappeared from the newspaper until March 1939, when an isolated article reminded readers that in East Africa it was necessary to maintain a clear separation 'between the dominant race and the dominated race, between the Aryan and the Semite, between the white and the black'; the mixing of those races would diminish the prestige of the colonisers and eventually bring them to decay.[58]

In a curt letter of February 1939, Ciano confirmed the regime's intention to expel Jews from the diplomatic service:

> With reference to previous communications on this subject, I shall wish to receive an urgent guarantee from Your Excellency that all Jewish personnel – whatever the level of their employment . . . – have been reported to this Ministry so that it is possible to proceed to dismissal.[59]

It is difficult, on the basis of very few documents on this subject, to measure the reaction of the Italian community to racial laws. According to De Felice's study of Italian anti-Semitism, both Italian diplomatic representatives and Fascist propaganda abroad tended to apply the racial laws with a light touch.[60] The London embassy and Italian consulates in Britain nevertheless carried out the census and respected the orders received from Rome. This was also because, as Ciano's letter made clear, it was the foreign ministry's prerogative to dismiss Jewish employees of embassies and consulates, since they were part of the diplomatic service. As Chapter 6 demonstrates, the racial laws complicated Grandi's relations with the British establishment. The hostile letters he received from British sympathisers who were nevertheless horrified by Italian anti-Semitism may also suggest that the relationship between the Italian community and British society was worsening. Unlike the BUF campaign, which since 1934 had been almost totally focused on anti-Semitism, the London *Fascio* had never demonstrated any interest in it. While BUF supporters saw the Jews as rich foreigners who were exploiting the British, the Italian Fascists in Britain do not seem to have made an issue of people of Jewish origin, be they Italian or British. The correspondence of the *Fasci* with the embassy and of the embassy with Rome, as well as the available files of the British Foreign Office and of MI5 give no indication of anti-Semitism within Italian communities. From the autobiographies of Italians who lived in London in the 1930s, it was evident that most Italians who embraced Fascism were at the same time, for obvious reasons, interested in maintaining good relations with Britain; none mention racial issues, nor the purported existence of a Jewish question.[61]

When the Italian authorities began to introduce anti-Semitic measures into the London community, even the secretary of the *Fascio* and the embassy seemed unwilling to persecute Italian Jews who were members of the *Fascio*. When Italians of Jewish origin had been good Fascists and were presently useful to the community, the authorities of the *Fascio* and of the Italian schools abroad could not understand why they had to get rid of them. Magnocavallo, director of school at the *Circolo del Littorio* and later secretary of the *Fascio*, was reluctant to sack an Italian teacher, who, besides being married to the director of the *Credito Italiano* in London, was the only teacher holding a teaching diploma in mathematics. Moreover, she had always discharged her duties admirably, and had even given her salary to Fascist charitable activities. He convinced consul Biondelli to ask the foreign ministry if she could remain in service at least for another year.[62] Similarly in December 1938, the secretary of the London *Fascio* obtained the support of both Grandi and the consul to ask the Italian ministry of the interior to make an exception in favour of a Jew who had been a member of the *Direttorio* and a former war volunteer.[63] Over the following months, Magnocavallo nevertheless continued his investigation into the racial origins of members of the *Fascio*.[64]

The atmosphere of surveillance within the community and of anxiety over international events was accompanied, especially in 1939, by a general worsening of the morale and economic conditions of Italians. Some emigrants were sufficiently alarmed to cease sending their children to Italian schools, and those who could afford it moved back to Italy. This led to a worsening of the financial conditions of the *Fascio*. By March 1939 the newspaper could not afford to buy propaganda photographs sent from Italy, and had to ask to the general secretary in Rome for financial support. In the same month the paper was reduced to four pages. In July the *Fascio* informed the general secretary that Italian Fascists in London were not sure that they could organise a journey to the Autarchic Exhibition in Turin because of the difficult conditions in which they were living.[65] The general secretary's request that the *Fascio* found a section of the GUF (the Fascist university students' association) in London likewise received a negative answer. After almost five months of attempts to find Fascist university students in the city, the *Fascio* had to explain its failure by the absence of 'Fascist elements'.[66] Even the corporations, the pride of the Fascist community in 1937 and 1938, began to appear weak and inefficient. Particularly after the international crisis of September 1938, when Germany's preparations to invade Czechoslovakia seriously threatened world peace, coffee-shop owners seemed less committed to their corporation than previously. A meeting of the organisation in January 1939 revealed that many members were ready to offer moral solidarity, yet were not as ready when the organisation requested financial solidarity in the form of the purchase of shares.[67] In June they were still discussing the same question: the organisation, from being a 'moral strength' had to become an 'economic strength', and what used to be 'feeling' had now to become 'interest'. The Fascist ideal of the London community remained a dream:

> We dream of the day when every Italian shop will be part of a corporation and will be able to satisfy all its needs directly from its own corporation . . . And we can see ever further . . . if one day the interests of one member, or of a group of members, or of the whole community, were threatened, our unity will be the best defence . . . At the same time the economic and numerical power of the organisation will render us more respected by the country in which we live.[68]

Fascistisation Must Continue: *Fasci* and Schools face the War

At the end of the 1930s, the *Fasci* still considered the Italian schools abroad as the most powerful element against 'de-nationalisation'.[69] Their programmes did not change significantly from the previous years, especially for younger children in the primary schools. However, for older children, especially those in the intermediate classes aged between nine and thirteen, the programmes showed increased attention to the teaching of history, geography and international events, which were used to highlight Italy's position in the world. This did not simply relate, as previously, to Italy's contribution to world civilisation, but extended to Fascist Italy's contribution to major changes in world politics and geography.

In 1938 the schools seemed to be working successfully. This reflected a period of improvement in Anglo-Italian relations: in March, Anthony Eden left the Foreign Office, in part due to a Grandi intrigue, and the ambassador was more than ever celebrated as the hero and the 'duce' of the community; in April, Britain recognised the Italian conquest of Ethiopia, as Neville Chamberlain implemented his policy of appeasement toward Italy, which *L'Italia Nostra* often acknowledged. Anti-British propaganda was less intense even in Italy; the massive number of anti-British publications from the Ethiopian War period was temporarily interrupted from 1938, to begin again in 1940. This reflected no substantial shift in foreign policy, but rather the belief that Italy was now in the position to face Britain on equal terms. The conquest and recognition of the empire and the campaign in Spain created a new confidence in Italy's universal mission. In a book published in 1938, the universal Fascist Asvero Gravelli underlined the inevitability of Italy's destiny as that of a civilisation re-born after thousands of years. The 'infallible hand of Providence', the 'infallible sign of the Divinity' emphasised by Mussolini's words for the schools abroad, was evident, Gravelli argued, in Ethiopia and in Spain. He defined Mussolini as 'eternal', 'infinite', and as the man who represented History as opposed to the rootless daily round. Unlike leaders in democratic countries, who were merely politicians, Mussolini was the reincarnation of an ancient glorious history and expression of a new age.[70] The shift in propaganda thus reflected this new self-perception, rather than any genuine pro-British feeling.

The situation of the Italian schools in London differed according to the areas in which they were situated. The school at the *Istituto del Littorio* continued to be celebrated as the finest example of a united, fascistised and imperial community. It was the only daily school in London, since the other schools were held in the evenings, no more than twice a week, and were situated in the poorer areas of the city where the majority of Italians lived. In January 1938, ninety-seven students were registered at the daily school.[71] If discipline caused no problems and most students spoke good Italian, this was entirely due to the fact that only children of rich families, Grandi's children included, went to the *Istituto*. Most of these children came from families of coffee-shop owners, who appeared to be the most fascistised social group in London. They were generally prosperous, occupied all day with their business, and happy to leave their children all day at the *Istituto*, where after school hours the children could take part in sports. Unlike poor Italian families, they did not need to put their children to work at an early age. This situation was certainly not a demonstration of the classless society of which the *Fasci* had always boasted, and as the Fascist organiser Ada Fantozzi remarked several times, was a serious limitation on the penetration of Fascism into the community. She often reminded the Italian consulate and the foreign ministry of the importance of creating a daily school in the area between Soho and Clerkenwell, because, although some families did not send children to the *Istituto* because it was far away and others did not because they were 'snobbish' and believed English schools to be better, for many Italians the problem was merely economic. Not only were registration fees high, but the refectory, books and bus service were expensive. In particular, the bus service was vitally important, because the school was situated in a non-Italian area, and the bus fee created further problems in convincing the parents to enrol their children. Another issue of concern for parents was the teaching of English, which according to the *Fascio* did not require more than one hour per day. On the contrary, several parents realised that, however important it was for their children to maintain *italianità*, they also needed to speak and write English as well as the natives in order to enjoy a chance of success in British society. A number of parents asked for an Italian school which taught in English. This the *Fascio* considered to be narrow-minded, a sign of not having understood the crucial role of the Italian schools in a foreign country.[72]

At the end of 1938, the students registered at the ten Italian night-schools in London numbered 906, 801 of whom were actually attending. The classes, normally held twice a week, took place in rooms supplied by the London City Council and the Catholic Church. According to Ada Fantozzi's reports, the schools were very successful: most students spoke good Italian and were acquainted with the major events in Italian history and of the Fascist 'revolution', as well as an understanding of the geography of the peninsula and its colonies.[73] The most effective means to create national consciousness among children who experienced a Fascist atmosphere only twice a week, and spent the rest of their time in difficult 'spiritual conditions', was the teaching of history linked with geography. This included, for example, programmes that linked the history of the *Risorgimento* to the age of Augustus and to the geography of *Alma Roma*.

A new school was founded in 1938. It was a 'secondary course', intended for girls only since it was held in the rooms of Don Bosco nuns. It was dedicated to girls of poor families who had to work and study at the same time. This created obvious attendance problems; indeed only two-thirds of the registered students were actually able to attend the courses regularly, and the school could only meet once a week. The aim of the course was 'Italian education': 'formation of a national consciousness, stimulus of desire for culture, appreciation of beauty'. According to Fantozzi, one of its major achievements was to stimulate the girls to start collecting Italian poems to teach their children once they became mothers: 'they have understood the national problem as a problem of language, and this gives us certainty that these girls will be good Italian mothers'.[74]

The programmes of Italian schools in 1938 and 1939 clearly reflected the recent changes in Italy's foreign policy: first and foremost, schools celebrated the empire. Alongside speeches by Mussolini and by other Fascists, readings assigned to pupils also drew on the writings of famous Italian poets such as Giosuè Carducci and Ugo Foscolo, and several stories set in Ethiopia. Most of them were politicised: they emphasised Italy's mission of civilisation in Africa and presented Badoglio and Graziani as Roman heroes of the renewed empire.[75] They described the continuity of Rome in history as a divine mystery and as a necessity for world order.[76] To remind the Italians abroad that they were part of this destiny, some readings included letters from mothers and wives of soldiers who had volunteered in East Africa and died for the empire, symbolising a sacrifice that embraced all, men as well as women. The imagery surrounding the Fascist widows was particularly used in the generation of emotions, as it had been for the widows of the martyrs of the 'Fascist revolution' after the March on Rome.[77] At the proclamation of the empire, Mussolini had reminded them that death was 'the sublime test of discipline'.[78] However, the school readings made no mention of the racial problem, of the racial laws in Italy, or of the purported existence of a Jewish question.[79]

If the final collapse of the Fascist community in London came with Italy's entry into the Second World War, it had in fact begun during the week of international crisis in September 1938. It was only temporarily alleviated by the international agreement at Munich between Britain, France, Germany and Italy, and seemed irreversible with the Pact of Steel, the military alliance between Italy and Germany signed by Ciano and the German foreign secretary von Ribbentrop in Berlin in May 1939, and with the outbreak of war in September 1939. The *Fasci* nevertheless continued their activities as if the international crisis were soon going to end. Italian diplomacy continued to work for the community's institutions, organising events as usual (schools, summer camps, *Befana Fascista* and political celebrations), and the Italian foreign ministry continued to finance those activities. Yet the community was changing. During the September crisis, Ada Fantozzi blamed the Italians for not being courageous enough. She divided the community into three categories: the cowards, who immediately left for Italy because alarmed by war preparations in Britain; the worried ones, who decided to withdraw their children from the Italian schools; and the good ones, who continued to send children to the schools with the usual enthusiasm. Her description of the 'few good Italians' suggested the idea of a return to the origins of the *Fasci* Abroad, when it was represented by only a handful of revolutionary pioneers. That ideal was proposed again by Gravelli in 1940, when he insisted that the PNF itself needed to return to the intransigence of its origins.[80] In a book published after the Second World War, Camillo Pellizzi, founder of the London *Fascio* in 1921 and the major intellectual of the *Fasci* Abroad, underlined once again that the Fascist 'missed revolution' was due to lack of revolutionary courage; as the situation in Britain demonstrated, Fascism needed the 'few good' patriots, not the 'cowards' or the uncertain.[81]

Despite the Fascist need for patriots, in times of difficulty and uncertainty about the future families worried about practical issues rather than about children's *italianità*. Italians were seeking to defend the results of their labour and were obviously worried that war might bring everything to an end. In poor and outlying areas such as Hackney, the *Fascio* complained that parents did not look after the children, who were free to do whatever they wanted. This resulted in lack of discipline and in irregular attendance at school. Fear of an international crisis was probably the cause of a shortage of teachers from Italy that was evident for the first time in 1939. During the school year of 1938–9 teachers were recruited mainly locally. The difficulty in finding Italians who could act as teachers was solved by the employment of nuns: three qualified teachers and nine nuns of the Don Bosco order worked in the London schools during that year.[82] The *Fascio* praised the nuns as missionaries of *italianità*, which showed the extent to which the Church and Fascism had come together. The Catholic Church thus came to rescue the most important Fascist institution, the schools, at the moment of their greatest difficulty. However, it was the Church rather than the *Fascio* that derived greater advantage from the situation. Indeed, following the racial laws, the alliance with Germany, the crisis in Anglo-Italian relations, and consequently the loss of support for Fascism from part of the Italians in Britain, the Church seized the opportunity to increase its own role in the community.[83] The nuns did not simply replace teachers previously sent from Rome, but apparently demonstrated an extraordinary degree of enthusiasm and dedication.[84]

Not only did the *Fascio* pretend that schools continued to work as usual, but it also blamed the British government for being excessively alarmist and for giving the 'impression of an imminent war' by distributing gas masks, preparing trenches and unleashing allegedly hysterical war propaganda from the newspapers during the first months of 1939. Even after the beginning of the war, the *Fascio* claimed that the British fear of German air attacks was exaggerated.[85] The history and geography of Italy continued to be the major topic taught in the schools throughout 1938–9. The *Fascio* continued to believe it important to commemorate all the glorious dates of Italy's history and to keep the students updated with 'the events which symbolise a step forward in the rise of imperial Italy'.[86] The records of the *Fascio* and of the schools give the impression that those responsible either believed that Italy would never become involved in the war, or that it would soon end. Until then, everything had to continue. While English schools closed, Italian schools had to remain open, with or without bombing. In October 1939, the Inspector of the *Fasci* in Britain, Patrizi, proudly recalled that, despite the conflict, the Italian government had never stopped assistance for and financing of the organisation of the *Fasci*, or of Italian schools, hospitals, welfare activities and summer camps. The outbreak of the war had not been enough, he argued, to interrupt such efficient and continuous activity. Because of the threat of a blitz over London, the daily primary school moved to the countryside, but the war was regarded as a temporary problem. For the moment it was enough to move the schools, or to provide a bus service for Italians now living outside London.[87] Since the city was completely blacked-out from five o'clock onward, it became impossible to hold classes in the evenings; the consulate reopened as morning schools six out of the eleven evening schools. Although only about 150 children were attending, this was nevertheless a remarkable achievement. Ada Fantozzi was proud to confirm that the *Fascio* had taken 150 children 'out of the streets, and now they live in an Italian atmosphere'.[88] It was a 'beautiful victory, an almost complete success, which gives us certainty of what the work of tomorrow will be'.[89] Apart from one qualified teacher, nuns were again doing most of the teaching. Since most families had moved to the countryside, it became necessary to pick up the children by bus every day from different areas outside London. Despite petrol rationing, thanks to the action of the consulate, buses continued to provide an efficient service. Drivers and assistants received instructions on how to act in case of bombing along the way. The refectory continued to be as good as it had been in the past. This situation lasted until May 1940, when military events made it necessary to shut down the schools, and a number of Italians were voluntarily repatriated. Even then, Ambassador Bastianini explained this measure by blaming increased danger in London, not the growing likelihood of Italy's intervention.[90]

Outside London

The spiritual and financial condition of Italian communities outside London was definitely worse than in the capital. Communities were qualitatively and quantitatively weaker: they received less attention from Rome; they lacked the presence of a 'mythical' Fascist such as Dino Grandi and of skilled intellectuals such as Camillo Pellizzi; and they were generally poorer, since they were situated in less prosperous areas of the country in a time of economic crisis and the threat of war.

In March 1938 the secretary of the Manchester *Fascio* informed the London *Fascio* that those who worked for his organisation numbered only a few volunteers without experience; they needed to do paid work, and so could dedicate little time to the *Fascio*. Yet even in 1939 this did not stop the organisation of celebrations and gatherings, for example the *Natale di Roma* or the *Befana Fascista*, nor the running of a primary school.[91] The Liverpool *Fascio* even managed to organise its first corporation, the *Associazione importatori ortofrutticoli ed agrumari*, and intended to create another one among coffee-shop owners.[92] However, consular reports showed that not only Manchester, but also Liverpool, Newcastle-on-Tyne and in general the whole of Northern England were showing serious symptoms of quantitative decline. Fewer Italians were arriving as emigrants and more were integrating into British society and leaving their community. The gravest sign of this crisis was the 'shocking decrease in the school population of all Italian schools of the area', where the Italians who were born in Italy were extremely few; most children had been born in England and had no interest in their parents' country. The fact that the children spoke Italian only during their few hours at school suggested that their parents did not care about their children's *italianità*, or simply that they worked all day and had no time to think about it. Moreover, if parents wanted the children to improve their social status, they knew that it was better for them not only to enter business as British subjects, but also to move to Southern England, where it was easier to find jobs.[93] Similar problems existed in Manchester, where the community was continuously diminishing, rendering it difficult to organise Fascist activities. The consulate could not even afford to maintain a proper *Casa d'Italia*, simply because it lacked the minimum number of members. The Fascists instead rented a room for their monthly meetings, and the premises were in such an unhealthy state that it was not possible to invite women. For this reason the consular agent in Manchester decided to transform part of his own house into a '*Casetta d'Italia*'.[94] Gatherings and celebrations were used as an attempt to reunite the otherwise dispersed community.[95]

The most difficult time before the war broke out was the Czech crisis of September 1938, during which many Italians applied for British citizenship. Among them, Patrizi sadly admitted, were several members of the *Fasci*. This happened especially in South Wales, an area particularly hit by the economic crisis.[96] Indeed, although the *Casa d'Italia* in Cardiff was operating and holding regular meetings, the Italians who lived in South Wales were dispersed in small communities and it was difficult for the *Fascio* to gather all of them for meetings and celebrations in Cardiff.[97] In addition, the financing of Italian schools, despite the Italian foreign ministry annual subscriptions, was creating problems because of the economic crisis and of unemployment in that area of Britain. The Cardiff consulate decided to reduce teachers' wages; they apparently accepted the reduction and collaborated with enthusiasm, yet further contributions from the foreign ministry were necessary in order to keep the schools open.[98]

Similar difficulties existed in Scotland, although the Glasgow *Fascio* was relatively well organised. *The Casa d'Italia* occupied a central position, since the community was dispersed in different areas of the city, due to the jobs of the emigrants, who were mainly shopkeepers (selling primarily fish or ice cream) and restaurant owners and could not establish their businesses all in the same area. In 1935 the *Fascio* bought a new and luxurious building for the *Casa d'Italia*; it also contained the *dopolavoro*, the Dante Alighieri Society, the GILE and the schools. Rooms for playing pool and for dancing were available, along with a restaurant. The area was safe, which was important because the children had to go to school on their own at night.[99] However, outside Glasgow the conditions of the *Fasci* were not as good. In February 1938 the Glasgow consul visited the cities of Aberdeen and Dundee, and his report to the foreign ministry showed that the situation was problematic. The community in Aberdeen, containing around 600 Italians, mainly consisted of fruit and fish merchants, and ice cream vendors. Very few were unemployed and the children had to help their parents in the shops, which generally remained open until late in the evening. That meant that the most important Fascist activities, such as the *dopolavoro*, the schools and the GILE, were almost non-existent. Most emigrants came from the same areas of Italy (Lucchesia and Liri valley) and were generally related to each other. That circumstance, along with their almost total lack of education, had made it impossible to find anyone who could act as a leader and give direction to the rest of the community. The school was not operating because the only teacher in the community was the wife of the secretary of the *Fascio*, and had moved to Italy. Yet the worst aspect, from a Fascist perspective, was that several Italians had recently acquired British nationality, and an entire generation was growing up with Scottish mentalities and habits. In general, the consul concluded, it was a good community, but needed firm direction from a talented teacher.

Even worse was Dundee, where the characteristics of the community were similar to those of Aberdeen, 'with an even greater state of neglect and indifference'. The *Fascio* had been 'for a long time in complete ruin'; the *dopolavoro*, the schools and the GILE did not exist. The 'best elements' of the community refused to accept Fascist positions at all, although they declared themselves to be good and loyal Italians. The only possible solution, according to the consul, was to send a Fascist teacher from Italy who could act at the same time as consular agent, secretary of the *fascio* and teacher of the school.[100] The main problem, especially in small and peripheral communities, thus seemed to be not anti-Fascism, which consular reports never mentioned, but a lack of interest in Fascism and a reluctance to become personally involved and to take on responsibilities. The Italian government was also responsible for this situation, since it had made little effort in the past to fascistise the small communities, certainly not to the extent evident in London and in other major British cities. Once this situation had existed for a number of years, the temptation to become more integrated into British society, and even to become British, increased strongly due in part to the international crisis and fear of war. Between the spring and autumn of 1939, Magnocavallo reported that from Aberdeen to Southampton the number of Italians who applied for British citizenship was increasing. This included several members of the *Fasci*, who were immediately expelled.[101]

Conclusion

Italians in Britain hoped that Mussolini could find a solution to the European crisis, or at least that Italian neutrality could last indefinitely. Some emigrants had sons in the British army and obviously saw the possibility of Italy's entrance in the war with horror. As Lucio Sponza has pointed out in a recent book on the Italians in Britain during the Second World War, the emigrants' hope that Italy would not become involved in the War was not simply due to practical concerns, but also to their divided loyalties (their desire to remain Italians and to integrate into British society at the same time) and to a dramatic sense of uncertainty, not only about their own future but also about their very identity.[102]

Such difficulties influenced the activity of the *Fasci*. The articles of *L'Italia Nostra* and the diplomatic correspondence make evident that even the Italian authorities in Britain hoped that Italy was not going to enter the war. Like the news of the Axis in 1936, news of the *Anschluss* and of the Pact of Steel were only briefly reported in the newspaper. The racial laws were applied mainly because of pressure from the foreign ministry in Rome rather than from any enthusiasm in Britain. *L'Italia Nostra* reflected the embassy's reluctance to persecute Jews. The newspaper supported racism with enthusiasm, yet that racism expressed itself not as open anti-Semitism, but rather claimed to seek the improvement of the Italian race, a viewpoint found in the newspaper throughout the 1930s. However this did not prevent the authorities from applying the racial laws, since control from Rome had increased due to the new centralised organisation of the *Fasci*.

The London consulate and the *Fascio* were first and foremost concerned with preserving the achievements of previous years. The *Fascio* sought to convince Italians that the coming war was not really going to affect the community. The Fascists required the Italian communities in Britain to continue their corporative organisation and to support the fatherland by introducing autarchy into their daily lives. Rather than asking Italians to resist the war in general, the *Fasci* presented the new measures as forms of resistance to British society; British war propaganda and later the outbreak of war were the principal reasons for the massive increase in the applications for naturalisation. The situation was more striking outside London, and in reality communities in other British areas tended to disappear from the pages of the newspaper. Fascist efforts against such a decline were mainly evident in London, and in the schools in particular. The reopening of schools, the maintenance of expensive services in time of war, and even a willingness to accept risks and drive children to school by bus under the threat of air attack were major examples. Such resistance activity inevitably involved a small section of the London community, and brought the *Fasci* back to the age of the pioneers, to the original idea of the Italians abroad, ready to make sacrifices for the fatherland in difficult times.

However, such spiritual and financial efforts did continue to play a role in the preparation of the Italians abroad for the war, which in Mussolini's mind, especially following the Pact of Steel, was clearly going to be a war against Britain and on the side of Germany. To the same end, the regime continued to organise summer camps for children even after Italy's entry into the war. The reorganisation of the *Fasci* Abroad in 1938 was part of that project. From diplomatic papers, and especially from the correspondence between Parini, Mussolini and Grandi, and from Ciano's diary, it is indeed possible to suggest that Parini's removal was due to the need to centralise the *Fasci*, and to increase the control of the foreign ministry over them as part of a wider attempt to strengthen totalitarianism and Mussolini's personal dictatorship along the road to war.

Notes

1. Mussolini, in *Letture classe quinta. Scuole italiane all'estero* (Rome: Fasci italiani all'estero, 1938), p. 27. I wish to thank Gerry Slowey for providing this book.
2. Parini to Mussolini, 7 January 1938, ASMAE, *DeF*, *CG*, b. 53, f. 128.
3. See Salvatore Lupo, *Il fascismo. La politica in un regime totalitario* (Rome: Donzelli, 2000), especially the chapter on 'Mussolini e i suoi uomini', pp. 398–413.

4. Parini to Mussolini, 12 January 1938, ASMAE, *DeF*, *CG*, b. 53, f. 128.
5. This may be seen as a lesser though significant example of Mussolini's cruelty and vindictiveness underlined by Denis Mack Smith in a recent criticism of De Felice's statement, in his biography of Mussolini, that 'the Duce was not a cruel man' (Mack Smith, 'Mussolini: Reservations about Renzo De Felice's Biography', *Modern Italy*, V, 2, November 2000, pp. 208–9).
6. Parini to Mussolini, 15 January 1938, ASMAE, *DeF*, *CG*, b. 53, f. 128.
7. Parini to Mussolini, 1 February 1938, ibid.
8. Parini to Grandi, 2 February 1938, ibid; Parini to De Revel, no date but attached to a letter sent to Grandi on 15 Oct 1938, ibid.
9. Galeazzo Ciano, *Diario 1937–1943* (Milan: Rizzoli, 1980; first ed. 1946), entry for 21 September 1937, p. 39.
10. Ibid., entry for 6 January 1938, p. 84.
11. De Cicco was a 'first hour' Fascist: *squadrista* at Foggia, he participated in the March on Rome, and was vice-director of the *Fasci* Abroad from August 1936. He remained general secretary of the *Fasci* until 1943 and joined the Salò Republic (Mario Missori, *Gerarchie e statuti del PNF. Gran Consiglio, Direttorio nazionale, Federazioni provinciali: quadri e biografie*, Rome: Bonacci, 1986, p. 197).
12. On Mussolini's attempt to accentuate the regime's totalitarian features, see Alberto Acquarone, *L'organizzazione dello stato totalitario* (Turin: Einaudi, 1965), pp. 307–9; Emilio Gentile, *La via italiana al totalitarismo. Il partito e lo Stato nel regime fascista* (Rome: La Nuova Italia Scientifica, 1995).
13. 'Bagni d'italianità – 18 mila giovani figli d'Italiani all'Estero in Patria', *Il Legionario*, n. 17, 20 June 1938, p. 6.
14. *Il Legionario* mentioned De Cicco only once, simply to inform about his appointment, on 31 August 1938, n. 24, p. 14.
15. *L'Italia Nostra*, 24 June 1938, p. 2; 'S.P.Q.R. – Cives Romani Sumus', ibid., 1 July, n. 491, p.1.
16. Bastianini to all Italian embassies and consulates, 14 February 1938, ASMAE, *AL*, b. 1015, f. 2.
17. 'Statuto dei fasci italiani all'estero', 1938, article n. 2, ibid.
18. *L'Italia Nostra*, 28 January 1938, n. 469, p. 4.
19. 'Segreteria Generale dei Fasci all'Estero – Circolare n. 859700-C', Attilio De Cicco to all secretaries of the *Fasci* abroad, to all embassies and consulates, June 1938, ASMAE, *AL*, b. 1015, f. 2. On the new phase of the PNF from 1938, see Paolo Pombeni, 'Il partito fascista', in Angelo Del Boca, Massimo Legnani and Mario G. Rossi (eds), *Il regime fascista. Storia e storiografia* (Rome and Bari: Laterza, 1995), p. 205; Paolo Pombeni, *Demagogia e tirannide. Uno studio sulla forma-partito del fascismo* (Bologna: Il Mulino, 1984).

20. De Cicco to all GILE commanders, to all embassies and consulates, 10 November 1938, ASMAE, *AL*, b. 1015, f. 2.
21. General secretary of the *Fasci* abroad to all GILE commanders, to all embassies and consulates, 10 November 1938, ibid.
22. Ciano to the general secretary of the *Fasci* abroad, 29 January 1938, ibid; De Cicco to all embassies and consulates, 'Circolare n. 50', no date but shortly after 29 January 1938, ibid.
23. Segreteria Generale dei Fasci Italiani all'Estero, *Disposizioni che regolano la vita e le attività delle organizzazioni fasciste all'estero* (1938), ibid.
24. The male *fascio* had 818 members and 187 applicants waiting to be accepted; the female *fascio* had 120 members and 33 applicants ('Verbale delle consegne al cambio della guardia del *fascio* Arnaldo Mussolini', Telesio and Patrizi to Grandi, 18 January 1938, ibid). See also 'Il cambio della guardia al *Fascio* 'Arnaldo Mussolini'', *L'Italia Nostra*, n. 468, 21 January 1938, p. 1.
25. 'Corporativismo in marcia – L'assemblea costitutiva dell'associazione fra gli importatori orto-frutticoli ed agrumari', *L'Italia Nostra*, 14 January 1938, n. 467, p. 1; 'Corporatismo in marcia – Verso l'associazione degli importatori di vini?', ibid., 4 February, n. 470, p. 4.
26. 'Verbale delle consegne al cambio della guardia del *fascio* Arnaldo Mussolini', Telesio and Patrizi to Grandi, 18 January 1938, ASMAE, *AL*, b. 1015, f. 2.
27. 'La collettività italiana "meravigliosa"', *L'Italia Nostra*, 18 March 1938, n. 476, p. 1.
28. Patrizi to Grandi, 6 May 1938, ASMAE, *AL*, b. 1015, f. 2.
29. Biondelli to foreign ministry and to the London embassy, 13 June 1938, ibid.
30. *L'Italia Nostra*, 18 February 1938, n. 472, p. 2.
31. 'La relazione dell'ispettore dei fasci delle isole britanniche', ibid., 1 April, n. 478, p. 1 (cont. at p. 4). A similar appeal to the Italians in Britain came also from *Il Legionario* ('Inghilterra', n. 11, 16 April 1938, p. 26).
32. War remained a central element of both internal and external colonies: in the first case it was a metaphorical war against nature, destined to educate the new generations to real wars. Piero Bevilacqua, 'Le bonifiche', in Mario Isnenghi, ed, *I luoghi della memoria. Simboli e miti dell'Italia unita* (Rome and Bari: Laterza, 1996), p. 412; Charles Burdett, 'Journeys to the *Other* Spaces of Fascist Italy', *Modern Italy*, V, 1, May 2000, pp. 16–19; Oscar Gaspari, 'Bonifiche, migrazioni interne, colonizzazioni (1920–1940)', in Piero Bevilacqua, Andreina De Clementi and Emilio Franzina (eds), *Storia dell'emigrazione italiana*, (Rome: Donzelli, 2001), pp. 323–41; Steen Bo Fraudsen, '"The War that We Prefer": the Reclamation of the Pontine Marshes and Fascist Expansion', in Robert Mallett and Gert Sørensen (eds), *International Fascism, 1919–45* (London: Frank Cass, 2002), p. 69–82.
33. 'La colonizzazione demografica in atto nell'impero', *L'Italia Nostra*, 15 April 1938, n. 480, p. 8; 'La costituzione di una commissione permanente per il

rimpatrio degli italiani dall'estero', ibid., 2 December 1938, n. 513, p. 1; 'Il rimpatrio di connazionali dall'estero. Un primo scaglione di mille italiani', ibid., 3 March 1939, p. 1. 'Rimpatrio degli italiani all'estero', *Il Legionario*, n. 32, 20 November 1938, p.1

34. Patrizi to the General Secretary, 18 March 1938, ASMAE, *AL*, b. 1015, f. 2.
35. Magnocavallo to Biondelli, 19 December 1938, ASMAE, *AL*, b. 1068, f. 1.
36. Magnocavallo to General Secretary, 17 January 1939, ibid; Patrizi to Capodanno, 6 February 1939, ibid.
37. Mimmo Franzinelli, *Delatori. Spie e confidenti anonimi: l'arma segreta del regime fascista* (Milan: Mondadori, 2001).
38. Franzinelli, *I tentacoli dell'OVRA. Agenti, collaboratori e vittime della polizia politica fascista* (Turin: Bollati Boringhieri, 1999), p. 170; see also Romano Canosa, *I servizi segreti del Duce. I persecutori e le vittime* (Milan: Mondadori, 2000). For an interesting comparison with Nazi Germany, see Robert Gellately, *The Gestapo and German Society: Enforcing Racial Policy, 1933–1945* (Oxford: Clarendon, 1990).
39. Magnocavallo to the Fascist Celeste Orsi, who was asked to be part of that commission, 25 January 1939, ASMAE, *AL*, b. 1068, f. 1.
40. Magnocavallo to Biondelli, 5 February 1939, ibid.
41. See for example the case of the ex-socialist Giuseppe Sinicco, wrongly classified as an ex-anarchist by Magnocavallo, who also mistook the year of Sinicco's conversion to Fascism, which did not happen in 1933 but during the Ethiopian War. 'Oggetto: Sinicco Giuseppe fu Luigi', Magnocavallo to London consulate, 6 April 1939, ASMAE, *AL*, b. 1068, f. 1; see also Sinicco, *Le memorie di un calzolaio da Borgognano a Londra* (Udine: Pellegrini, 1950); ACS, *CPC*, b. 4829, f. 3597.
42. 'Oggetto: Beschizza Angelo di Lazzaro', Magnocavallo to consulate, 11 April 1939, ASMAE, *AL*, b. 1068, f. 1.
43. Magnocavallo to General Secretary, 5 July 1939, ibid.
44. Ciano to all employees of the foreign ministry administration, 23 September 1938, ASMAE, *AL*, b. 1095, f. 2, sf. 'Personale locale. Censimento razza ebraica'.
45. Grandi to consulates in London, Glasgow, Liverpool and Cardiff, 24 November 1938, ibid.
46. Michele Sarfatti, *Mussolini contro gli ebrei. Cronaca dell'elaborazione delle leggi del 1938* (Turin: Zamorani, 1994), p. 8; David Bidussa, *Il mito del bravo italiano* (Milan: Il Saggiatore, 1994), p. 10.
47. Emilio Gentile, *Fascismo. Storia e interpretazione* (Rome and Bari: Laterza, 2002), p. 28.
48. Aaron Gillette, *Racial Theories in Fascist Italy* (London and New York: Routledge, 2002), p. 42; p. 53.

49. 'Come il mondo si orienta verso Roma', *L'Italia Nostra*, 7 January 1938, n. 466, p. 1.

50. 'Il duce e la razza', ibid., 5 August 1938, n. 496, p. 2.

51. De Felice, *Storia degli ebrei italiani sotto il fascismo* (Turin: Einaudi, 1961), p. 387.

52. 'La difesa della razza – Concezione italiana e fascista', *L'Italia Nostra*, 12 August 1938, n. 497, p. 2 (originally in *Il Legionario*, n. 21, 1 August 1938, p. 1). As underlined by Paola Di Cori, anti-Semitism began to threaten Italian Jews from 1935 onward, due to the colonial adventure in Africa, which stimulated the emergence of a detailed ideology about the purity of Italian race ('Le leggi razziali', in Isnenghi, ed, *I luoghi della memoria*, p. 469).

53. Gillette, *Racial Theories*, pp. 38–40.

54. 'La politica razziale del fascismo – La statura media degli italiani in progressivo aumento', *L'Italia Nostra*, 26 August 1938, n. 499, p. 3; 'Mussolini e l'idea della razza', *Il Legionario*, n. 26, 20 September 1938, p. 17.

55. 'Il problema ebraico', ibid., n. 29, 20 October 1938, p. 5.

56. 'Il clima è maturo per il razzismo italiano', *L'Italia Nostra*, 12 August 1938, n. 497, p. 2.

57. For the anti-Semitic stance of *Il Legionario*, see in particular: 'Gli ebrei in Italia', n. 6, 26 February 1938, p. 9; 'Il fascismo e i problemi della razza', n. 20, 20 July 1938, p. 4; 'La difesa della razza e il problema ebraico in Italia', n. 25, 10 September 1938, p. 4.

58. 'La colonizzazione italiana in A.O.', ibid., 10 March 1939, n. 527, p. 2.

59. Ciano to all embassies and consulates, 6 February 1939, ASMAE, *AL*, b. 1095, f. 2, sf. 'Personale locale. Censimento razza ebraica'.

60. De Felice, *Storia degli ebrei italiani*, p. 386.

61. Elena Salvoni, *Elena: A life in Soho* (London: Quartet Books, 1990); Calisto Cavalli, *Ricordi di un emigrato* (London: La Voce degli Italiani, 1973); Charles Forte, *Forte: The autobiography of Charles Forte* (London: Sidgwick & Jackson, 1986).

62. 'Insegnante di aritmetica presso la Scuola media', Biondelli to foreign ministry, 22 September 1938, ASMAE, *AS* (1936–45), b. 87 ('Gran Bretagna 1938–40'), f. III, sf. 3 ('Londra').

63. London *Fascio* to Augusto Assettati (Bastianini's capo di Gabinetto), 9 December 1938, ASMAE, *AL*, b. 1068, f. 1.

64. See Magnocavallo to consulate, 31 March 1939, ibid.

65. Magnocavallo to General Secretary of the 'Agenzia d'Italia e dell'Impero', 3 March 1939; Magnocavallo to Rampagni, 28 June 1939; Magnocavallo to General Secretary, 3 July 1939, ibid.

66. Magnocavallo to General Secretary, 23 January 1939; Magnocavallo to General Secretary, 14 June 1939, ibid.

67. 'Relazione dell'assemblea generale dell'Associazione Caffettieri Italiani di Londra tenuta il 19 gennaio alla Casa del Littorio', *L'Italia Nostra*, 3 February 1939, n. 522, p. 5.

68. 'La fondazione dell'Associazione Caffettieri Italiani di Londra', ibid., 23 June 1939, n. 542, p. 1.

69. This was perceived also outside London: see 'Scuola italiana di Liverpool', Giovanni Palmeri (secretary of the Liverpool *Fascio*) to Liverpool consul Count Ottavio Gloria, 1 June 1938, ASMAE, *AS, (1936–45)*, b. 87, f. III, sf. 7.

70. Asvero Gravelli, *Uno e molti. Interpretazioni spirituali di Mussolini* (Rome: La Nuova Europa, 1938), p. 12; p. 24.

71. They were divided according to age: 13 at the *Casa dei bambini* (kindergarden), 15 in the first class, 16 in the second, 25 in the third, and 28 between the forth and the fifth classes. 'Prima relazione trimestrale sul funzionamento della scuola elementare diurna', Ada Fantozzi (director of the schools) to foreign ministry – Direzione Generale Scuole, and to London consulate, 27 January 1938, ASMAE, *AS (1936–45)*, b. 87, f. III, sf. 3.

72. Ibid.

73. 'Scuole serali', Biondelli to foreign ministry and to London embassy, 10 June 1938, ibid.

74. 'Relazione finale sul funzionamento delle scuole serali italiane di Londra', report signed by Ada Fantozzi and carrying the stamp of the consulate-general, no date but attached to report of 11 August 1938, ibid.

75. See especially 'Vigilia d'impero', in *Letture classe quinta*, pp. 22–4; 'La vita al campo del maresciallo Badoglio', ibid., pp. 231–5; 'Diavolo ed Arcangelo' (about Graziani), ibid., pp. 242–3.

76. 'Roma', ibid., pp. 146–7.

77. See Mabel Berezin, *Making the Fascist Self: the Political Culture of Interwar Italy* (Ithaca and London: Cornell University Press, 1997), p. 73.

78. 'Le voci del sacrificio', *Letture classe quinta*, pp. 87–91.

79. Only one reading hinted at the superiority of the European race over the African race ('La prossima volta', ibid., pp. 48–50). The programmes of the school year 1938–9 are in ASMAE, *AS (1936–45)*, b. 87, f. III, sf. 3.

80. See Gravelli's foreword to Partito Nazionale Fascista, *Vademecum dello stile fascista. Dai fogli di disposizioni del segretario del partito*, edited by Gravelli (Rome: La Nuova Europa, 1940), pp. 5–14.

81. Camillo Pellizzi, *Una rivoluzione mancata* (Milan: Longanesi, 1948), p. 137.

82. 'Iª relazione trimestrale sul funzionamento delle scuole serali', Ada Fantozzi to General Direction of the Italians Abroad and the Schools, 30 January 1939, ASMAE, *AS (1936–45)*, b. 87, f. III, sf. 3.

83. According to Francesco Malgeri, the long relationship between Fascism and the Church seemed, toward the end of the 1930s, to reward mostly the Church.

While the regime was losing public support, the Church was often able to strengthen its position ('Chiesa cattolica e regime fascista', in Del Boca, Legnani and Rossi (eds), *Il regime fascista*, p. 176). See also Stefano Pivato, 'Strumenti dell'egemonia cattolica', in Simonetta Soldani and Gabriele Turi, *Fare gli italiani. Scuola e cultura nell'Italia contemporanea* (Bologna: Il Mulino, 1993), vol. II, pp. 361–88.

84. 'Relazione finale sul funzionamento delle scuole serali di Londra durante l'anno scolastico 1938–39', signed by Ada Fantozzi, 27 June 1939, ASMAE, *AS (1936–45)*, b. 87, f. III, sf. 3.

85. At the time, 70 per cent of Londoners carried gas masks, waiting 'for the blow from the air which they have been told to expect' (Richard Overy, *The Battle of Britain: The Myth and the Reality*, New York: Norton, 2001, p. 4).

86. 'Relazione finale sul funzionamento delle scuole serali di Londra durante l'anno scolastico 1938–39', signed by Ada Fantozzi, 27 June 1939, ASMAE, *AS (1936–45)*, b. 87, f. III, sf. 3.

87. Patrizi to foreign ministry, 24 October 1939, ibid.

88. 'Scuole serali. Corsi d'italiano', Ada Fantozzi to General Direction of the Italians Abroad, no date but shortly before Christmas 1939, ibid.

89. Ada Fantozzi to General Direction of the Italians Abroad, 22 December 1939, ibid.

90. 'Chiusura scuole', telegram from Bastianini to foreign ministry, 14 May 1940, ibid.

91. C. Floriani (secretary of the *Fascio* of Manchester) to the Inspector of the London *Fascio*, 23 March 1938, ASMAE, *AL*, b. 1015, f. 2; Floriani to Patrizi, 11 February 1939, ibid.

92. From Liverpool consulate to London consulate and embassy, and to the foreign ministry, ibid.

93. 'Visita alla collettività italiana di Newcastle-on-Tyne Fasci del distretto del R. Vice Consolato GILE', consul of Liverpool to foreign ministry and to the London embassy, 11 March 1938, ibid.

94. 'Casa d'Italia', consular Agency of Manchester to Count Ottavio Gloria (consul of Liverpool), 28 March 1938, ibid; '*Fascio* di Manchester – Casa d'Italia', consul of Liverpool to the foreign ministry and to the London embassy, 8 April 1938, ibid.

95. Consul of Liverpool to foreign ministry and to the London embassy, 31 May 1938, ibid.

96. Patrizi to General Secretary, 4 November 1938, ibid.

97. 'Dopolavoro', consul of Cardiff to foreign ministry and to the London embassy, 16 September 1938, ibid.

98. Cardiff consulate to foreign ministry and London embassy, 5 November 1938, ASMAE, *AS*, b. 87, f. III, sf. 2.

99. 'Organizzazioni dopolavoristiche all'estero e case d'Italia', Glasgow consul to foreign ministry and to the London embassy, 2 March 1938, ASMAE, *AL*, b. 1015, f. 2.

100. 'Visita consolare ad Aberdeen e Dundee', Glasgow consulate to foreign ministry and to the London embassy, 22 February 1938, ibid.

101. Magnocavallo to the General Secretary, 6 March 1939, ASMAE, *AL*, b. 1068, f. 1; 'Riservata – Oggetto: Sezione di Southampton. Nazionali che hanno chiesto la cittadinanza inglese', Magnocavallo to consulate, 21 September 1939, ibid.

102. Lucio Sponza, *Divided Loyalties: Italians in Britain during the Second World War* (Bern: Peter Lang, 2000), pp. 55–6; p. 69.

— 6 —

The End of an Era: Grandi between London and the Axis, 1938–39

We will turn the Berlin-Rome Axis Pact into a Berlin axes Roma fact.[1]

Between the end of 1937 and the beginning of 1938, anti-British propaganda in Italy persisted as intensely as during the period of sanctions. After Italy's conquest of Ethiopia, Lord Lloyd had prepared a memorandum together with the British Foreign Office urging a visit to Rome, which the Conservative Italophile hoped might convince Mussolini of the necessity for an Anglo-Italian agreement on Mediterranean issues and on propaganda. The British proposal included a deal over the exchange of information about Italian and British forces in the Mediterranean, and a request for the Italians to stop anti-British propaganda. The visit did not materialise, but the British ambassador to Rome, Eric Drummond, now Lord Perth, thought that Lloyd's memorandum might still be useful. Perth suspected that the Italians were using anti-British propaganda as a bargaining counter during any conversation that might take place. Both the Foreign Office and the ambassador believed that the Italians considered propaganda as a means of pressure on Britain in order to demonstrate that it would be better for the British if Italy were not hostile. Perth commented: 'it is bad psychology on their part and smacks to our mind of blackmail, but it is typically Italian'.[2]

A record of a conversation between Grandi and Neville Chamberlain at the beginning of February 1938 shows a similar perception of Mussolini's foreign policy. It reveals Grandi's difficulty in discussing matters such as the withdrawal of Italian troops from Spain or Italy's commitment to Austria. Without any precise commitment from Italy on these crucial matters it was difficult for the British government to contemplate any agreement with Italy. Grandi told the British that 'Italy must choose between Germany and Great Britain', which was, the British Foreign Office memorandum reported, 'exactly what Giolitti told the allies in 1914'. Moreover, the British suspected that Mussolini was saying 'the same thing in Berlin'. Grandi told them that Italy would be even more bound to Germany if they did not agree soon. The memorandum continued: 'but how can this be? How much closer can the Axis be? Italy has never found any difficulty in betraying her allies when she thought it was in her interest'.[3]

As a result of the continued confrontation in Anglo-Italian relations, *L'Italia Nostra* kept on stirring up anti-British propaganda in London, mainly by attacking the foreign secretary, Eden (until his resignation in February 1938), along with the Anglican Church. The Italian newspaper believed that the Church, after having allegedly supported the League against Italy, was now supporting Eden's anti-Italian foreign policy. In January, the claim made by the bishop of London that Britain's function in the world was comparable to that of a policeman unleashed an indignant protest from *L'Italia Nostra*:

> Why? And who has entrusted the British Empire with such a duty? . . . There existed an era in world history which has taken its name from a glorious Queen of England . . . That time has gone . . . We do not recognise for England the function of international policeman. One would need strong hands. The English no longer have them.[4]

The following week, the newspaper informed its readers that the average Englishman was no longer the traditional blonde and tall type. The average Englishman tended now to have dark hair, dark eyes and to be only about one metre and 69 centimetres tall; moreover, he suffered from rheumatism.[5] Opposed to this modest example, *L'Italia Nostra* represented the new Germans as a disciplined and proud people who had risen thanks to 'the Führer's miracle'. Since the newspaper had almost never mentioned Italo-German friendship before, it became necessary in February to give a summary of its major stages, from the Ethiopian War to the Spanish Civil War, from the Axis to the present commitment to anti-Communism.[6]

Although the Spanish Civil War continued to complicate Anglo-Italian relations, two events interrupted *L'Italia Nostra*'s anti-British propaganda in 1938: Eden's resignation in February and the British recognition of the Italian empire in Ethiopia with the Easter agreement in Rome. For his contribution to Eden's fall, Neville Chamberlain was praised as a hero by the newspaper.

The shifts in the propaganda of *L'Italia Nostra* – anti-British until February 1938, pro-British until the end of the year and later almost neutral – reflected the complicated balance between Grandi's relationship with Chamberlain and the British Right on the one hand, and Italy's pro-German foreign policy on the other. Grandi's failure was reflected in the last speech he gave to the Italian community of London before leaving Britain, based on a written text for which Mussolini and Ciano had given instructions and which they had carefully checked; it was violently anti-French and was addressed to a German-Italian gathering at the embassy.

Grandi between Ciano and Chamberlain

During the growing crisis over Austria in February 1938, Ciano had explained to Grandi that it was safe for Italy to improve relations with Britain and that Grandi should seek to convince the British to open discussions with Italy. Grandi saw Ciano's request as a consequence of problems with Germany, as an 'S.O.S. to London', and a mistake because it was important to give the British the impression that the Axis was strong. He did not want Eden to seek an agreement with Germany without consulting Mussolini.[7] Grandi was in favour of a pact with Britain, but knew that this was impossible while Eden remained at the Foreign Office. His efforts were therefore directed towards an agreement with Chamberlain that could bring Eden's fall.[8] Ciano thought that Grandi's enthusiasm was exaggerated, and saw it as an attempt by the ambassador to claim the role of peacemaker with Britain, 'an image that many Italians might even like'. But peace and war, Ciano emphasised, were entirely in Mussolini's hands; no one could take upon themselves a personal role. At heart, Ciano believed, Grandi was dying for a rapprochement with the British and disliked the Germans.[9] That the relationship between Grandi and Ciano in 1938 and 1939 was one of competition and distrust is evident from both figures' diaries. In February, Grandi confided to his diary that he had to take decisions without consulting Ciano and the Duce because they were not eager to make an agreement with Chamberlain. As a result, when Eden left the Foreign Office as a consequence of the conflict with Chamberlain over the policy toward Italy, the ambassador believed that Chamberlain and he had played the greatest part in an event which led to a genuine improvement in Anglo-Italian relations. Ciano thought it was important not to present Eden as a victim of Fascism, and decided that the press should explain Eden's fall as a normal development within British government.[10] Unlike Ciano, Grandi regarded it as an unforgettable event which marked the beginning of a new era. On the night of 19/20 February, he wrote in his diary that his happiness was immense, and concluded: 'Chamberlain is tough'.[11] From that moment onward, his cooperation with Chamberlain continued to be very close. Often Grandi did not even inform Rome of his activities because he believed his superiors would not understand the necessity for diplomacy: 'they would have stopped me'.[12] He recalled the moment when Eden entered the British Foreign Office in 1935 as an immensely sad day, but the day Eden left as one of the happiest moments in his life. Yet Grandi knew he now had to pay for it. Rome did not recognise his role, and Mussolini ignored him. Ciano had first asked for his help, and now that Grandi had succeeded, Ciano acted as if Eden's departure had been something bound to happen anyway.[13]

Anti-Eden propaganda in Italy had been so intense in the previous months that, despite Ciano's order to the press not to talk about it, Eden's resignation created the impression of a real shift in Anglo-Italian relations among part of the Italian population. Schoolteachers in Italy made the children pray to God to thank him for having eliminated the British Minister, 'deadly enemy of Fascist Italy'.[14] Former *squadristi*, universal Fascists and 'first hour' revolutionary Fascists wrote letters to Grandi expressing their admiration, as though the ambassador had started a new era in the history of the regime. Eugenio Coselschi, president of the Action Committees for the Universality of Rome (CAUR), praised Grandi's courage, 'really worthy of a volunteer and of a Fascist', and his 'wisest and most inspired finesse'.[15] Those who acknowledged Grandi's role were drawn mainly from among British Conservative Italophiles and Italian former *squadristi* from the Romagna. The latter saw Grandi as the Fascist ambassador who continued the Revolution that had begun before the March on Rome. While to the British Conservatives Grandi was a moderate and pro-British diplomat, to his Italian supporters he was a Fascist revolutionary capable of imposing Italy's rights over Britain. Old friends from the Romagna were proud that the Duce had chosen from among the men of his land – their own land – the one who could 'keep high, above all coalitions of peoples, states, and parties, Italy's flag'. The feeling that they somehow represented 'the people', that they came from a province that had given birth to the 'chosen men' who would lead Italy created a sense of comradeship between them and the ambassador.[16] Camillo Pellizzi, the cleverest intellectual among the Italians abroad, who lived in London and worked with Grandi, acknowledged the measure among Grandi's 'enormous success', but doubted that Britain intended to respect and continue the new friendly relationship.[17]

According to *L'Italia Nostra*, a new era had indeed begun after Eden. Anglo-Italian relations were now different in the present, thanks to Neville Chamberlain, but also with reference to the past: the newspaper began once again to recall the *Risorgimento* and the traditional friendship of Britain and Italy, which it had declared dead until shortly before. Yet distrust of the British persisted, and friendship was conditional:

> yet the Italian people expects that . . . all the rapid but profound evolution that occurred in recent years be acknowledged . . ., years during which Italy had been able to find again its radiant European and world destiny . . ., clenched in the fist of a Man who in himself contains, defines, and represents the most passionate strength of the Italic race and genius which had never been extinguished.[18]

One condition of that friendship was the relationship with Germany. *L'Italia Nostra* presented the news of the *Anschluss* on 18 March 1938 on the second page, in a short article and in a detached tone. Without having ever discussed the Austrian situation before, it assumed that Austria had always been part of German history. Mussolini's favourable attitude toward Hitler showed that the Rome-Berlin Axis had overcome its most crucial trial. The Italian people, it was alleged, realised that the *Anschluss* was a historical necessity: unlike Britain and France at the time of the Ethiopian War, Italy had not acted in a hypocritical manner, but had accepted German expansion as inevitable: 'history is made by the strong; we want and must be very strong'.[19] In the same issue, the newspaper published the text of a letter Hitler had sent to Mussolini a week earlier:

Whatever the consequence of forthcoming events, I have drawn a clear German frontier facing France and I am now drawing an equally clear one toward Italy. It is the Brenner Pass. That decision is beyond doubt, and will not change. Nor did I take that decision in 1938, but immediately after the end of the Great War, and I have never been secretive about it.

The Führer had concluded by apologising for the short notice and by declaring to the Duce his everlasting friendship.[20]

Ciano knew that the *Anschluss* was not a great advantage for Italy. Nonetheless he believed that Italy should not ally itself with France and Britain against Germany, since to do so would be anachronistic. He therefore rejected an appeal from France:

After sanctions, after failing to recognise the Empire, and after the misconduct against us from 1935 onward, do they want to rebuild Stresa in one hour, with Hannibal on the doorstep? France and England have lost Austria by their policy. It is not good for us either. But in the meanwhile we have taken Ethiopia.[21]

Only three weeks later, German propaganda in Alto Adige had begun to worry Mussolini and Ciano. Friction with Germany now favoured agreement with Britain. At the beginning of April Mussolini asked Ciano to start the talks with Perth.[22] However, Grandi continued to believe that it was his own initiative in London that led to the Anglo-Italian agreement signed in Rome on 16 April. On 26 April, he wrote in his diary that thanks to his diplomatic activity with Chamberlain he had managed to bring Mussolini and Chamberlain together (even by forging friendly messages from Mussolini to Chamberlain). Grandi had persisted despite Mussolini, who, according to Grandi, had never wanted an agreement with London. Grandi recalled that in the summer of 1937 Mussolini had thought it might be possible to 'drag Germany into war against Britain' in the Mediterranean.[23] The British Foreign Office indeed suspected that Mussolini had such a plan in his mind as early as 1936, when information considered to be reliable suggested that Italy was increasing its armaments, and that the *Fasci* Abroad were warning Italians living in the United Kingdom to liquidate their investments there and to send their money to the United States. The main reason for this, the British gathered, was that Mussolini intended to attack Britain in the Mediterranean and in North Africa at the first favourable opportunity.[24] However, after the *Anschluss*, Mussolini found it safer to accept Perth's proposal for agreement with Britain, quite independent of Grandi's activity in London. To Grandi, Perth was 'the ambassador of the enemy'[25] and Ciano the one who cynically exploited the situation to achieve the honour of having made a pact with Britain. The ambassador received neither letters nor phone calls from the Duce. Grandi underwent a moral collapse, evident from the pages of his diary which are filled with expressions of sorrow, disappointment and suffering caused by the apparent loss of the Duce's trust and approval. He blamed

Ciano for this outcome, because when the latter was not in Rome, Grandi still received letters of encouragement from Mussolini. Several weeks later, Grandi was still torturing himself with the unbearable truth: the Duce knew that one word from him would have made Grandi satisfied and happy, 'he could have got away with it cheaply. Yet he uttered no word. Nothing'. Grandi could never forget the way Mussolini received him on the night of the foundation of the Empire: 'it was the last time'; a few weeks later he made Ciano foreign secretary; 'after that, it was over'.[26] However, Grandi did remain in personal contact with Mussolini during 1938–9, although these contacts were less frequent than during previous years.

The British legate to the Holy See, Francis d'Arcy Godolphin Osborne, wrote to Grandi that although he had not taken part in preparing and signing the treaty, it would never have been possible without his diplomacy in London: 'I think we all, in both countries, owe you a great debt of gratitude'.[27] Grandi's reply that 'these three nightmare years are over and the skies are again blue and sunny, even in our misty London' is, however, difficult to believe.[28] Indeed, less than two months later, the Italian government made it clear that it would not withdraw the Italian volunteers from Spain at such a critical point in the Civil War. Perth sought to convince Ciano that Italy should propose an armistice in Spain, but the Italian minister considered that compromise was impossible in a civil war.[29] Thus the agreement did not officially take effect until the following November, when Mussolini finally withdrew Italian troops from Spain, which was one major condition in the treaty.

Again, the letters of congratulations received from Italy came from Grandi's loyal friends from Romagna and northern Italy ('extremely few from Rome, of course').[30] The *camerati romagnoli* and the *Camicie nere della vigilia* who wrote in Pedrazza's newspaper *Il Resto del Carlino* expressed 'Fascist enthusiasm' and gratitude for the former *ras* of Bologna. The use of Fascist slogans, such as *alalà*, served to underline their belief that Grandi was in London as a *camicia nera* rather than as a traditional ambassador, and that his role in the creation of the Anglo-Italian pact had been a revolutionary role.[31]

The Italian community in London celebrated the treaty at the *Casa del Littorio*, where the consul relayed Grandi's message because the ambassador could not be present in person. The main aspect of the treaty, went the message, was that Britain solemnly and finally acknowledged Italy's empire and Italy's interests as a great Mediterranean, European and world power. The agreement allegedly brought tension between Britain and Italy to an end, and sanctioned the beginning of a historic age of fertile and peaceful collaboration between the Fascist empire and the British Empire.[32] *L'Italia Nostra* placed the agreement in the context of the change in Anglo-Italian relations already stressed at the time of Eden's resignation. According to the newspaper, the treaty was based on the central assumption that for Britain the Mediterranean was merely 'a highway' while for Italy it meant 'life'. The spirit of the agreement relied on a completely new form of friendship between the two countries. The 'ancient friendship' derived from a 'sentimental and often sloppy inclination of the English for Italy as the most beautiful country of all [*il bel paese*], for its mandolin serenades, its spaghetti, its *dolce far niente* and other similar rhetorical or nineteenth-century bits and pieces.'

The new friendship was allegedly between two strong nations which had looked into each other's eyes and shaken hands. The newspaper concluded optimistically that Britain 'has now acknowledged this new Italy, resounding with factories and building yards, filled with bayonets and cannon, with a thousand prows and a thousand wings'.[33] Grandi believed that Chamberlain was the first British prime minister to overcome the usual commonplaces of the traditional friendship, and saw Italy as it was in the present, as remade by Mussolini.[34] But *L'Italia Nostra* did not simply praise Britain for having understood Italy's greatness. It even expressed admiration for Britain for the first time: no longer the decadent country of the 'average men' of a few months before, Britain was reborn, in April 1938, as a great country run by steady and strong leaders. All this was due to Chamberlain, a 'wonderful type of dictator'. Chamberlain was great precisely because, despite the existence of a liberal parliamentary system, he was able to govern his country with the same style as if he was running a dictatorship. In order to understand British realism, it was enough to compare Britain with France, a country which continued to pursue a 'feminine policy'.[35] *L'Italia Nostra* thus anticipated the new line of Italian foreign policy, in which hostility to France took the place of anti-British sentiment.[36]

Ciano indeed informed Grandi shortly afterward in a long secret letter that Mussolini did not intend to rest, but had a new direction in mind for Italy's foreign policy, moving from hostility to Britain to hostility toward France. The new situation needed to be analysed, Ciano explained, under the light of the new imperial achievements of the regime. Since the political, military and geographical conditions of Italy had changed, future conversations with France could not continue as they had done in the past. The aims Italy had kept concealed in its breast for a long time could now be discussed openly: Tunisia, Djibouti and the Suez Canal. In the case of Tunisia, Italian labour, Ciano explained to Grandi, was the only active white workforce of the region. It was too early to ask for territorial cession, but it was time to establish a 'sort of a joint ownership that could allow a safe and fertile development of our activities'. This was particularly evident in the case of Djibouti: 'it is obvious that we cannot continue to feed French companies with our work and our commerce'. Mussolini intended to ask for control of the railway from Djibouti to Addis Ababa, while the harbour could be jointly operated by both Italy and France. Ciano relayed the Duce's claim that without Italy's cooperation Djibouti was bound to wither on the vine. As to the third question, Ciano pointed out that now Italy's commerce in the Red Sea area, the Indian Ocean and the Pacific had multiplied, and Italy no longer intended to accept its extreme exploitation by the Suez Canal Company. The reason why Grandi needed to know about these future developments was because Italy, again, required his contribution. Ciano now sought to flatter Grandi by saying that the Duce wished to enlist his very personal and particular abilities to inform the British about the changed direction of Italian policy. Mussolini wanted Grandi to talk about it with the British from time to time, 'dropping the word at the opportune moment', and if possible preparing British opinion to accede to Italy's new requests. At the moment Ciano could not say when and how all this would happen: it depended on the course of events. But the Duce had these aims fixed in his mind, and that was enough, Ciano concluded, to be certain that they would be realised.[37]

Less than two months later, Ciano gave a similar warning to Ribbentrop. Other questions, which he had not mentioned to Grandi, were 'historic in character' and concerned those territories that 'geographically, ethnically, and strategically' belonged to Italy, namely Corsica and Nice. Such questions could not be solved by purely diplomatic means and therefore could not be made public at the moment. However, Italy's interest in those French territories was made clear by Italian propaganda publications.[38]

Grandi had long shared these anti-French views. As early as May 1938, he had realised that Germany did not simply want the Sudetenland; Czechoslovakia was merely the beginning of expansion toward Romania and Russia. He was convinced that the Germans were going to achieve their aims, and that the British were not going to interfere. Grandi was convinced of this because British acquiescence appeared to be the only way to ensure peace in Europe. Indeed, in his view Britain did not merely accept German expansionism, but was actually assisting the development of German ambitions. Such a course was, Grandi felt certain, the only way to save Western Europe from the 'German avalanche'. The choice was between the Germans in Paris, Flanders and the Adriatic Sea, or the Germans in the Ukraine, Budapest and perhaps even Romania. Russia was going to pay; one nation had to pay for the peace of the other nations, and Grandi felt it was better that it should be Russia. Grandi assumed that Chamberlain understood this reasoning. Unlike Britain, Grandi believed that France was on Russia's side, since it was supporting 'the Reds in Barcelona'. In this way, France was slowing down possible implementation of the Anglo-Italian agreement of April 1938, which was, according to Grandi, its ultimate aim. He had no doubt that an anti-Fascist plot existed between Left-wing British politicians, the French and Moscow, and as a result believed that 'the Duce is right in attacking France'.[39] The situation became more problematic at the beginning of June 1938. Grandi admitted that Chamberlain had been doing his best to keep the Italo-British agreement alive, while Italy had done nothing to support Chamberlain against the attacks of the British Left or to reinforce the Rome agreement. He reflected on possible reasons for Italian behaviour: 'fear of irritating Berlin?' he wondered. British friends of Italy appeared to be cooling day after day; they had now begun to regret that they had gone so far in establishing friendship with such an unreliable country.[40]

At the end of the summer of 1938 Grandi became convinced that Churchill, followed by the British Left, was taking part in an international Bolshevik plot against Chamberlain. In his mind, all the forces of anti-Fascism were seeking to exploit the Czechoslovak crisis in order to regain the initiative and cause a major European war. Instead of blaming Germany for its aggression, Grandi accused the French and the Czechoslovaks of threatening European stability, and believed that only by reinforcing Anglo-Italian relations and supporting Chamberlain was it possible to prevent the Communists from unleashing war. He was thus convinced that the ultimate chance for peace rested with Mussolini, since Mussolini did not want a war at that moment. Grandi intensified his connections with British Conservatives and Italophiles to convince them that an agreement with Italy was still possible. The outcome of the Munich conference convinced Grandi once again that he had been the major figure responsible for securing peace, since he had succeeded once again in bringing Mussolini and Chamberlain together. At the time of the conference he wrote in his diary: 'Mussolini has triumphed. It is he whom millions and millions of mothers must bless today'. On that historic night, returning home after having been to the cinema with his wife and his children, Grandi walked among the crowds of London, who were celebrating in the streets, after the first newspapers came out announcing: 'it is peace'. Grandi concluded the page of his diary with the sentence: 'Viva il Duce! . . .'[41]

The Italian community in London celebrated the sudden outbreak of the peace at the *Fascio* and at the *Dopolavoro Mazzini e Garibaldi*. The authorities of the consulate, the embassy and the *Fascio* cheered both Chamberlain's wisdom and Mussolini's greatness. Yet they warned the Italians not to cultivate illusions: the western powers now recognised Italy's role, but this did not necessarily imply that they were ready to offer Mussolini the concessions Italy really deserved.[42] As usual, Grandi received no thanks from Rome, although he did receive many letters from landowners and former *squadristi* from northern Italy.[43] Ciano's diary makes almost no mention of Grandi's role; in his view, Munich had shown Italy's crucial role among the great powers. To Mussolini, the crisis had demonstrated that 'even at a high price, we could have crushed France and Britain forever. We now have overwhelming proof of that'.[44]

Although De Felice, Nello and Quartararo explain the period before Munich as an attempt by Mussolini to intensify friendship with Britain and to create a new relationship with France, Grandi's diary, Ciano's diary and *L'Italia Nostra* suggest a wholly different interpretation of the months between February and September 1938.[45] Although Grandi's activity had been important in February in convincing Chamberlain that it would be possible, if Eden resigned, to improve Anglo-Italian relations, and that Mussolini could be persuaded to withdraw Italian troops from the Spanish Civil War, he certainly exaggerated when he claimed that his own role in the Easter agreement, and later at Munich, had been indispensable.[46] On the one hand, as Grandi suggested, it was difficult to believe that Mussolini wanted suddenly to inaugurate a pro-British foreign policy, after he had been stoking the fires of anti-British resentment within Italy for at least the previous two years. On the other, German pressure at the Brenner Pass convinced the Duce that an agreement with Britain was nevertheless temporarily convenient. Mussolini did not help convene the Munich conference, as the ambassador liked to believe, because of Grandi's action, nor because the Duce had become committed to Britain and France, but rather because Italy was not ready for war.[47] When the Anglo-Italian agreement was finally implemented in November 1938, Mussolini told Ciano that such an agreement did not alter Italy's foreign policy: 'In Europe, the Axis remains fundamental. In the Mediterranean, co-operation with the British as long as it is possible. France is out: toward France our claims are now defined.'[48]

Grandi, the BUF and the Italophiles

The relationship between the Italian embassy and the BUF never recovered after the Ethiopian War. From time to time, the embassy reported to the Italian foreign ministry on Mosley's activities, which were not very successful. From 1938 in particular, the BUF was first and foremost committed to Germany, and wanted to avoid a war between Britain and Germany. British fascists spoke publicly against Eden, whom they considered responsible for Britain's international isolation. As a consequence of his policy, the British Empire was now facing a hostile Germany in the North Sea, Japan in East Asia, and a problematic situation in the Mediterranean, where there were no fewer than three enemies: the new fascist Spain, the Arab populations and Italy between them. Mosley praised Chamberlain for recognising the past mistakes of British foreign policy and for starting a necessary rethinking.[49] In 1939, despite the efforts of some BUF members to create anti-war committees and to spread pro-German propaganda by emphasising that Britain did not need to fight for Poland, Mosley's movement continued to enjoy little success in Britain. It also showed little interest in Italy, and was thus irrelevant to Italian Fascism in Britain. The British Council Against European Commitments, created in 1938 by BUF members, took the view that Britain and Germany were the two countries responsible for bringing world civilisation forward. A war between Britain and Germany, they believed, meant 'Bolshevism in both countries, and the loss of everything for which both countries stand . . . It is worth fighting to save civilisation, but not to kill it'.[50]

In 1939, the BUF position on British foreign policy thus demanded agreement with Germany. BUF propaganda focused on anti-Semitism and on the bizarre notion of an international Bolshevik plot organised in Britain by politicians such as Churchill and Baldwin, who supported 'international Jewish finance'.[51] While Mosley's autobiography tended to explain his support for Germany as merely a question of foreign policy (Germany could expand into the East and Britain could reinforce its empire without need for war), the idea of a common British and German civilisation had at this stage become a central aspect in his movement's propaganda. Unity Mitford, Mosley's sister-in-law, gave the most dramatic example of loyalty to a German-British fascist ideal when she shot herself, after hearing that Britain had declared war upon Germany in September 1939.[52]

It was evident that propaganda of this sort from the BUF did not assist Grandi's efforts toward rapprochement with Britain. The Italian government now considered BUF activity to be virtually useless, and no longer showed interest in it. As explained in Chapter 4, after 1935 the relationship between the Italian government and Mosley's movement, which had been characterised by exchange and collaboration in the previous three years, swiftly cooled, and BUF offices in Italy shut down as the result of a decision by the BUF in London. Although the BUF in Britain had supported the Italian campaign in Ethiopia both through public demonstrations and in the pages of *The Blackshirt*, life for British citizens in Italy became difficult during those months of intense anti-British propaganda. Very few documents exist about Anglo-Italian fascist relations after 1935; yet some British Foreign Office records for 1938 confirm what Italian foreign ministry records had suggested in 1935. From that year, the BUF in Italy no longer existed, but British fascists resident in Italy were still to be found and did not stop their efforts to organise Anglo-Italian fascism. In 1935, after BUF offices in Italy were closed, these British subjects founded a new group called the British Union of Friends of Italy. No evidence exists as to whether they continued to receive money from the BUF. The organisers were the same people, the most active of whom was John Celli, who had started his work for the BUF in Italy on behalf of Mosley in 1932. Their activity was convenient to the Italian government since it promoted pro-Italian activities and Anglo-Italian events. Even during the paroxysm of anti-British propaganda within Italy at the time of the Ethiopian War, these Britons continued to criticise British foreign policy publicly, an attitude which the British Foreign Office regarded as a form of treason: it was permissible behaviour for Englishmen living in Britain, but it savoured of disloyalty when conducted by Englishmen in the enemy's country.[53] Given the rationalist outlook of the BUF, it was likely that the British fascists shared this view. The British fascists in Italy were not very active, at least during the difficult months in Anglo-Italian relations which followed the conquest of Ethiopia. They genuinely believed in Anglo-Italian friendship, and reappeared in 1938 when, after Eden's resignation, the relationship between the two countries appeared to improve. When Eden resigned, they wrote to Grandi assuming that his role in London had been essential:

Your work will never be forgotten by Englishmen who love Italy, and you will remain
a lasting memory in our hearts. May old sores be wiped out and a happier era of better
relations a better understanding of your Revered Chief by my People result from Mr
Chamberlains [*sic*] great Statesmanlike action [*sic*].[54]

They also organised public meetings, most of them in Milan, where Celli had lived
since 1934. The Italian ministry of popular culture and the CAUR backed these
events. At a crowded public meeting held in Milan shortly before the Easter
agreements, Celli described the British press as not really free because it was
owned by high finance and the Jews. A British Foreign Office informant reported
that Celli depicted the British people as 'good honest folk who had been led
terribly astray but who were gradually beginning to see the light'. On the contrary,

Fascist Italy, secure in her great glory, was begged to be long-suffering and to exercise
magnanimity towards a friend who had erred and strayed (largely as a result of the
pernicious influence of 'one of the most dangerous men that had ever appeared on the
European stage . . .') but who was well-meaning at heart and deserving of pity and good-
will.

Celli, the report concluded, was in good faith but 'too uneducated to be able to
avoid a grotesque simplification of the issue involved'.[55]

After the Easter agreements, the British fascists in Italy sent a letter to Chamberlain praising the prime minister's wisdom and courage; fifty-four British subjects
who lived in Italy signed it. They believed that over the last eighty years the most
stable element in European politics had been friendship between Britain and Italy.
'It was indeed lamentable', they remarked, 'from the point of view of both peoples,
when events occurred which impaired that friendship and brought us almost within
sight of hostilities . . . We, who live in Italy, could see how deeply the Italians felt
the change that had come about.'[56]

The British Foreign Office believed that the British Union of Friends of Italy
was genuine in its aim of improving Anglo-Italian relations, but also judged that
its leaders were 'ignorant' and 'idiots', and therefore bound to fail. Other prominent figures in the movement included Captain Ernest Platt, Harry Brittain, the
universal fascist James Strachey Barnes and Colonel Rocke. The Foreign Office
described them as not very clever individuals who had pursued an anti-British
campaign throughout the previous years (Colonel Rocke was even on the blacklist
of the British embassy in Rome). Despite the leaders, the group secured the support
of several distinguished Italophiles such as Charles Petrie and Leo Amery. That
support was facilitated by a change of name in July 1938, from British Union of
Friends of Italy to the Anglo-Italian Cultural Association. The reason for this
change, in Celli's view, was that Anglo-Italian understanding was now an
accomplished fact and therefore required activities of a purely cultural nature. This

belief sometimes gave Celli the confidence to seek support from the British consulate in Milan and even from the British embassy in Rome. For example, he suggested in September 1938 to the British consulate in Milan that it investigate the possibility of arranging for unemployed Britons to fill the positions left vacant by British Jews who might need to leave Italy in the next six months. The consul took the opportunity of making plain to Celli that he could not count on the support of the British government for any of his activities.[57]

Grandi no longer had contacts with the BUF, although he continued to work with Conservative Italophile MPs. They also believed that after Eden's resignation a new era in Anglo-Italian relations could begin. They were particularly supportive of Grandi's activities, which they considered had been fundamental in achieving Eden's dismissal. One of the first to congratulate Grandi on that occasion was Mottistone. On behalf of Italy's many English friends, he expressed gratitude for Grandi's 'ceaseless efforts in the cause of Italian-English friendship' and expressed the hope that 'all will go well, and if and when friendship is completely restored it will be in the first degree due to you'. Grandi replied that he too believed that 'all will eventually be well between our two countries, and I am happy to think that our work will have helped to further the lasting friendship which is so near to both our hearts'.[58] Kenneth de Courcy, on behalf of the Imperial Policy Group, wrote to Grandi to express the group's collective view that Europe owed him a special debt for his 'diplomacy, courtesy, and statesmanship throughout the last two years'. Grandi, de Courcy wrote, had helped to safeguard the imperial interests of both countries, and had also demonstrated that they were 'not incompatible with friendship'.[59]

The Italophiles likewise expressed gratitude for Grandi's efforts in bringing about the Easter agreement in Rome. They thanked the ambassador for the 'splendid Easter present you and Signor Mussolini have given us'.[60] According to Petrie, Grandi was the individual who more than anyone else deserved to feel real satisfaction from the outcome. Sir Ronald Graham, Sir Edward Grigg, Admiral Taylor, Petrie himself and a few others were thinking about forming a new body to further good relations between Britain and Italy.[61] Grandi's English friends thus conveyed to the ambassador the gratitude and loyalty that he did not receive from Ciano and the Duce. While the latter had, in Grandi's view, been ungrateful and unfair, the English Italophiles had shown themselves sincere friends who had rallied to his side at a difficult moment.[62] After the vote to approve the Anglo-Italian agreement, another pro-Italian MP, George Lambert, took the occasion in congratulating Grandi to also thank him for facilitating his visit to Italy the previous month. The favourable conditions he found in Italy made him even more convinced that he had acted rightly in voting in favour of the agreement: all social classes received him 'with the most charming courtesy' and he was greatly impressed by the vast improvement in Italian conditions: not only were the trains punctual, but the hotels were admirable, 'and there was an absence of those parasites on the streets who made the stranger's life a burden in days gone by'.[63] At the beginning of April 1938 the Conservative MP Sir Philip Dawson, well known for his pro-Italian feelings, organised a meeting at Westminster among Conservatives in order to constitute an Anglo-Italian Parliamentary Committee.[64]

The correspondence between the British Conservatives and Grandi during the weeks preceding the Munich conference was filled with tension, hope and anxiety, but also mutual expressions of solidarity and friendship. Neville Chamberlain realised that as long as the Spanish Civil War persisted it was impossible to implement the Anglo-Italian agreement, but thought that thanks to Grandi's help a chance existed that 'reason would prevail'.[65] The Italophiles regarded the prospect of Italy's support for Germany in the event of war with terror and dismay. Their relationship with Grandi continued to be excellent, but the Axis was a daunting presence. In a dramatic letter preceding Munich, Petrie expressed to the ambassador his sympathy even in the current difficult circumstances and confirmed his devoted friendship with the promise that, whatever happened in the international situation, such feelings would never change:

> If by an unhappy chance Italy adopts what, if you will forgive me for saying so, I consider to be the suicidal policy of supporting Germany in the event of war, I can assure you that this will make no difference in the feelings of affection which I have for so long entertained for yourself. I can say no more, but I think you will understand.[66]

Grandi maintained friendship with Petrie and with other Italophiles well into the period after the Second World War. Grandi, Petrie and Beaverbrook in particular continued to share their worries with each other: Grandi about the alleged advance of Communism in Italy, Beaverbrook and Petrie about the collapse of the British Empire.[67]

However, while the Italophile MPs continued their work with the Italian embassy, the activity of the intellectuals, journalists and writers who had so earnestly supported Italy during the Ethiopian War by publishing articles and books, was becoming less intense. This was clearly because of Italy's increasing closeness to Germany, since these Italophiles were and had always been anti-Nazi. *The English Review*, which was their principal publication, was pro-Italian but anti-German. Figures such as Petrie and Jerrold had always stressed the importance of the Roman tradition in Italian Fascism, and being Catholics they believed they belonged to the same civilisation. The Germans remained in their view little more than barbarians, and Nazism was the ultimate expression of their barbarism.[68] In 1937 *The English Review* was incorporated into *The National Review*, a right-wing publication but not specifically Italophile; the usual Italophile contributors then disappeared. In 1938 and 1939, the only article signed by anyone connected to the

Italophiles was by Luigi Villari, who explained the reasons for Italy's intervention in the Spanish Civil War. He wrote it in May 1938, after the Anglo-Italian talks in Rome; only now that Anglo-Italian relations had improved, was it possible to set forth Italy's position 'in its true light'. In his opinion, every patriotic Briton should realise that Italy had fought for British interests as well, because Britain did not want a 'Russian colony' in the Mediterranean.[69] This notion was certainly common among the Italophiles, who obviously hoped for Franco's victory against the Republicans. However, the Spanish Civil War also helped to move Italy closer to Germany, the power they dreaded above all others. The *Bulletin of International News*, rather than the *National Review*, continued to express the Italophiles' views over Italo-German relations, but after Hitler's invasion of Austria, the *Bulletin* began to criticise Italy although only with regard to foreign policy. Even the racial laws of February 1938 raised no difficulties for the Italophiles. In March 1938 the *Bulletin* explained that Italy had emerged 'weakened and embarrassed' from the Ethiopian conflict, and by no means 'able to withstand German pressure in Austria without the friends who had been alienated'.[70] News of the Anglo-Italian agreement of April 1938 came as a momentary relief between the *Anschluss* and Hitler's visit to Rome in May, on which occasion the Italian and the German dictators raised a toast to the 'natural frontiers which Providence and history have visibly drawn between our two peoples'. The two leaders also drank to the meeting of two revolutionary countries, some two thousand years after Romans and Germans had met for the first time in history.[71] The *Bulletin* remained pessimistic even during Chamberlain's visit to Italy in January 1939. Beside the news that the Italian press wholeheartedly welcomed the Prime Minister, the article relayed information about Virginio Gayda's anti-French declarations, 'that the Italian claims on France were based on documentary rights as well as on essential political and moral reasons'.[72] In March, the *Bulletin* condemned Germany's destruction of Czechoslovakia, and emphasised that the Italian official position was that the Czechs had 'asked to be annexed'. It also reported a speech by Mussolini in which the dictator had stressed that what happened in Eastern Europe was 'fated to happen' and that the Axis was a relationship not between states but between revolutions. Mussolini then added a number of violently anti-French remarks, mentioning the questions of Tunisia, Djibouti and the Suez Canal. Among his Mediterranean claims, the *Bulletin* observed, the Duce included 'that gulf which is called the Adriatic', indicating future problems with the Slavs.[73]

Leo Amery believed that the German claims had represented a danger for the world's stabilisation for a long time; in 1939 he recalled his visit to Germany as early as 1899, when he found the Germans already hostile to the Britons out of jealousy of the British Empire. Since then, he believed, Germany had always wanted to build an even greater empire, and Hitler was the ultimate expression of that aggressive spirit, which was typical of German history.[74] He never mentioned

Italy as a problem, although in the same year he contributed to a book on the German threat to Britain, in which the Axis powers, and not Germany alone, now figured as a challenge to the British Empire.[75]

Among the Italophiles, only Francis Yeats-Brown continued to be optimistic even in 1939, when he published a book on European politics that confirmed once more his romantic and idealised view of 'the Land of the Caesars'. His favourite region was the Duce's Romagna, a land which besides bearing abundant fruits had given the world 'so many saints and scoundrels':

> One expects to meet a *condottiere* or a poet round every corner, and one understands why a glory of great men have come out of Italy down the centuries. Since the days of Dante, she has produced a world-genius in almost every generations; and now, through Mussolini, himself so clearly Roman in shape and soul, she may have again set her course upon the steep and difficult path of Empire.

He concluded that such thoughts came naturally to the traveller to Predappio.[76] He felt certain that Mussolini was a sincere friend of Britain; Italians were ambitious and brave, but disliked the idea of being second to Germany in world conquest, and were not going to risk their own existence in a war in which Germany 'would reap most of the profits'.[77]

The Axis in London

In 1938 and 1939 Grandi received a large number of letters from ordinary British citizens, both pro-Italian and anti-Italian. The pro-Italian letters came from British citizens and from organisations which worried about the possibility of war and hoped for a peaceful relationship with Italy. The correspondents generally believed that Hitler was a mystic and a criminal maniac, and that the German people had been kept in complete ignorance of his real aims. They hoped that Grandi would be able to convince Mussolini to try to bring Hitler to his senses before it was too late, and that Grandi should ensure that the Italian people were not kept in ignorance. They reminded Grandi that England, France and Russia were bound to intervention in case Germany invaded Czechoslovakia.[78] After Munich, ordinary British citizens wrote to Grandi to thank him and Mussolini for their immeasurable service to humanity at the Munich conference; women wrote to him as 'English mothers' to thank Mussolini for purportedly saving the peace.[79]

At the same time, Grandi also received hostile letters from student unions and other organisations as well as from individuals. He collected all these letters in a file entitled 'Anonymous. Fanatics. Envious . . .' Left-wing clubs passed resolutions in favour of the Soviet Union and Czechoslovakia, and called Italy and Germany imperialist aggressors and murderers. They hated Chamberlain and demanded a stronger prime minister who would support the League of Nations and collective security.[80] Most letters indicated that the British complaints against Italy were its aggression against Ethiopia, which was considered a cowardly rape of a poor country, and its intervention in the Spanish Civil War. While some letters were signed by British organisations or gentlemen who clearly explained their reasons, others were written by less educated individuals who simply wished to protest. A hand-written anonymous note stated that 'England will never be friendly to Italy, while you have old Mussolini we know him to [*sic*] well for what he is (bad to the core). He made war on the poor Ethiopians, but it was no victory'. In a more literate tone, a British soldier protesting against Italy's behaviour in the Spanish conflict expressed a similar disgust:

> A soldier can only view with the uttermost contempt the policy you have followed whilst the murderous excesses you have fostered in Spain deserves [*sic*] the sternest condemnation and is that of unmitigated blackguard . . . the murderous crimes inflicted on harmless women and children in the cities of Spain, actions that apparently receive the blessing of the Vatican.[81]

Another major source of discontent was the racial laws, which occasionally caused deep disappointment for British travellers to Italy:

> Dear Sir, I had arranged to spend my holiday in Italy with my wife as I have done during the past two years. As a self respecting Englishman however I cannot visit a country that indulges in the luxury of religious persecution. I hope others will express to you their disapproval and disgust.[82]

Another British traveller thought it impossible to continue to visit because of the rumours about Italian atrocities in Spain: 'These are grave insinuations and as one who cherishes happy memories of a recent visit to Italy and had, until recently, the intention of repeating the visit, I should be grateful if you would inform me if there is any substance in these rumours.'[83]

One letter in particular was significant on an issue likely to worry Grandi most, Italy's fate should it continue its alliance with Germany. It was cast as a satirical letter from Hitler to Grandi, containing German stereotypes about Italy. The fact that it was written by a Briton obviously suggested that the British shared those stereotypes: Italy was unreliable, always changed alliances, based its policies on bluff and was falling increasingly under German domination. The false 'Hitler' asserted that if Mussolini had had his former allies (France and Britain) still with him, he could certainly have stopped Hitler at the Brenner, despite the Axis. But without them he was too weak, since he had wasted all his forces in the Ethiopian and Spanish campaigns. Italy, the letter continued, was not trustworthy, and Germany was ready 'to wreak on Musso [*sic*] and Italy as a revenge for Italy's betrayal in the last great European War'. In fact what the Germans liked most about the capture of Austria was that they were now on the Italian border, 'ready to deal Italy one death blow and make Italy and her Colonies part of our Great German Empire'. The Rome-Berlin Axis had been invented for Germany alone, and indicated what the conclusion would be: 'We are going to put the Hypocrite Pope and Musso', the 'dirty double-crosser', 'in a Concentration Camp. We will turn the Berlin-Rome Axis Pact into a Berlin axes Roma fact'.[84]

Such notions about Italo-German relations clearly did worry Grandi, as well as other Fascist *gerarchi* such as Bottai, De Bono and Balbo, and universal Fascists, in particular Gravelli and Pellizzi, who continued to see the alliance with Germany as good only so long as Italy's primacy was respected.[85] Throughout his diary, Grandi emphasised that the relationship with Britain was the only possible way to avoid war; he saw alliance with Germany as a favourable option only if it brought advantages to Italy. This perception remained present not only in his diary but also in *L'Italia Nostra*, and marked Grandi's activity in London from 1937 onward.

The celebration of the Munich agreement in London coincided with the celebration of the March on Rome and of victory in the Great War. In November 1938 *L'Italia Nostra*, unlike its practice in previous years, described the celebration of victory in the Great War in terms of foreign policy rather than as an Italian community event. This was due both to the crisis of the community after September 1938 and to Grandi's hopes for an improvement in Anglo-Italian relations, which *L'Italia Nostra* continued to support. The celebration in November 1938 brought together Italian and British organisations, and Grandi's speech to the community focused on the new friendship between two countries which had been allies in the Great War. The period of crisis and difficulty between Italy and Britain, Grandi argued, had lasted four years, but was ended with British recognition of the Italian empire. A new era of loyal friendship between the two nations was now beginning. As he had done in 1936, he now praised the Italians in Britain for their contribution to foreign policy; they had shown themselves to be the 'new Italians' that Mussolini wanted, at home and abroad:

> Every time I took my children to the Italian school, I stopped to watch the children of Italians in London: they are able to march with the same confident smile with which their elder brothers, the *Legionari d'Africa*, marched under the tropical sun toward the enemy and onward to the conquest of empire.[86]

L'Italia Nostra saw Mussolini's meeting with Chamberlain in Rome in January 1939 as the reconsecration, on the soil of Rome, of an ancient Anglo-Italian friendship. The newspaper expressed the pious wish that Italians would now forget the events of the recent difficult years. Chamberlain and Mussolini were 'distinguished men who founded their policies on reality'. One sentence by Mussolini was reported in huge characters, and underlined the historic meaning of that meeting for the Italian people: 'We do not govern the nation for today's Italians alone, which would be remarkable in itself, but also for future generations, because the Fatherland will live for centuries and millennia'.[87] During the same period, the newspaper was filled with photographs of Franco's victory in the Spanish Civil War and of the crowds in Rome listening to Mussolini's speech celebrating the event.

News of Italy's invasion of Albania appeared in *L'Italia Nostra* in April 1939; until that date, the newspaper had never mentioned either Albania or Italian interests in that region. The average reader of *L'Italia Nostra* might have been puzzled by the explanation that the event was a 'fated conclusion of a natural and historic process, caused by the very condition of Albania'. The newspaper claimed that the invasion had not been decided on the spur of the moment, although the policy leading to it had developed over a short period of time. In its account, Italy had been invited there by Albanian patriots who disliked their government and by Italian citizens who lived there and were continuously threatened by groups of armed Albanian bandits. Italy intended now to contribute directly 'to the elevation of the Albanian people on the paths of work and of civil progress'.[88] Unlike the invasion of Ethiopia, which the newspaper had publicised in advance by publishing maps and articles, the invasion of Albania did not receive the patriotic and unanimous approval of the Italian communities in Britain. The newspaper coverage suggests that in the case of Albania the *Fasci* did not even attempt to make a similar appeal to the communities. The embassy organised only one public meeting for the celebration of the event at the *Casa del Littorio*. There the authorities explained how the invasion of Albania had been a peaceful gift of civilisation to a country that aspired to link its destiny to the fate of immortal Rome. The supposed absence of violence and cruelty during the conquest did not mean that Italy had refrained from using military means: 'when one needs to break a chain, one must have the courage to break it'. Although only one battalion was employed in the operation, *L'Italia Nostra* claimed that Italy's military campaign had been so extensive, precise and perfect that the whole world admired it: 'things never seen before, not even in dreams: an entire army coming to Tirana from the air'. The freedom and independence of Albania, rather than being diminished, was now beginning once it had become part of the ancient and imperial Roman family.[89]

During the last months of Grandi's work in London, the *Fascio*'s newspaper no longer mentioned Anglo-Italian relations and ignored the Axis, but instead continued to report on autarchy, summer camps and schools. The paper described the invasion of Albania as a logical event, but never referred to the possibility of war in Europe. German aggression against Czechoslovakia was ignored and the broader German threat never mentioned. Yet this was not the view of the general secretary of the *Fasci* Abroad. Unlike *L'Italia Nostra*, *Il Legionario* continued to propagate news about the Italo-German alliance and about Germany's alleged right to expand in the East. The bulletin of the Italian *Fasci* Abroad went so far as to explain that Czechoslovakia was a mere invention of Versailles diplomacy.[90] Reporting on the Pact of Steel included an attack against Britain for its failure to understand the wider perspective of the new alliance, which was the expression of a spiritual change in the world.[91] The divergence between the newspaper of the *Fasci* in Britain, controlled by the Italian embassy, and the organ of the Italian *Fasci* Abroad, controlled by the foreign ministry, reflected the divergence between Grandi and Ciano, which was not simply a personality clash but had become a political issue.

This was particularly evident after the signature of the Pact of Steel. On 22 May 1939 Grandi simply noted in his diary without comment: 'signature in Berlin of Italo-German Pact'. A day later he sent an invitation to the German ambassador for 25 May asking him to a reception to celebrate the Pact. According to Grandi, a number of journalists knew about the event and sent the news to Rome. Grandi claimed in his diary that this happened by chance, but it is likely that Grandi wanted Mussolini to know about it. The following day Ciano phoned Grandi to tell him that Mussolini was pleased to be told about such an invitation. The Duce took the occasion to order Grandi to extend the invitation to the representatives of the Italian and German communities in Britain and to prepare a speech to mark the occasion. The speech, Mussolini emphasised, had to be violent, it had to attack directly the democracies, especially France. Ciano, to the immense annoyance of Grandi, added: 'you have seen . . . what French newspapers have written about you and your opposition to Axis policy even during the last few days'; and concluded by ordering Grandi to be extremely tough and explicit. Grandi replied that he had not read the French newspapers, and concluded by saying that the Duce would simply be obeyed. A day later he knew that Mussolini had ordered the Italian press to attach great importance to what he was going to say. Grandi thus extended the invitation to all Italian and German Fascist and Nazi organisations in London, to the personnel of the Italian and German embassies, and to Italian and German journalists, gathering in total about 300 people. Before giving the speech on 25 May, he sent a written draft to Rome so that Ciano and Mussolini had time to check it.[92]

Grandi began with the usual explanation of the alliance as the necessary corollary to Axis policy, as a sign of the 'indivisible communion of two States, two Peoples and of two Empires', but also of two leaders and of two revolutions. Grandi even referred to the Italian *Risorgimento*, which he had previously used to demonstrate traditional Anglo-Italian friendship, but which he now used to recall that the first alliance of the newly unified Italy had been concluded with Prussia.

Following that (and forgetting about the Italo-German clash in the First World War), he emphasised that the first alliance of the reborn Roman Empire had been concluded with Nazi Germany. Grandi, as he always did in his speeches, then turned his thoughts to the Italian community, which was now becoming an Italo-German community:

> Italians living in London wish to-day, together with their German friends and in unison with our comrades living in the Fatherland, to express their sentiments of solidarity, of joy for the historic event and of gratitude to the Duce . . . Italians living in Great Britain . . . perhaps more and better than any other, are in a position to appreciate the value of the deep significance and decisive importance that the Italo-German Pact has for the future of our two countries.

Grandi then attacked the alleged campaign of the democracies against Italy and Germany, and in particular the purported lies of the Western press. For example, he continued, French newspapers had recently presented Grandi himself as the most resolute adversary of the Italo-German alliance. He insisted that the French had lied, and accused them of acting in bad faith. He then extended his polemic to the whole period between 1918 and 1935, attacking Versailles and Geneva, and warning that Italy would never forgive or forget. In conclusion, he claimed that the Italo-German pact had already been successfully tested both in the political field with the Rome-Berlin Axis, and in the military field with the Spanish Civil War.[93]

After the speech, the German journalists present appeared most embarrassed. They could not understand the reason behind Grandi's anti-French diatribe, which at that point ran the risk of embarrassing German diplomacy. The German journalists indeed asked Grandi not to publish the speech, and informed him that they themselves did not plan to report it. Grandi replied that the decision rested with Mussolini alone. The following day, Ciano phoned Grandi to tell him that the Duce liked his speech immensely; it was exactly what the dictator had wanted.[94] Yet Grandi was not convinced that the speech had been such a good idea, and as a result nothing appeared in *L'Italia Nostra*. However, *Il Legionario* came out on 30 May with a long article about Grandi's speech, showing again the different perception of foreign policy between Ciano and Grandi. The article included the attacks against the democracies in general and France in particular. It also emphasised the Italo-German character of the London gathering, giving the impression of the existence in Britain of a strong Italo-German community, whose members felt themselves to be part of a common revolution and a common destiny. The meeting concluded, ran the report, with the two communities acclaiming both the Duce and the Führer, and singing the Italian and German national anthems.[95]

Nevertheless, the British Italophiles understood Grandi's intentions and were still eager to cooperate. Grandi again saw himself as the man who could rescue

Italy – and therefore Europe – at the eleventh our, and despite Mussolini. But this time Mussolini gave him no chance. Without consulting him, the Duce declared Grandi's mission in London at an end. Although Grandi officially left the embassy in July, Mussolini's decision came after the speech at the embassy, when Ciano asked Grandi to return to Rome, where Grandi learned from Mussolini that he was to be appointed minister of justice.[96]

Conclusion

In 1939 the divergence between Grandi's and the Italophiles' beliefs on the one hand and Italy's propaganda and foreign policy on the other persisted. The attitude of the *Fasci* Abroad reflected this divergence. Despite the increased centralisation of the *Fasci* under the control of the foreign ministry from 1938 onward, *L'Italia Nostra* continued to reproduce Grandi's views on Italian foreign policy. The London newspaper became pro-British after Eden's resignation, and avoided giving excessive weight to news about Italy's aggressiveness and closeness to Germany.

Two years after Grandi had left London, while Britain was at war with Italy, Douglas Jerrold insisted that even at the eleventh hour Italy would have preferred an alliance with Britain and France but was 'committed, by virtue of her fear and hatred of Bolshevism, to the cause of General Franco', in which Jerrold had shared.[97] His view was widespread among the Italophiles during the Second World War. For Muriel Currey, Charles Petrie and Harold Goad Italy remained an ideal second country, and they regretted that events such as Ethiopia, the League's sanctions and the Spanish Civil War had allegedly dragged Mussolini toward a purportedly unwanted alliance with Germany.[98] In the same year, their Italian friend Luigi Villari published a book in which he sought to demonstrate that the British had never really been able to understand Italy, and how the Anglo-Saxon struggle in the Second World War was 'essentially a struggle against Western civilisation and patriotism'.[99] Contemporary anti-British Italian publications reiterated Villari's perception. A book by Virginio Gayda about Italy's foreign policy aspirations was, despite its Italian title, actually written in German.[100]

Notes

1. Anonymous letter, without date but 1938, addressed to 'Dear Dago Grandi' and signed 'Hail Hitler', ASMAE, *DeF*, *CG*, b. 53, f. 131.

2. Perth to Sargent, 31 December 1937 and Sargent to Perth, 10 January 1938, PRO, *FO*, 371/22402, R89/23/22.

3. 'Memorandum on conversation of Grandi with British Government', 15 February 1938, in Lord Harvey of Tasburgh Diaries, BL Manuscripts, Add. 56401, ff. 63–8.

4. 'Polizia e poliziotti', *L'Italia Nostra*, 14 Jan 1938, n. 467, p. 2.

5. 'The average man', ibid., 28 January 1938, n. 469, p. 3.

6. 'Cinque anni di regime nazista', ibid., 4 February 1938, n. 470, p. 2.

7. Dino Grandi, *Diario di Londra*, ASMAE, *DeF*, *CG*, b. 151, f. 199, sf. 2, ins. 3, pp. 2–3, entry for 18 February 1938. See also Paolo Nello, *Un fedele disubbidiente. Dino Grandi da Palazzo Chigi al 25 luglio* (Bologna: Il Mulino, 1993), p. 287.

8. Renzo De Felice, *Mussolini il duce*, II (Turin: Einaudi, 1974), p. 445.

9. Galeazzo Ciano, *Diario 1937–1943* (Milan: Rizzoli, 1980; first edition 1946), p. 95, entry for 7 February 1938; p. 96, entry for 9 February 1938.

10. Ibid., p. 102, entry for 21 February 1938; Egidio Ortona, 'La caduta di Eden nel 1938', *Storia Contemporanea*, XV (1984), 3, pp. 477–94.

11. Grandi, *Diario di Londra*, ASMAE, *DeF*, *CG*, b. 151, f. 199, sf. 2, ins. 3, p. 16, entry for 19–20 February 1938.

12. Grandi, *Diario di Londra*, ibid., sf. 4, pp. 6–8.

13. Grandi, *Diario di Londra*, ibid., sf. 2, ins. 3, pp. 20–4, entry for 21 February 1938.

14. See the pages of diary of a *Piccola Italiana* from Naples, who sent her diary to Grandi on 21 February 1938, ASMAE, *DeF*, *CG*, b. 53, f. 126.

15. Coselschi to Grandi, 12 February 1938, ibid.

16. Letter sent by three old friends from Imola, 27 February 1938, ibid. See also Vittorio Gambillo to Grandi, 27 February 1938, ibid.

17. Camillo Pellizzi to Grandi, 28 Feb 1938, ibid.

18. 'Italia e Inghilterra', *L'Italia Nostra*, 11 March 1938, n. 475, p. 1.

19. 'Le conseguenze', ibid., 18 March 1938, n. 476, p. 2

20. 'Asse Roma-Berlino – La lettera di Hitler al Duce', ibid., 18 March 1938, n. 476, p. 3.

21. Ciano, *Diario*, p. 111, entry for 11 March 1938.

22. Ibid., p. 120, entry for 3 April 1938.

23. Grandi, *Diario di Londra*, ASMAE, *DeF*, *CG*, b. 151, f. 199, sf. 2, ins. 3, pp. 10–14, entry for 26 April 1938.

24. Wickham Steed to Sargent, 20 July 1936, PRO, *FO*, 371/20411, R4375/226/22.

25. Grandi, *Diario di Londra*, ASMAE, *DeF*, *CG*, b. 151, f. 199, sf. 2, ins. 3, p. 13, entry for 20 April 1938.

26. Grandi, *Diario di Londra*, ibid., pp. 5–7, entry for 20 April 1938; 4 May, p. 4; 11 May, p. 5.

27. Osborne to Grandi, 27 April 1938, ASMAE, *DeF*, *CG*, b. 53, f. 126.

28. Grandi to Osborne, 3 May 1938, ibid.

29. Ciano, *Diario*, p. 150, entry for 20 June 1938.

30. Grandi, *Diario di Londra*, ASMAE, *DeF*, *CG*, b. 151, f. 199, sf. 2, ins. 3, pp. 1–2, entry for 1 May 1938.

31. Piero Pedrazza (headed letter 'Il Resto del Carlino') to Grandi, 11 May 1938, ASMAE, *DeF*, *CG*, b. 53, f. 126.

32. Grandi to Biondelli, 30 April 1938, ASMAE, *AL*, b. 1015, f. 2.

33. 'Pasqua di pace', *L'Italia Nostra*, 15 April 1938, n. 480, p. 1.

34. Grandi to foreign ministry, 5 May 1938, ASMAE, *DeF*, *CG*, b. 55, f. 144.

35. Agostino Nasti, 'La politica di Chamberlain', *L'Italia Nostra*, 15 April 1938, n. 480, p. 2.

36. See Virginio Gayda, *Italia e Francia. Problemi aperti* (Rome: il Giornale d'Italia, 1938); Ettore Rota, *Italia e Francia davanti alla storia: il mito della sorella latina* (Milan: Industrie Grafiche Nicola, 1939); Enrico Serra and Jean Baptiste Duroselle, *Italia e Francia, 1939–1945* (Milan: Angeli, 1984).

37. 'Segreta', Ciano to Grandi, 14 November 1938, ASMAE, *DeF*, *CG*, b. 43, f. 107 (1935–8).

38. Ciano to Ribbentrop, manuscript – draft, 2 January 1939, ASMAE, *Gab* 29, f. 2. See in particular Gioacchino Volpe, *Storia della Corsica italiana* (Milan: ISPI, 1939) and Gayda, *Italia e Francia*.

39. Grandi, *Diario di Londra*, ASMAE, *DeF*, *CG*, b. 151, f. 199, sf. 2, ins. 3, entry for 14 May 1938, pp. 1–3; entry for 16 May 1938, pp. 1–3; entry for 20 May 1938, pp. 1–3.

40. Grandi, *Diario di Londra*, ibid., sf. 4, pp. 1–2.

41. Grandi, *Diario di Londra*, ibid., entry for 30 September 1938, p. 24; p. 34; p. 41. As to the role played by the Italophiles, Grandi was particularly grateful to Graham for his help in the attempt to convince Chamberlain; see Grandi to Graham, 30 September 1938, ASMAE, *DeF*, *CG*, b. 53, f. 128.

42. 'La celebrazione della pace al nostro Fascio e al dopolavoro Mazzini e Garibaldi', *L'Italia Nostra*, 14 October 1938, n. 506, p. 1; see also 'La parola della pace', ibid., 30 September 1938, n. 504, p. 1; 'La vittoria della pace il trionfo del Duce', ibid., 7 October 1938, n. 505, p. 1.

43. See in particular Marcello Cerioli to Grandi, 30 September 1938, ASMAE, *DeF*, *CG*, b. 53, f. 128.

44. Ciano, *Diario*, p. 186, entry for 28 September 1938.

45. Nello, *Un fedele disubbidiente*, p. 345; De Felice, *Mussolini il Duce*, II, p. 536; Quartararo, *Roma tra Londra e Berlino*, p. 404.

46. Grandi's view has been supported by Ortona, 'La caduta di Eden in 1938'; see also Nick Smart, *The National Government, 1931–1940* (London and Basingstoke: MacMillan, 1999), pp. 156–7.

47. Giorgio Rochat, in Angelo Del Boca, Massimo Legnani and Mario G. Rossi (eds), *Il regime fascista* (Rome and Bari: Laterza, 1995), pp. 160–2. However, it is not at all clear if Mussolini realised that until later. See Enzo Collotti, *Fascismo e politica di potenza. Politica estera 1922–1939* (Milan: La Nuova Italia, 2000), pp. 361–74.

48. Ciano, *Diario*, p. 213, entry for 16 November 1938.

49. 'Discorso di Sir Oswald Mosley a Leeds', London embassy to foreign ministry, 28 February 1938, ASMAE, *AP*, *GB*, b. 34, f. 2, sf. 2.

50. Viscount Lymington, *Should Britain fight?* (London: British Council Against European Commitments, 1938), SUL, *Special Collections and Archives*, *BU Collection*, 3/LYM.

51. 'Discorso di Mosley all'Earls Court', London embassy to foreign ministry, 17 July 1939, ASMAE, *AP*, Gran Bretagna, b. 34, f. 2, sf. 2.

52. Mosley, *My Life* (London: Nelson, 1968), p. 366; *Mosley: the Facts* (London: Euphorion Distribution, 1957), p. 10; Diana Mosley, *A Life of Contrasts: the Autobiography of Diana Mosley* (London: Hamilton, 1977), p. 159.

53. 'Activities of Mr John Celli', Foreign Office minutes as comments to a letter by Perth to British Foreign Office, 5 May 1938, PRO, *FO*, 371/22434, R5157/395/22.

54. Ernest Platt, Vice-President of the British Union of Friends of Italy, to Grandi, February 1938, ASMAE, *DeF*, *CG*, b. 53, f. 126.

55. Report by Mr Sedgwick on the meeting held in Milan on 7 April 1938, sent to the Foreign Office on 22 April, PRO, *FO*, 371/22434, R4622/395/22.

56. Many British subjects living in Italy (54 signatures) to Neville Chamberlain, 1 May 1938, ASMAE, *DeF*, *CG*, b. 53, f. 126.

57. British consulate in Milan to the chargé d'affaires at British embassy in Rome, 9 September 1938, PRO, *FO*, 371/22434, R7656/395/22; British consulate in Milan to Perth, 25 July 1938, ibid., R6960/395/22.

58. Mottistone to Grandi, 11 February 1938 and Grandi to Mottistone, 18 February 1938, ASMAE, *DeF*, *CG*, b. 53, f. 126.

59. Kenneth de Courcy to Grandi, 23 February 1938, ASMAE, *DeF*, *CG*, b. 53, f. 129.

60. Lloyd to Grandi, 18 April 1938 and Phillmore to Grandi, Easter Sunday 1938, ASMAE, *DeF*, *CG*, b. 53, f. 126.

61. Petrie to Grandi, 20 April 1938, ibid.

62. Grandi to Lord Phillmore, 19 April 1938 and Grandi to Petrie, 25 April 1938, ibid.

63. George Lambert to Grandi, 3 May 1938, ibid.

64. 'Gruppo parlamentare anglo-italiano', Grandi to foreign ministry, 8 April 1938, ASMAE, *DeF*, *CG*, b. 55, f. 144.

65. Neville Chamberlain to Grandi, 19 September 1938, ASMAE, *DeF*, *CG*, b. 53, f. 127.

66. Petrie to Grandi, 28 September 1938, ibid.

67. Petrie to Beaverbrook, 16 April 1956, HLRO, *Lord Beaverbrook Papers*, Correspondence with Charles Petrie, 1929–1963, C/270; Grandi to Beaverbrook, 21 July 1960; Grandi to Beaverbrook, 31 July 1962; Grandi to Beaverbrook, 15 January 1964, ibid., Correspondence with Dino Grandi, C/145.

68. Richard Griffiths, *Fellow Travellers of the Right: British Enthusiasts for Nazi Germany, 1933–39* (London: Constable, 1980), p. 23.

69. Luigi Villari, 'Italian – and other – intervention in Spain', *The National Review* (incorporating *The English Review*), vol. 110, n. 663, May 1938, p. 593; p. 596.

70. 'Austria and Germany', *Bulletin of International News*, vol. XV, n. 5, 5 March 1938, p. 177.

71. 'The Speeches in Rome on May 7', ibid., vol. XV, n. 10, 21 May 1938, p. 441.

72. 'Mr Chamberlain's Visit to Rome', ibid., vol. XVI, n. 2, 28 January 1939, p. 60.

73. 'The Economic Value of Czecho-Slovakia to Germany', ibid., vol. XVI, n. 6, 25 March 1939, p. 265; 'Signor Mussolini's Speech on Sunday, March 26', ibid., p. 316.

74. Leo Amery, *The German Colonial Claim* (London and Edinburgh: W. & R. Chambers, 1939), p. 9; pp. 75–6; pp. 131–2.

75. Richard Michael Keane (ed), *Germany – What Next? Being an Examination of the German Menace in so far as it Affects Great Britain* (Harmondsworth: Penguin, 1939). See in particular General Tilho (Académie des Sciences), 'The Axis in Africa', p. 222.

76. Francis Yeats-Brown, *European Jungle* (London: Eyre and Spottiswoode, 1939), p. 69.

77. Ibid., p. 89.

78. Adrian Brunel to Grandi, 28 September 1938; Orion S. Playfair (secretary of the 'New Europe Group') to Grandi, 29 September 1938, ASMAE, *DeF*, *CG*, b. 53, f. 127.

79. See letters from Sheffield and from Middlesex, 30 September 1938 and 4 October 1938, ibid.

80. From a meeting of university students and left-wing clubs on 18 March 1938; they sent a summary of their resolutions to Grandi, no date, ASMAE, *DeF*, *CG*, b. 53, f. 131; see also Windhill Co-operative Society to Grandi, date not readable, ibid.

81. Handwritten note, anonymous and without date, ibid; anonymous from Birmingham, 1 February 1938, to Mussolini, but sent to Grandi, ibid.

82. Handwritten, to Grandi, no date, ibid; John D. Hunt to Grandi, no date, ibid.

83. Mr S. G. Hum, from Essex, 3 Feb 1938, ibid.

84. Anonymous letter, without date but 1938, addressed to 'Dear Dago Grandi' and signed 'Hail Hitler', ibid.

85. Emilio Gentile, *La grande Italia. Ascesa e declino del mito della nazione nel ventesimo secolo* (Milan: Mondadori, 1997), p. 194; Ruggero Zangrandi, *Il lungo viaggio attraverso il fascismo* (Milan: Feltrinelli, 1962), p. 217.

86. 'La serata dei combattenti al Criterion. Il discorso di S. E. l'ambasciatore', *L'Italia Nostra*, 11 November 1938, n. 510, p. 4; London consulate to foreign ministry, ASMAE, *AL*, b. 1015, f. 2, 8 November 1938.

87. 'L'esito del convegno di Roma', *L'Italia Nostra*, 20 January 1939, n. 520, p. 1.

88. 'L'Italia in Albania', ibid., 14 April 1939, n. 532, p. 1

89. 'L'Unione dell'Albania all'Italia – La celebrazione dell'avvenimento a Londra', ibid., 21 April 1939, n. 533, p. 1.

90. 'La parola dell'Italia fascista per la risoluzione della questione dei Sudeti', *Il Legionario*, 20 September 1938, n. 26, p. 8.

91. 'Dal discorso di Cuneo al patto italo-germanico', ibid., 30 May 1939, n. 15, p. 1.

92. Grandi, 'Appunto circa mio discorso all'ambasciata, ordinatomi da Mussolini, dopo Patto alleanza italo-tedesca (Maggio 1939)', ASMAE, *DeF*, *CG*, b. 56, f. 153.

93. Grandi, speech of 25 May 1939, attached to the notes of Grandi's diary, ibid.

94. Grandi, 'Appunto', ibid.

95. 'Londra – Manifestazione italo-tedesca all'Ambasciata d'Italia. Vibrato discorso di S. E. Grandi', *Il Legionario*, 30 May 1939, n. 15, p. 21.

96. Grandi, *Memorie: i sette anni a Londra*, ASMAE, *DeF*, *CG*, b. 153, f. 200, sf. 1, ins. 3, pp. 184–94.

97. Douglas Jerrold, *Britain and Europe, 1900–1940* (London: Collins, 1941), p. 144.

98. Muriel Currey to Lord Cecil, 31 August 1941, BL Manuscripts, *Lord Cecil Papers*, Add. 51187, part II, f. 424.

99. Luigi Villari, *L'Italia come non è. Polemica con gli Anglosassoni* (Rome: Tosi, 1941), p. 276.

100. Gayda, *Che cosa vuole l'Italia* (Rome: il Giornale d'Italia, 1940).

Conclusion

Grandi's era in London had begun with a novel attempt to transform the Italian communities in Britain. The ambassador's activity toward fascistisation of the Italians was symbolised by his visit to the children gathered in London for departure to summer camps in Italy in July 1932. After seven years, the conclusion of his mission coincided with another gathering: that of an Italo-German community celebrating the Pact of Steel at the Italian embassy in July 1939. That development poses some crucial questions, in particular about Grandi's role in the transformation of the Italian communities, the role of the *Fasci* Abroad, the manipulation of those communities in the service of Italian foreign policy, and consequently the relationship between Rome and London during those years. When Grandi began his mission, neither he nor the London *Fascio* had a plan to transform the Italian community into an Italo-German community. Yet although an Italo-German community in London in fact did not and never had existed, that was the image given by the Italian press for the *Fasci* Abroad at the end of the 1930s.

The role of imagery was fundamental to the fascistisation of the communities abroad. The Fascist press, public rituals and the organisation of programmes for the education of the Italians were all elements that contributed to the creation of a new image of the Italians in Britain. This book attempts to measure the gap between such Fascist aspirations and their success among the communities, namely the actual belief of the Italians in Fascist ideology, and the extent to which such education of the Italians created a microcosm of what Fascism did to Italian society as a whole.

The Italian *Fasci* Abroad did not simply attempt to fascistise the emigrants. One of their main roles was to transform them into new Italians, but their interest was not only in the Italians themselves. They wanted to expand fascism in other countries and, by creating Italian Fascist communities, they played a part in Italy's foreign policy: by creating fifth columnists in crucial areas and by disseminating Fascist ideology. Mussolini's declaration in 1933 that fascism could be exported abroad, together with the more general expansion of European fascism, transformed the *Fasci* Abroad into an important instrument in the attempt to create a fascist international. It was therefore only when Mussolini became interested in expanding fascism abroad that the *Fasci* became an essential element in fascist foreign policy. Although fascist international meetings were organised by 'universalists' and groups such as the CAUR, the *Fasci* joined their efforts by creating networks of contacts and activities between them and foreign fascist movements.

The British-Italian case is a clear example of this, since contacts between Italian and British fascism were organised by the *Fasci* in Britain, and in Italy by the local BUF branches, which hoped to develop into an equivalent institution. These contacts also occurred in other countries in the 1930s because it was only during that decade that foreign fascist movements began to appear in any number. The increased relevance of the *Fasci* for Italian foreign policy is also demonstrated by the large number of publications about the *Fasci* Abroad in the 1930s, compared to the 1920s. Their work in the 1930s, as the British case demonstrated, remained a revolutionary one: the development of schools and summer camps meant the realisation of Mussolini's plans for the education of the new Italians.

When Italy's foreign policy became openly aggressive from 1935 onward, these institutions played an even greater role. The mobilisation of Italians abroad during the Ethiopian campaign was an example of the attempt to transform emigrant communities into totalitarian colonies. The accent on totalitarianism coincided with the explosion of anti-British propaganda. The separation of community life from the rest of British society appeared to realise the Fascist dream of the new Italians abroad. In Britain in particular, *L'Italia Nostra* claimed to represent a community which was supposed to be living after 1935 in a metaphorical trench, surrounded by enemy territory.

The myth of Rome also played an important role in Fascist imagery of the community. For emigrants from small villages who had probably never visited Rome even when they had lived in Italy, the celebration of the new Rome represented a step toward nationalisation. The identification of the new Rome with Mussolini served the creation of the myth of the Duce as a new Augustus, and was reflected in London by the creation of a subsidiary 'myth' surrounding Grandi. The ambassador was the visible link between the community and Mussolini; at the same time, Grandi had been one of the founders of Fascist Italy. He mixed with Italian Londoners, sent his children to the Italian school, and acted as a local 'duce' at public events. It was also the case that when Grandi first arrived in London, a new secretary of the *Fascio* was appointed: the incoming secretary, Camagna was not only young, but self-consciously saw himself as a *squadrista*.

Summer camps were the most important point of identification with the regime for many Italian families, because it was also an institutional link, recognised by the authority of the *Fascio* and of the regime. The Fascist press described the Italians in Britain as heroes who were required to act in a revolutionary manner, but also to observe local laws and pursue private rather than public interests: a dichotomy between Fascism and family – between being pioneers and warriors, and being good fathers and mothers. This imagery tended to change from 1935 onward, when the whole community was called upon to mount a major battle against sanctions. Mussolini's slogan 'many enemies much honour' was reflected in the renewed pride of a community living in an enemy country and facing local hostility. By that point, the *Fasci* Abroad considered integration into British society almost as a sort of treason. *Il Legionario* and *L'Italia Nostra* worked in unison to persuade Italians to strengthen their links with each other, and never to mix with the native population. In 1935 all were required to act as heroes: the war volunteers; the women, who had to support the war through propaganda and education; and the children who had to act as little soldiers, in schools, in sport activities after school, and in the summer camps, the *colonie*. The imperial image was widespread. While volunteers left for the *colonia* in Africa, Italian children left for their own *colonie* in Italy itself.

The myth of repatriation after the conquest of empire seemed to reward Fascism for its fight against sanctions and against the great powers. That myth was deeply felt in Britain: allegedly, Italians could now leave the country which had exploited them and had attempted to deny Italy its living space. The illusion was sustained that Italy had actually won a war against Britain, and that Italians had at last obtained their own living space. They were able to move there and live as employers rather than employees.

The belief that Italy had won a war against the British Empire was linked with the idea of the Italian as a proletarian. In that case, another major dichotomy was involved. Italians were always described in the Fascist press as working-class communities, people who worked all day every day of their lives, and who sacrificed themselves for their families and for the wealth and reputation of their fatherland. At the same time, while continuously celebrating *'la comunità lavoratrice'*, *L'Italia Nostra* reported daily on a social life in London which was evidently restricted to an Italian élite. The community was supposed to be proud of those Fascist notables who had achieved success in British society. This clearly contradicted the regime's propaganda on the classless society, which was alleged to be spreading from Italy into Italian communities abroad. The schools were meant to fill this gap, for example by teaching Italian to children of families who had never spoken Italian, but rather dialect. That conflict in the self-image of the Italians was again apparently solved with the conquest of empire: the new *Casa d'Italia* in London symbolised the new status of the whole community. 'Little Italy' was once and forever destroyed. The belief that all this had happened through victory in a war against the British Empire was in large part due to Grandi's speeches to the community. He repeated the idea in his letters to Rome. He believed he had played a crucial role in challenging British pride. In 1938 he also came to believe in the importance of his role in bringing about agreement with the British Empire, which was presented to Italian communities as the re-establishment of an equal relationship between Italy and Britain.

The Ethiopian War was the most crucial event in the relationship between Fascism and the Italian communities. The rebirth of the Roman imperial dream and the myth of Italy's power had a remarkable influence in creating a sense of belonging to a Fascist community. The use of the *Fasci* by the Italian government also involved the organisation of fifth columnists and the creation of an intense propaganda against the democratic states, which continued, against Britain in particular, after 1936, and spread throughout the British Empire, mostly in the Mediterranean basin. By isolating Italian communities from British society and by organising espionage activity, the *Fasci* certainly contributed to Italy's preparation for war against Britain. Yet the Italian community itself was not prepared to follow Fascism to that extreme end. In this sense, the community remained loyal to its ambassador rather than to Mussolini's policies. It is possible to see in *L'Italia Nostra* and in Grandi's diary for 1938, the anxieties of a community which hoped that Italy would never go to war against Britain.

The *Fascio* found itself in a difficult position from 1938 onwards. On the one hand, it was under the control of the secretary of the *Fasci* in Rome, and, after Parini's fall, under that of Ciano, and therefore effectively an instrument in the hands of Italy's foreign policy. On the other, it had to deal locally with an Italian community worried from September 1938 about the serious prospect of war, a community whose members increasingly shrank from their Fascist mission and in some cases chose even to apply for British citizenship. The *Fascio* also had to deal with the lack of response from the Italians to the racial laws and the alliance with Germany.

One attempt made by the *Fascio* was to call for radicalisation, which inevitably involved a small section of the London community and returned the *Fasci* to the age of the pioneers, to the original idea of the Italians abroad, ready to make sacrifices for the fatherland in difficult times. That raises the question of radicalism within the *Fasci* Abroad and within Fascism itself. It is simplistic to conclude that the founders of the *Fasci* were radical Fascists linked with the Party in the 1920s and that in the 1930s they were forced to accept a process of normalisation.[1] Farinacci's Party in 1925, and later the tendencies led by Roberto Farinacci, Pietro Marsich and other supporters of intransigent Fascism (among which very different interpretations of Fascism nevertheless existed) were never linked with the organisation of the *Fasci* Abroad, at least so far as research on the *Fasci* has demonstrated. In the 1930s in particular, different views existed as to which was 'the' revolutionary current. Representatives of racism and supporters of the Axis who advocated a revolutionary foreign policy considered themselves to be extreme and intransigent, pure Fascists of the first hour. At the same time, after his efforts toward a rapprochement with Britain and a less pro-German foreign policy, Grandi was hailed by former *squadristi* from the Romagna as the true representative of Fascism 'of the origins', the revolutionary ambassador, under whose guidance Italy had been able to assert and maintain a position of parity with Britain. The London *Fascio*, whose major figure was the 'revolutionary' Pellizzi, was always on Grandi's side. From this point of view, the book demonstrates that the idea of the pioneers never disappeared, and that its myth was crucial in the organisation of a revolutionary youth, through summer camps, schools and athletics training for young Italians. The fact that the *Fascio* expanded its members toward the mid-1930s was a consequence of the growth in the success of these activities and myths within the community, which reached its peak with the proclamation of the empire in 1936 and with the splendid new *Casa d'Italia* in 1937.

The threat of war and the general worsening of economic conditions in Britain sapped the vitality of the Fascist myth after 1938: the few who remained loyal to Fascism and were ready to risk their lives for it recreated the myth of the pioneers and of the origins, a myth that had never really disappeared, perpetuated throughout the years by resistance to sanctions, and by propaganda for autarchy and corporativism. Such attempts to build a micro-totalitarian Italy within British communities reflected the wider attempt to intensify totalitarianism within Italy.

Another aspect analysed by the book, the collaboration between Italian and British fascism, raises several issues about the nature of the fascist international and the existence of Anglo-Italian fascist relations. In 1933 Italian Fascist universalism considered it a duty to support British fascists, who professed to believe in the 'universality of Roman ideas'. Only two years later, the major representative of universal Fascism, Asvero Gravelli, began to distinguish between a Protestant (German and British) and a Roman (Italian) type of fascism. Such a variation in the Italian perception of British fascism clearly reflected a shift in BUF's role model from Italy to Germany. The cultural origins of British fascism, with its strong relationship to the Italian movement, ensured regular contacts between British and Italian fascists, which continued until the identification with a 'Roman' form of fascism became complicated by the growth of Nazi Germany. The violence at Olympia in 1934 was hardly comparable to what had happened in Germany during the 'night of the long knives', but rather showed a similarity to Italian *squadrismo* before the March on Rome. At the time, Italian imagery about the BUF represented the latter as a *squadrista* movement, and Mosley as a sort of *ras*, analogous to the provincial chieftains of the Italian Fascist movement. BUF propaganda up to 1934 reflected the belief that British fascism was part of universal fascism, and that Rome was its origin. The shift from Italophilia to admiration for National Socialism in 1935 was associated with two main issues: the role of British pride in the attempt to establish a fascism 'better' than the Italian, and the shift from a Roman to a Teutonic model of fascism, linked with the new concept of complementary Anglo-German roles in the creation of the new European order. While Mussolini continued to favour the expansion of fascism in other countries, he made clear that the new European civilisation was Mediterranean, since it had developed from Rome and had once more been made universal by Rome. In October 1935, while Italy was unleashing aggressive anti-British propaganda and Anglo-Italian relations were worsening, the BUF decided to shut down all its offices in Italy.

Grandi's shift from an anti-British attitude in 1935–6 to collaboration with the British Conservatives coincided with a worsening relationship with the BUF. Relations between the London *Fascio* and the BUF cooled. Hitler's shadow always seemed to be present in Grandi's mind as a threat to European order, and also in the mind of British Conservative Italophiles. Like Mosley, the Italophiles were extreme nationalists and believed that Britain had to become 'great again', but through the organisation of a corporativist system which did not necessarily imply a dictatorship. At the same time, they recognised the Fascist rebirth of Italy as the rebirth of ancient Rome, which they continued to consider as the basis of European civilisation. Thus instead of working with Mosley for the growth of fascism in Britain, they worked with the Italian embassy in an attempt to support the cause of Italy and to improve Anglo-Italian relations. Although less interested in fascism in Britain, the Italophiles in fact supported the cause of Fascism and Mussolini more than the BUF did. Their role also grew after 1935 because of the BUF's shift toward German Nazism. Their idealisation of Italy, which perpetuated nineteenth-century romantic images, did not fit in with the type of fascism that the BUF wanted.

When Grandi wrote his memoirs in 1943, Mussolini was no longer Italy's dictator. Grandi had been one of the major figures responsible for the change in regime on 25 July 1943, and felt the need to explain his seven years in London as reflecting a clear anti-German and pro-British policy, which Mussolini, Ciano and the Germans had brought to an end. That version was only partially true: Grandi's activity was in fact anti-British during the period of the Ethiopian War, although in 1938 and 1939 he became worried by the German alliance and by Rome's continued hostility toward London. He became convinced that peace in Europe could only be maintained by agreement between Italy and Britain, which did not imply a withdrawal from the Axis, but could act as a balancing force between France and Russia on the one side and Germany on the other. According to his memoirs, after the Pact of Steel both he and British Conservatives believed that the possibility still existed that war could be prevented. However this plan could only have succeeded if Grandi had remained in London and continued his work with the British Conservative Italophiles. The storm began with Ciano's phone call in May 1939 ordering Grandi to give his anti-French speech at the London embassy after the signature of the Italo-German alliance. Grandi saw no means of escape: he had to give the speech.

L'Italia Nostra, even though strongly anti-British from 1935 onward, showed little enthusiasm for Nazi Germany and favoured rapprochement with Britain once Eden resigned in 1938, proclaiming that Chamberlain was almost a fascist. The London *Fascio*, despite the attempts from Rome to reorganise it in a more centralised way, continued to follow Grandi rather than Ciano. The centralisation of the *Fasci* in Rome after the Ethiopian War gave an indication of the direction of Italian foreign policy; the move toward totalitarianism with the direct control of the *Fasci* by Ciano from 1938 was the final blow. The fact that the Italian Fascist press in Britain tended to talk about Germany as little as possible indicated that Grandi had a different plan in mind. His removal from the London embassy was final confirmation of the division between the London embassy and the Italian foreign ministry. In contrast, *Il Legionario* showed Italy's foreign policy as it actually was, suggesting what was evident both in Ciano's diary and in the correspondence between Ciano and Grandi, that the Axis was Italy's fundamental alliance. Ciano's pro-German position in 1938–9, at least until Grandi's resignation, made Grandi the most important figure in Anglo-Italian relations; even though he failed, and could not possibly have succeeded since Mussolini no longer approved of his policy in London, he remained for the British Italophiles and those who wanted peace with Italy the only viable way to collaborate with Italy.

Note

1. As argued by Luca De Caprariis in 'Fascism for export? The Rise and Eclipse of the *Fasci Italiani all'Estero'*, *Journal of Contemporary History*, XXXV, 2 (April 2000), 151–83.

Bibliography

1. Archival Sources

Archivio Centrale dello Stato, Rome:

Carte di Personalità, Archivi Privati, Carte Grandi, Fondo E. Susmel
Casellario Politico Centrale
Ministero della Cultura Popolare
Segreteria Particolare del Duce, Carteggio Ordinario
Segreteria Particolare del Duce, Carteggio Riservato

Archivio Storico Diplomatico del Ministero degli Affari Esteri, Rome:

Ambasciata di Londra
Affari Politici (1931–45), Gran Bretagna
Archivio De Felice, Carte Dino Grandi
Archivio di Gabinetto del Ministro (1923–43)
Archivio Scuole (1929–35)
Archivio Scuole (1936–45)

Biblioteca Comunale 'Sormani', Milan:

Il Legionario, 1932–39

British Library:

British Library Manuscripts
Bulletin of International News, 1935–9
The English Review, 1935–7

British Library, Newspaper Library, Colindale:

The Blackshirt, 1932–5
The British-Italian Bulletin, 1935–6
L'Italia Nostra, 1932–9

British Library of Political and Economic Science:

BLPES Archive, League of Nations Union
Documenti Diplomatici Italiani
New Times and Ethiopia News, 1936–9
Pamphlet Collection

House of Lords Record Office:

Lord Beaverbrook Papers

Public Record Office, Kew, London:

Foreign Office Correspondence
Home Office 45
Home Office 144

Sheffield University Library:

Special Collections and Archives, British Union Collection, Memoirs of Members
of the BUF

2. Printed Primary Sources

Amery, Leopold Stennet, *The Forward View* (London: Jeoffrey Bles, 1935)
——, *Hitler's Claim for Colonies* (London: Trustees for Freedom, 1936)
——, *The German Colonial Claim* (London and Edinburgh: W. & R. Chambers,
    1939)
Balbo, Italo, *Diario 1922* (Milan: Mondadori, 1932)
Bastianini, Giuseppe, *La gloria di Roma* (Rome: G. Berlutti, 1923)
——, *Rivoluzione* (Rome: G. Berlutti, 1923)
——, *Gli italiani all'estero* (Milan: Mondadori, 1939)

Bollough, Edward, *Irredentism and the War* (London: British-Italian League, 1917)

——, *The Trentino* (London: British-Italian League, 1917)

Borsa, Mario, *Gli inglesi e noi* (Milan: Fasani, 1945)

Canevari, Emilio, *La conquista inglese dell'Africa* (Rome: Istituto Grafico Tiberino, 1935)

——, *Graziani mi ha detto* (Rome: Magi-Spinetti, 1947)

——, *La guerra italiana. Retroscena della disfatta*, 2 vols (Rome: Tosi, 1948)

Caporilli, Pietro, *L'educazione giovanile nello stato fascista* (Rome: Sapientia, 1930)

Chamberlain, Austen, *The Austen Chamberlain Diary Letters. The Correspondence of Sir Austen Chamberlain with his Sisters Hilda and Ida, 1916–1937*, edited by Robert C. Self, Camden Fifth Series, Vol. 5 (Cambridge: Cambridge University Press, 1995)

Chesterton, Arthur Kenneth, *Oswald Mosley. Portrait of a Leader* (London: Action Press, 1937)

Chiurco, G. A., *Storia della rivoluzione fascista, 1919–1922* (Florence: Vallecchi, 1929)

Ciano, Galeazzo, *Diario 1937–1943* (Milan: Rizzoli, 1980)

Claremoris, Maurizio, *Noi e la Francia*, foreword by Roberto Farinacci (Cremona: Cremona Nuova, 1939)

Coselschi, Eugenio, *L'universalità di Roma* (Florence: Vallecchi, 1933)

Currey, Muriel, *An Englishwoman's Impressions of Tigrai under Italian Rule. A Broadcast*, pamphlet (Rome: 1936)

——, *A Woman at the Abyssinian War* (London: Hutchinson & Co, 1936)

——, *Insurance and Social Welfare in Italy*, pamphlet (London: 1938)

Di Marzio Cornelio, *Fascisti all'estero*, in *La civiltà fascista*, introduction by Benito Mussolini (Turin: U.T.E.T., 1928)

Drennan, James, *B.U.F.: Oswald Mosley and British Fascism* (London: John Murray, 1934)

Farinacci, Roberto, *Squadrismo* (Rome: Ardita, 1933)

Fiaccadori, Aldo, *La supremazia economica inglese e le origini della sua decadenza* (Milan: Hoepli, 1940)

Fuller, John Frederick Charles, *The First of the League Wars. Its Lessons and Omens* (London: Eyre and Spottiswoode, 1936)

Gario, Gino, *Italy: 1914–18* (London: T. G. Norris, 1937)

Gayda, Virginio, *Italia e Francia. Problemi aperti* (Rome: il Giornale d'Italia, 1938)

——, *Che cosa vuole l'Italia* (Rome: il Giornale d'Italia, 1940)

Giannini Amedeo, *I rapporti italo-inglesi* (Rome: Istituto nazionale fascista di cultura, 1936)

——, *L'Albania dall'indipendenza all'unione con l'Italia 1913–1939* (Milan: Istituto studi di politica internazionale, 1940)

Gioventù (La) Italiana all'Estero al mare e ai monti della patria (Rome: Fasci italiani all'estero, 1929)

Goad, Harold, *What is Fascism?: an Explanation of its Essential Principles* (Florence: Italian Mail and Tribune, 1929)

——, *The Making of the Corporate State. A Study of Fascist Development* (London: Christophers, 1932)

—— and Catalano, Michele, *Education in Italy* (Rome: Laboremus, 1939)

—— and Currey, Muriel, *The Working of a Corporate State. A Study of National Cooperation* (London: Nicholson & Watson, 1933)

Grandi, Dino, *Dino Grandi racconta l'evitabile Asse* (Milan: Jaka Book, 1984)

——, *Il mio paese. Ricordi autobiografici* (Bologna: Il Mulino, 1985)

——, *La politica estera dell'Italia dal 1929 al 1932* (Rome: Bonacci, 1985)

Gravelli, Asvero, *Europa, con noi!* (Rome: La Nuova Europa, 1933).

——, *Il Fascismo inglese* (Rome: La Nuova Europa, 1933)

——, *Panfascismo* (Rome: La Nuova Europa, 1935)

——, *Uno e molti. Interpretazioni spirituali di Mussolini* (Rome: La Nuova Europa, 1938)

Guida generale degli italiani a Londra (London: Edward Ercoli & Son, 1933)

Jerrold, Douglas, *They That Take the Sword. The Future of the League of Nations* (London: John Lane, 1936)

——, *Georgian Adventure* (London: Collins, 1937)

——, *Britain and Europe, 1900–1940* (London: Collins, 1941)

Joyce, William, *Fascism and India*, pamphlet (London: 1933)

Keane, Richard Michael (ed), *Germany – What Next? Being an Examination of the German Menace in so far as it Affects Great Britain* (Harmondsworth: Penguin, 1939)

Letture classe quinta. Scuole italiane all'estero (Rome: Fasci italiani all'estero, 1938)

Masi, Corrado, *Italia e italiani nell'Oriente vicino e lontano* (Bologna: Cappelli, 1936)

Miles, A. C., *Mosley in Motley*, pamphlet (London: 1937)

Morelli Emilia, *Mazzini in Inghilterra* (Florence: Studi e documenti di storia del Risorgimento, 1938)

Mosley, Diana, *A Life of Contrasts. The Autobiography of Diana Mosley* (London: Hamilton, 1977)

Mosley, Oswald, *The Greater Britain* (London: BUF, 1932).

——, *Fascism: 100 Questions Asked and Answered* (London: BUF, 1936).

——, *Tomorrow We Live* (London: BUF, 1939)

——, *My Answer* (Ramsbury: Mosley Publications, 1946)

——, *A Policy for Britain* (Ramsbury: Mosley Publications, 1947)

——, *The European Situation: the Third Force* (Ramsbury: Mosley Publications, 1950)

——, *Automation: Problems and Solution. The Answer of European Socialism* (London: Sanctuary Press, 1956)

——, *My Life* (London: Nelson, 1968)

Mosley: the Facts (London: Euphorion Distribution, 1957)

Movimenti fascisti esteri (Rome: Ministero degli Affari Esteri, 1934)

Mussolini, Benito, *Opera Omnia*, edited by Edoardo and Duilio Susmel (Florence: La Fenice, 1959)

Orani A., *La legislazione fascista nelle scuole italiane all'estero* (Turin: 1928)

Orano, Paolo, *Avanguardie d'Italia nel mondo* (Rome: Fasci italiani all'estero, 1938)

Pareti, Luigi, *Tre secoli di ingerenze inglesi* (Rome: Latium, 1941)

——, *L'anglicanesimo contro la Chiesa e Roma* (Venice: Edizioni popolari, 1944)

Parini, Piero, *I fasci italiani all'estero*, in *Il decennale. X anniversario della vittoria. Anno VII dell'era fascista* (Florence: Vallecchi, 1929)

——, *Fasci italiani all'estero: 45 morti, 283 feriti* (Rome: Fasci italiani all'estero, 1932).

——, *I figli degli italiani all'estero in patria* (Rome: Fasci italiani all'estero, 1934)

——, *Gli italiani nel mondo* (Milan: Mondadori, 1935)

Partito Nazionale Fascista, *Vademecum dello stile fascista. Dai fogli di disposizioni del segretario del partito*, edited by Gravelli (Rome: La Nuova Europa, 1940)

Pellizzi, Camillo, *Problemi e realtá del fascismo* (Florence: Vallecchi, 1924)

——, *Fascismo-Aristocrazia* (Milan: Alpes, 1925)

——, *Italy* (London: Longmans Green, 1939)

——, *Italiani nel mondo*, edited by Jolanda de Blasi (Florence: Sansoni, 1942)

——, *Una rivoluzione mancata* (Milan: Longanesi, 1948)

Petrie, Charles, *Mussolini* (London: The Holme Press, 1931)

——, *The British Problem* (London: Ivor Nicholson and Watson, 1934)

——, *Lords of the Inland Sea. A Study of the Mediterranean Powers* (London: Lovat Dickson Limited, 1937)

——, *Monarchy in the Twentieth Century* (London: Dakers, 1952)

——, *The Carlton Club* (London: Eyre and Spottiswoode, 1955)

——, *The Modern British Monarchy* (London: Eyre and Spottiswoode, 1955)

Pigli, Mario, *Italian Civilisation in Ethiopia* (Rome: Dante Alighieri, 1936)

Piovene, Guido, *Italy* (London: Alec Tiranti, 1956)

——, *In Search of Europe* (New York: St Martin's Press, 1975).

Pitigliani, Fausto, *The Italian Corporative State* (London: P. S. King & Son, 1933)

Polson Newman, E. W., *The New Ethiopia* (London: Rich and Cowan, 1938)

Pomba, Giuseppe Luigi (ed), *La civiltà fascista illustrata nella dottrina e nelle opere* (Turin: Utet, 1928)

Preti, Luigi, *Gli inglesi a Malta. Una politica errata, la cui fine contribuirebbe a migliorare i rapporti anglo-italiani* (Milan: Bocca, 1938)

Re-Bartlett, Lucy, *Italy, the Pioneer of Peace* (London: British-Italian League, 1921)

Rossi, Ettore, *Lingua italiana, dialetto maltese e politica britannica a Malta* (Livorno: Giusti, 1929).

Rota, Ettore *Italia e Francia davanti alla storia: il mito della sorella latina* (Milan: Industrie Grafiche Nicola, 1939)

Rudlin, W. A., *The Growth of Fascism in Great Britain* (London: Allen & Unwin, 1935)

Saracino, Giovanni, *L'impero italiano e l'Inghilterra* (Milan: Impresa Editoriale Italiana, 1936)

Serventi, Gaetano Nino, *Inglesi 1935* (Rome: Edizioni del Secolo fascista, 1935)

Signoretti, Alfredo, *Italia e Inghilterra durante il Risorgimento* (Milan: Istituto di studi di politica internazionale, 1940)

Sinicco, Giuseppe, *Le memorie di un calzolaio da Borgognano a Londra* (Udine: Pellegrini, 1950)

Squire, John, *Reflections and Memoires* (London: William Heinemann, 1935)

Suvich, Fulvio, *Memorie 1932–36* (Milano: Rizzoli, 1984)

Villari, Luigi, *The Awakening of Italy. The Fascista Regeneration* (London: Methuen, 1924)

——, *The Fascist Experiment* (London: Faber & Gwyer, 1926)

——, *Italy* (London: Ernest Benn, 1929)

——, *The war on the Italian Front* (London: Cobden-Sanderson, 1932)

——, *Italy, Ethiopia and the League* (Rome: Dante Alighieri Society, 1936)

——, *L'Italia come non è. Polemica con gli Anglosassoni* (Rome: Tosi, 1941)

——, *Storia diplomatica del conflitto italo-etiopico* (Bologna: Zanichelli, 1943)

Villari, Pasquale, *Scritti e discorsi per la Dante* edited by Felice Felicioni (Rome: Società Dante Alighieri, 1933)

Vindicator (pseud.), *Fascists at Olympia: a Record of Eye-Witnesses and Victims* (London: Gollancz, 1934).

Volpe, Gioacchino, *Storia della Corsica italiana* (Milan: ISPI, 1939)

Walter, Karl, *Co-operation in Changing Italy* (London: P. S. King & Son, 1934)

——, *The Class Conflict in Italy* (London: P. S. King & Son, 1938)

Wrench, John Evelyn, *Francis Yeats-Brown, 1886–1944* (London: Eyre and Spottiswoode, 1948)

Yeats-Brown, Francis, *Bengal Lancer* (London: Victor Gollancz, 1930)

——, *European Jungle* (London: Eyre and Spottiswoode, 1939)

3. Secondary Sources

Affron, Matthew and Antliff, Mark (eds), *Fascist Visions: Art and Ideology in France and Italy* (Princeton: Princeton University Press, 1997)

Acquarone, Alberto, *L'organizzazione dello stato totalitario* (Turin: Einaudi, 1965)

Adams, Ralf James Q., *British Politics and Foreign policy in the Age of Appeasement, 1935–39* (London and Basingstoke: MacMillan, 1993)

Anderson, Edward, *Towards Fascism: the Italian Community and the Italian Press in London, 1920–1922* (MA dissertation, Birkbeck College, 2002)

Baker, David, *Ideology of Obsession: A. K. Chesterton and British Fascism* (London: I. B. Tauris, 1996)

Baldoli, Claudia, 'Ho cambiato il cielo ma non l'animo . . . I Fasci Italiani all'Estero e l'educazione degli italiani in Gran Bretagna (1932–1934)', *Studi Emigrazione. International Journal of Migration Studies*, 134, June 1999, pp. 243–81

——, 'Le Navi. Fascismo e vacanze in una colonia estiva per i figli degli italiani all'estero', *Memoria e Ricerca*, n. 6, July-December 2000, pp. 163–76

——, 'The Remaking of the Italian Community in London: *L'Italia Nostra* and the Creation of a Little Fascist Italy during the 1930s', *The London Journal*, vol. 26, n. 2, 2001, pp. 23–34

Barone, Arturo, *Italians First: From A to Z* (Kent: Norbury, 1989)

Beckett, Francis, 'The Rebel Who Lost His Cause', *History Today*, 1994, 44 (5), pp. 36–42

Beloff, Max, *Il problema di Roma nella politica della Gran Bretagna* (Rome: Istituto per la storia del Risorgimento Italiano, 1970)

Benewick, Robert, *Political Violence & Public Order: a Study of British Fascism* (London: Allen Lane, 1969)

Berezin, Mabel, *Making the Fascist Self: the Political Culture of Interwar Italy* (Ithaca and London: Cornell University Press, 1997)

Bernabei, Alfio, *Esuli ed emigrati italiani nel Regno Unito 1920–1940* (Milan: Mursia, 1997).

Berselli, Aldo, *L'opinione pubblica inglese e l'avvento del fascismo (1919–1925)* (Milan: Angeli, 1971)

Bertonha, João Fábio, 'Emigrazione e politica estera: la "diplomazia sovversiva" di Mussolini e la questione degli italiani all'estero, 1922–1945', *Altreitalie*, July–December 2001, pp. 39–53

Bevilacqua, Piero, De Clementi, Andreina and Franzina, Emilio, *Storia dell'emigrazione italiana. Partenze* (Rome: Donzelli, 2001)

Bezza, Bruno(ed.), *Gli italiani fuori d'Italia. Gli emigrati italiani nei movimenti operai dei paesi d'adozione* (Milan: Angeli, 1983)

Bidussa, David, *Il mito del bravo italiano* (Milan: Il Saggiatore, 1994).

Blaniston, Noel, *La fine del potere temporale nella coscienza religiosa e nella cultura della Gran Bretagna* (Rome: Istituto per la storia del Risorgimento italiano, 1970)

Blinkhorn, Martin (ed.), *Fascists and Conservatives. The Radical Right and the Establishment in Twentieth-Century Europe* (London: Unwin Hyman, 1990)

Bolech Cecchi, Donatella, *L'accordo di due imperi. L'accordo italo-inglese del 16 aprile 1938* (Milan: Giuffré, 1977)

Bosworth, Richard J. B., *Italy, the Least of the Great Powers: Italian Foreign Policy before the First World War* (Cambridge: Cambridge University Press, 1979).

—— and Romano, Sergio (eds.), *La politica estera italiana (1860–1985)* (Bologna: Il Mulino, 1991)

Brand, Charles Peter, *Italy and the English Romantics. The Italianate Fashion in Early Nineteenth-Century England* (Cambridge: Cambridge University Press, 1957).

Brewer, John D., *Mosley's Men. The British Union of Fascists in the West Midlands* (Aldershot: Gower, 1984)

Briani, Vittorio, *Il lavoro italiano all'estero negli ultimi 100 anni* (Rome: Italiani nel mondo, 1970)

Bridge, Carl, *Holding India to the Empire. The British Conservative Party and the 1935 Constitution* (London: Oriental University Press, 1986)

Brunetta, Gian Piero, *Cent'anni di cinema italiano* (Rome and Bari: Laterza, 1991)

Bruti Liberati, Luigi, *Il Canada, l'Italia e il fascismo* (Rome: Bonacci, 1984)

Burdett, Charles, 'Journeys to the *other* spaces of Fascist Italy', *Modern Italy*, V, 1, 2000, pp. 7–21

Burgwyn, James H., *Italian Foreign Policy in the Interwar Period 1918–1940* (Westport: Praeger, 1997)

——, 'Grandi e il mondo teutonico: 1929–1932', *Storia Contemporanea*, XIX (1988), 2

Cannistraro, Philip V., *Blackshirts in Little Italy. Italian Americans and Fascism, 1921–1929* (West Lafayette: Bordighera, 1999)

Canosa, Romano, *I servizi segreti del Duce. I persecutori e le vittime* (Milan: Mondadori, 2000)

Carlton David, *Anthony Eden. A Biography* (London: Allen Lane, 1981)

Carpenter, L. P., 'Corporatism in Britain, 1930–45', *Journal of Contemporary History*, 11 (1976), pp. 3–24

Casali, Luciano, 'Tristi rottami di un triste passato', *Italia Contemporanea*, 1984 (155), pp. 93–9

Cavalli, Calisto, *Ricordi di un emigrato* (London: La Voce degli Italiani, 1973)

Cerruti, Mauro, *Fra Roma e Berna. La Svizzera italiana nel ventennio fascista* (Milan: Angeli, 1986)

Chabod, Federico, *L'Italia contemporanea 1918–1948* (Turin: Einaudi, 1961)

——, *Storia della politica estera italiana dal 1870 al 1896*, vol. II (Bari: Laterza, 1965)

Chisholm, Anne, *Beaverbrook: a Life* (London: Hutchinson, 1992)

Colarizi, Simona, *L'opinione degli italiani sotto il regime*, 1929–1943 (Rome and Bari: Laterza, 1991)

Collotti, Enzo (with Labanca, Nicola, and Sala, Teodoro), *Fascismo e politica di potenza. Politica estera 1922–1939* (Milan: La Nuova Italia, 2000)

—— and Klinkhammer, Lutz, *Il fascismo e l'Italia in guerra. Una conversazione fra storia e storiografia* (Rome: Ediesse, 1996)

Colpi, Terri, *The Italian Factor. The Italian Community in Great Britain* (Edinburgh: Mainstream, 1991)

——, *Italians Forward. A Visual History of the Italian Community in Great Britain* (Edinburgh: Mainstream, 1991)

Cowling, Maurice, *The Impact of Hitler. British Politics and British Policy 1933–1940* (Cambridge: Cambridge University Press, 1975)

Cresciani, Gianfranco, *Fascismo, antifascismo e gli italiani in Australia, 1922–1945* (Rome: Bonacci, 1979)

Cronin, Mike (ed.), *The Failure of British Fascism: the Far Right and the Fight for Political Recognition* (London and Basingstoke: Macmillan, 1996)

Cross, Colin, *The Fascists in Britain* (London: Barrie & Rockliff, 1961)

Cullen, Stephen M., 'Political Violence: the Case of the British Union of Fascists', *Journal of Contemporary History*, 1993, 28 (2), pp. 245–67

De Caprariis, Luca, 'Fascism for export? The Rise and Eclipse of the *Fasci Italiani all'Estero*', *Journal of Contemporary History*, XXXV, 2 (April 2000), pp. 151–83

Del Boca, Angelo, *Gli italiani in Africa Orientale. La caduta dell'impero* (Rome and Bari: Laterza, 1982)

—— (ed), *Le guerre coloniali del fascismo* (Rome and Bari: Laterza, 1991)

——, Legnani, Massimo and Rossi, Mario G. (eds.), *Il regime fascista. Storia e storiografia* (Rome and Bari: Laterza, 1995)

De Felice, Renzo, *Storia degli ebrei italiani sotto il fascismo* (Turin: Einaudi, 1961)

——, *Mussolini il duce. I. Gli anni del consenso 1929–1936* (Turin: Einaudi, 1974)

——, *Mussolini il duce. II. Lo stato totalitario 1936–1939* (Turin: Einaudi, 1974)

Dogliani, Patrizia, *L'Italia fascista, 1922–1940* (Milan: Sansoni, 1999)

Duroselle, J. B. and Serra, E. (eds.), *Il vincolo culturale tra Italia e Francia negli anni Trenta e Quaranta* (Milan: Angeli, 1986)

Falasca-Zamponi, Simonetta, *Fascist Spectacle: the Aesthetics of Power in Mussolini's Italy* (Berkeley – Los Angeles: University of California Press, 1997)

Fasano Guarini, Elena, 'Il 'Times' di fronte al fascismo (1919–1932)', *Rivista Storica del Socialismo*, 1965 (25), pp. 155–85

Febvre, Lucien, *Il Reno* (Rome: Donzelli, 1998)

Forte, Charles, *Forte. Autobiography of Charles Forte* (London: Sidgwick & Jackson, 1986)

Franzina, Emilio, *L'immaginario degli emigranti: miti e raffigurazioni dell'esperienza italiana all'estero fra i due secoli* (Treviso: Pagus, 1992)

——, *Stranieri d'Italia. Studi sull'emigrazione italiana dal Risorgimento al Fascismo* (Vicenza: Odeon, 1994)

——, *Gli Italiani al nuovo mondo: l'emigrazione italiana in America, 1492–1942* (Milan: Mondadori, 1995).

—— and Sanfilippo, Matteo (eds), *Il fascismo e gli emigrati. La parabola dei fasci italiani all'estero* (Rome and Bari: Laterza, 2003)

Franzinelli, Mimmo, *I tentacoli dell'OVRA. Agenti, collaboratori e vittime della polizia politica fascista* (Turin: Bollati Boringhieri, 1999)

——, *Delatori. Spie e confidenti anonimi: l'arma segreta del regime fascista* (Milan: Mondadori, 2001)

Gaeta, F., *Nazionalismo italiano* (Rome and Bari: Laterza, 1981, first ed. 1965)

Gallerano, Nicola, *Storia e uso pubblico della storia*, in Id. (ed.), *L'uso pubblico della storia* (Milan: Angeli, 1995)

Galli, Giorgio (ed.), *Il fascismo nella Treccani*, (Milan: Terziaria, 1997)

Gattari, Nicola, *La strada per Addis Abeba. Lettere di un camionista dall'impero (1936–1941)*, edited by Sergio Luzzatto (Turin: Paravia, 2000)

Gellately, Robert, *The Gestapo and German Society: Enforcing Racial Policy, 1933–1945* (Oxford: Clarendon, 1990)

Gentile, Emilio, *Il culto del littorio. La sacralizzazione della politica nell'Italia fascista* (Rome and Bari: Laterza, 1993)

——, *La via italiana al totalitarismo. Il partito e lo Stato nel regime fascista* (Rome: La Nuova Italia Scientifica, 1995)

——, 'La politica estera del partito fascista. Ideologia e organizzazione dei Fasci italiani all'estero (1920–1930)', *Storia Contemporanea*, XXVI (1995), 6, 897–956

——, *La grande Italia. Ascesa e declino del mito della nazione nel ventesimo secolo* (Milan: Mondadori, 1997)

——, *Fascismo. Storia e interpretazione* (Rome and Bari: Laterza, 2002)

Gillette, Aaron, *Racial Theories in Fascist Italy* (London and New York: Routledge, 2002)

Goglia, Luigi, 'La propaganda italiana a sostegno della guerra contro l'Etiopia svolta in Gran Bretagna nel 1935–36', *Storia Contemporanea*, XV (1984), 5, pp. 845–908

Goldman, Aaron L., 'Sir Robert Vansittart's Search for Italian Cooperation against Hitler', *Journal of Contemporary History*, 1974, 13, pp. 93–130

Griffin, Roger, *The Nature of Fascism* (London: Pinter Publisher, 1991)

—— (ed), *International Fascism: Theories, Causes, and the New Consensus* (London: Arnold, 1998)

Griffiths, Richard, *Fellow Travellers of the Right. British Enthusiasts for Nazi Germany, 1933–39* (London: Constable, 1980)

Higginbottom, Melvyn David, *Intellectuals and British Fascism: a Study of Henry Williamson* (London: Janus, 1992)

Holmes, Colin, *Anti-Semitism in British Society 1876–1939* (London: Arnold, 1979)

——, '"Germany Calling". Lord Haw-Haw's Treason', in *Twentieth Century British History*, 1994, 5 (1), pp. 118–21

Howarth, Patrick, *Squire. Most Generous of Men* (London: Hutchinson, 1963)

Inghilterra e Italia nel '900 (Florence: La Nuova Italia, 1973)

Ishida, Ken, 'Mussolini and Diplomats in the Ethiopian War. The Foreign Policy Decision-Making Process in Fascist Italy', *Journal of Law and Politics of Osaka City University*, 42, 4 (1996), pp. 1–11

Isnenghi, Mario, *L'educazione dell'italiano: il fascismo e l'organizzazione della cultura* (Bologna: Cappelli, 1979)

——, 'Per una mappa linguistica di un "regime di parole". A proposito del convegno "Parlare fascista"', *Movimento operaio e socialista*, 2 (1984)

—— (ed.), *I luoghi della memoria*, 3 vols (Rome and Bari: Laterza, 1996)

——, *L'Italia del Fascio* (Florence: Giunti, 1996)

—— and Lanaro, Silvio, 'Fascismo esorcizzato: cinque schede sulla "rivolta piccoloborghese"', *Belfagor*, XXV (1970), n. 2, pp. 219–29

Kennedy, Paul and Nicholls, Anthony (eds), *Nationalist and Racialist Movements in Britain and Germany before 1914* (London and Basingstoke: MacMillan, 1981)

Knox, MacGregor, *Mussolini Unleashed, 1939–1941: Politics and Strategy in Fascist Italy's Last War* (Cambridge: Cambridge University Press, 1982)

——, *Common Destiny. Dictatorship, Foreign Policy, and War in Fascist Italy and Nazi Germany* (Cambridge: Cambridge University Press, 2000)

——, *Hitler's Italian Allies. Royal Armed Forces, Fascist Regime, and the War of 1940–1943* (Cambridge: Cambridge University Press, 2000)

——, 'I testi "aggiustati" dei discorsi segreti di Grandi', *Passato e presente*, n. 13, 1987, pp. 98–117

——, 'In the Duce's Defence. Unconvincing Efforts to Blame the British for Mussolini's Alliance with Hitler', in *The Times Literary Supplement*, 26 February 1999, pp. 3–4

Kushner, Tony and Lunn, Ken (eds), *Traditions of Intolerance: Historical Perspectives on Fascism and Race Discourse in British Society* (Manchester: Manchester University Press, 1989)

Lamb, Richard, *Mussolini and the British* (London: Murray, 1997)

Lanaro, Silvio, *Patria. Circumnavigazione di un'idea controversa* (Venice: Marsilio, 1996)

Larsen, S. U., Hagtvet, B and Myklebust, J. P., (eds.), *Who Were the Fascists. Social Roots of European Fascism* (Oslo: Universitetsforlaget, 1980)

Lebzelter, Gisela C., *Political anti-Semitism in England 1918–1939* (London and Basingstoke: The Macmillan Press, 1978)

Ledeen, Michael, *Universal Fascism. The Theory and Practice of the Fascist International, 1928–1936* (New York: Howard Fertig, 1972)

Lewis, David Stephen, *Illusions of Grandeur: Mosley, Fascism and British Society, 1931–81* (Manchester: Manchester University Press, 1987)

Linehan, Thomas P., *East London for Mosley: the British Union of Fascists in East London and South-West Essex, 1933–40* (London: Frank Cass, 1996)

——, *British Fascism, 1918–39: Parties, Ideology and Culture* (Manchester: Manchester University Press, 2000)

Longo, Gisella, ' I tentativi per la costituzione di un'internazionale fascista: gli incontri di Amsterdam e di Montreux attraverso i verbali delle riunioni', *Storia Contemporanea*, XXVII (1996), 3, pp. 475–570

Lunn, Kenneth and Thurlow, Richard C. (eds), *British Fascism: Essays on the Radical Right in Inter-War Britain* (London: Croom Helm, 1980).

Lupo, Salvatore, *Il fascismo. La politica in un regime totalitario* (Rome: Donzelli, 2000)

Mack Smith, Denis, *Mussolini's Roman Empire* (New York: Penguin, 1977)

——, 'Mussolini: Reservations about Renzo De Felice's Biography', *Modern Italy*, V, 2, November 2000, pp. 193–210

Mallett, Robert, *The Italian Navy and Fascist Expansionism 1935–1940* (London: Frank Cass, 1998)

—— and Sørensen, Gert (eds), *International Fascism 1919–45* (London: Frank Cass, 2002)

Mandle, W. F., *Anti-Semitism and the British Union of Fascists* (London: Longmans, 1968)

Marin, Umberto, *Italiani in Gran Bretagna* (Rome: Centro Studi Emigrazione, 1975)

Martellone, Anna Maria, *La 'questione' dell'immigrazione negli Stati Uniti* (Bologna: Il Mulino, 1980)

Martinet, Gilles and Romano, Sergio, with Canonica, Michele, *Un'amicizia difficile. Conversazioni su due secoli di relazioni italo-francesi* (Florence: Ponte alle Grazie, 2001)

Mazzatosta, Maria Teresa, *Il regime fascista tra educazione e propaganda* (Bologna: Cappelli, 1978)

Mills, William C., 'The Chamberlain-Grandi Conversations of July-August 1937 and the Appeasement of Italy', *International History Review*, 19, 3 (1997), pp. 594–619

Minniti, Fortunato, 'Il "nemico vero". Gli obiettivi dei piani di operazione contro la Gran Bretagna nel contesto etiopico (maggio 1935–maggio 1936)', *Storia Contemporanea*, XXVI (August 1995)

——, *Fino alla guerra. Strategie e conflitto nella politica di potenza di Mussolini 1923–1940* (Naples: Edizioni Scientifiche Italiane, 2000)

Missori, Mario, *Gerarchie e statuti del PNF. Gran Consiglio, Direttorio nazionale, Federazioni provinciali: quadri e biografie* (Rome: Bonacci, 1986)

Morelli, Anne, *Fascismo e antifascismo nell'emigrazione italiana in Belgio* (Rome: Bonacci, 1987)

Mosse, George L., (ed.), *International Fascism: New Thoughts and New Approaches* (London: Sage Publications, 1979)

Nello, Paolo, *Un fedele disubbidiente. Dino Grandi da palazzo Chigi al 25 luglio* (Bologna: Il Mulino, 1993)

Nolte, Ernst, *Three Faces of Fascism: Action Francaise, Italian Fascism, National Socialism* (London: Weidenfeld and Nicolson, 1965)

O'Connor, Maura, *The Romance of Italy and the English Political Imagination* (New York: St Martin's Press, 1998)

Ortona, Egidio, 'La caduta di Eden nel 1938', *Storia Contemporanea*, XV (1984), 3, pp. 477–94

Overy, Richard, *The Battle of Britain. The Myth and the Reality* (New York: Norton, 2001)

Palla, Marco, *Fascismo e Stato corporativo. Un'inchiesta della diplomazia britannica* (Milan: Angeli, 1991)

Passerini, Luisa, *Mussolini immaginario. Storia di una biografia 1915–1939* (Rome and Bari: Laterza, 1991)

Perfetti, Francesco, *Il movimento nazionalista in Italia (1903–1914)* (Rome: Bonacci, 1984)

Peters, Anthony R., *Anthony Eden at the Foreign Office 1931–1938* (Aldershot: Gower, 1986)

Pisa, Beatrice, *Nazione e politica nella Società 'Dante Alighieri'* (Rome: Bonacci, 1995)

Pombeni, Paolo, *Demagogia e tirannide. Uno studio sulla forma-partito del fascismo* (Bologna: Il Mulino, 1984)

Pryce-Jones, David, *Unity Mitford. A Quest* (London: Weidenfeld & Nicolson, 1976)

Quartararo, Rosaria, *Roma tra Londra e Berlino. La politica estera fascista dal 1930 al 1940* (Rome: Bonacci, 1980)

Rochat, Giorgio, *Militari e politici nella preparazione della campagna d'Etiopia. Studio e documenti 1932–1936* (Milan: Angeli, 1971)

——, *Guerre italiane in Libia e in Etiopia. Studi militari* (Treviso: Pagus, 1991)

Rosoli, Gianfausto, 'Santa Sede e propaganda fascista all'estero tra i figli degli emigrati italiani', *Storia Contemporanea*, 1986, 17 (2), p. 315

Rumi, Giorgio, *Alle origini della politica estera fascista (1918–1923)* (Bari: Laterza, 1968)

Rusconi, G. E. (ed.), *Germania: un passato che non passa. I crimini nazisti e l'identità tedesca* (Turin: Einaudi, 1987)

Sabatini, Davide, *L'internazionale di Mussolini. La diffusione del fascismo in Europa nel progetto politico di Asvero Gravelli* (Tusculum: Grottaferrata, 1997)

Salvemini, Gaetano, *Prelude to World War II* (London: Gollancz, 1953)

——, *Memorie di un fuoruscito*, in *Scritti vari (1900–1957)*, ed. by G. Agosti e A. Galante Garrone (Milan: Feltrinelli, 1978)

Salvetti, Patrizia, *Immagine nezionale ed emigrazione nella Società 'Dante Alighieri'* (Rome: Bonacci, 1995)

Salvoni, Elena and Fawkes, Sandy, *Elena. A Life in Soho* (London: Quartet, 1990)

Santarelli, Enzo, 'I fasci italiani all'estero (Note ed appunti)', *Studi urbinati di storia filosofia letteratura*, XLV (1971), 1–2, 1323

Santinon, Renzo, *I fasci italiani all'estero* (Rome: Settimo Sigillo, 1991)

Sapelli, Giulio, *Tra identità culturale e sviluppo di reti. Storia delle Camere di Commercio italiane all'estero* (Soveria: Mannelli, 2000)

Sarfatti, Michele, *Mussolini contro gli ebrei. Cronaca dell'elaborazione delle leggi del 1938* (Turin: Zamorani, 1994)

Sebastian, Peter, *I servizi speciali britannici e l'Italia: 1940–1945* (Rome: Bonacci, 1986)

Serra, Enrico and Duroselle, Jean Baptiste, *Italia e Francia, 1939–1945* (Milan: Angeli, 1984)

—— and Seton-Watson, Cristopher, *Italia e Inghilterra nell'età dell'imperialismo* (Milan: Angeli, 1990)

——, 'Diplomazia italiana, propaganda fascista e immagine della Gran Bretagna, *Rivista di storia contemporanea*, XV, 3 (1986)

Silei, Gianni, 'I conservatori britannici e il fascismo (1929–1935). La parabola discendente di una "storica amicizia"', *Il Politico*, LVII, 1992, 3, pp. 527–8

Skidelsky, Robert, *Oswald Mosley* (London and Basingstoke: Macmillan, 1975)

Smart, Nick, *The National Government, 1931–40* (London and Basingstoke: MacMillan, 1999)

Soldani, Simonetta and Turi, Gabriele (eds.), *Fare gli italiani: scuola e cultura nell'Italia contemporanea*, 2 vols (Bologna: Il Mulino, 1993)

Spark, Muriel, *The Prime of Miss Jean Brodie* (London: Penguin, 1961)

Sponza, Lucio, *Italian Immigrants in Nineteenth-Century Britain. Realities and Images* (Leicester: Leicester University Press, 1988)

——, *Divided Loyalties. Italians in Britain during the Second World War* (Bern: Peter Lang, 2000)

Stone, Marla Susan, *The Patron State: Culture and Politics in Fascist Italy* (Princeton: Princeton University Press, 1998)

Strazzabosco, Stefano (ed.), *Guido Piovene tra ideali e ragione* (Venice: Marsilio, 1996)

Suzzi Valli, Roberta, 'Il fascio italiano a Londra. L'attività politica di Camillo Pellizzi', *Storia Contemporanea*, XXVI (1995), 6, pp. 957–1001

Taylor, Alan J. P., *Beaverbrook* (London: Hamilton, 1972)

Thorpe, Andrew (ed.), *The Failure of Political Extremism in Inter-War Britain* (Exeter: University of Exeter, 1989)

Thurlow, Richard, *Fascism in Britain: A History 1918–1985* (Oxford and New York: Blackwell, 1987)

——, 'British Fascism and State Surveillance, 1934–45', *Intelligence and National Security*, 1988, 3 (1), pp. 77–99

——, *Fascism in Modern Britain* (Gloucestershire: Sutton Publishing, 2000)

Tosi, Arturo, *L'Italiano d'oltremare. La lingua delle comunità italiane nei paesi anglofoni* (Florence: Giunti, 1991)

Trythall, Anthony John, *'Boney' Fuller: the Intellectual General, 1878–1966* (London: Cassell, 1977)

Waley, Daniel, *British Public Opinion and the Ethiopian War 1935–36* (London: Temple Smith, 1975)

Webber, G. C., *The Ideology of the British Right: 1918–1939* (London and Sidney: Croom Helm, 1986)

Weber, Eugen, *Varieties of Fascism. Doctrines of Revolution in the Twentieth Century* (Malabar, Florida: Krieger, 1982)

Woolf, Stuart J., *Fascism in Europe* (London-New York: Methuen, 1981)

Watso, James L. (ed), *Between Two Cultures. Migrants and Minorities in Britain* (Oxford: Blackwell, 1977)

Zangrandi, Ruggero, *Il lungo viaggio attraverso il fascismo* (Milan: Feltrinelli, 1962)

Index